Pathfinder Operations

*FM 3-21.38

Field Manual
No. 3-21.38

Headquarters
Department of the Army
Washington, DC, 25 April 2006

Pathfinder Operations

Contents

		Page
PREFACE		viii
Chapter 1	**INTRODUCTION**	**1-1**
	Employment	1-1
	Capabilities	1-2
	Limitations	1-2
	Equipment	1-2
	Communications Security	1-5
	Training	1-5
Chapter 2	**PLANS, ORGANIZATION, CONDUCT, AND THREAT**	**2-1**
	Section I. PLANS	**2-1**
	Warning Order	2-1
	Initial Preparations	2-1
	Coordination	2-2
	Linkup with Supported Unit	2-4
	Final Preparations	2-4
	Section II. ORGANIZATION FOR COMBAT	**2-4**
	Insertion	2-4
	Overland Movement	2-5
	Stay-Behind Operation	2-6
	Section III. CONDUCT OF OPERATIONS	**2-6**
	Daylight Assault	2-6
	Night Assault	2-6
	Extraction	2-6
	Staging Areas	2-7
	Artillery Displacement	2-7
	Support of Ground Operations	2-7
	Support of Air Force	2-7
	Mixed Operations	2-7
	Radio Communications	2-8

Distribution Restriction: Approved for public release; distribution is unlimited.

*This publication supersedes FM 3-21.38, 1 October 2002.

Contents

    Terminal Guidance by Supported Units.. 2-9
  Section IV. HIGH-THREAT ENVIRONMENT **2-9**
    Control and Navigation 2-9
    Tactical Instrument Flights 2-9
    Air Routes 2-10

Chapter 3   **AIR TRAFFIC CONTROL**.. **3-1**
  Section I. PATHFINDER AIR TRAFFIC **3-1**
    Safety 3-1
    Voice Control 3-1
    Formats... 3-2
    Numbers 3-3
    Phrases and Terms 3-4
  Section II. LANDINGS **3-6**
    Traffic Patterns... 3-6
    Methods of Entry.. 3-6
    Traffic Pattern Legs 3-8
    Advisory Service 3-8
    Spacing Techniques 3-9
    Final Landing Instructions.. 3-10
    Taxiing Aircraft... 3-10
    Minimum Aircraft Separation Requirements... 3-11
  Section III. GROUND-TO-AIR COMMUNICATIONS **3-12**
    Electronic Warfare Environment 3-12
    Ground-to-Air Transmissions... 3-13

Chapter 4   **HELICOPTER LANDING ZONES**.. **4-1**
  Section I. SELECTION OF LANDING SITES **4-1**
    Considerations.. 4-1
    Alternate Sites 4-10
  Section II. ORGANIZATION AND DUTIES **4-10**
    Control Center 4-10
    Landing Site Party 4-12
  Section III. LANDING SITE OPERATIONS.. **4-13**
    Communications.. 4-13
    Flight Formations 4-14
    Landing Zone and Obstacle Markings.. 4-14
    Air Assaults.. 4-14
    Intercept Headings.. 4-23
  Section IV. LANDING ZONE OPERATIONS **4-23**
    Communications Checkpoint 4-23
    Air Control Points 4-25
  Section V. NIGHT OPERATIONS.. **4-25**
    Tactical Landing Lights 4-26
    External Loads... 4-28
    Multihelicopter Operations 4-28
    Night Vision Goggles 4-28

Section VI. ENVIRONMENTAL CONSIDERATIONS 4-29
Pilot Input 4-29
Cold Weather 4-29
Jungle 4-32
Desert 4-33
Mountains 4-34

Section VII. APPROACH PATH CONSIDERATIONS 4-35
Vertical Air Currents 4-36
Escape Routes 4-36
Terrain Contour and Obstacles 4-36
Position of the Sun 4-36

Chapter 5 EXTERNAL LOADS 5-1
Landing Points 5-1
Types of Loads 5-1
Unit Responsibilities 5-2
Equipment 5-2
Service Life of Aerial-Delivery Slings 5-10
Aircraft Load Limitations 5-15
Standard Weights 5-18
Air Items Required For Common Standard Loads 5-19
Slingload Theory 5-20
Hookup and Release Procedures 5-21
Slingload Inspection Record 5-29

Chapter 6 DROP ZONES 6-1

Section I. SELECTION FACTORS 6-1
Airdrop Airspeeds 6-1
Drop Altitude 6-2
Type of Load 6-3
Methods of Delivery 6-4
Obstacles 6-6
Access 6-8
Size 6-9
Approach and Departure Routes 6-18

Section II. DROP ZONE SUPPORT TEAM 6-18
Organization 6-18
Missions 6-18
Equipment Familiarization 6-18
Coordination 6-24
Support Requirements 6-25
Duties of the Leader 6-27
Control Center 6-29
Signals 6-29
Determination of Release Point Location 6-31
Ground-Marked Release System 6-32
Army Verbally Initiated Release System 6-37
Air Force Verbally Initiated Release System 6-40

Contents

          Air Force Computed Air Release Point 6-40
          Assault Zone Availability Report 6-46
          AF IMT 3823, Drop Zone Survey 6-46
          AF IMT 4304, Drop Zone/Landing Zone Control Log 6-53

Appendix A   **CLOSE AIR SUPPORT AND CLOSE COMBAT ATTACK** **A-1**
          Definitions A-1
          Purpose A-1
          Types of Aircraft A-2
          Target Types A-3
          Weapons Effects A-3
          Aircraft Weapons Types A-4
          Risk Estimated Distances A-5
          Target to Weapons A-5

Appendix B   **OPERATIONAL FORMATS** **B-1**
          Planning Format B-1
          Landing Zone and Drop Zone Control Records B-2
          Troop-Leading Procedures B-5

Appendix C   **ARMY HELICOPTER SPECIFICATIONS** **C-1**
          Observation Helicopters C-2
          Attack Helicopters C-4
          Utility Helicopters C-8
          Cargo Helicopters C-12

Appendix D   **DIGITIZATION SUPPLEMENT** **D-1**
          Definition D-1
          Purpose, Advantages, and Capabilities D-1

Appendix E   **AIR FORCE INSTRUCTION** **E-1**
          Airdrop Airspeeds E-1
          Drop Zone Size E-2
          Ground Marked Release System E-3
          Point of Impact E-4

GLOSSARY **Glossary-1**

REFERENCES **References-1**

INDEX **Index-1**

Figures

Figure 2-1.	En route communication procedures with pathfinders in a landing zone.	2-8
Figure 2-2.	Comparison of air routes with and without a high-threat environment.	2-11
Figure 3-1.	Air traffic patterns.	3-7
Figure 3-2.	360-degree turnout.	3-9
Figure 3-3.	Traffic pattern extension.	3-10
Figure 3-4.	Minimum separation requirements.	3-11
Figure 4-1.	Landing point sizes.	4-2
Figure 4-2.	Standard flight and landing formations.	4-4
Figure 4-3.	Determination of ground slope.	4-6
Figure 4-4.	Maximum angle of approach (daylight).	4-7
Figure 4-5.	Maximum angle of approach (night).	4-8
Figure 4-6.	Approach and exit path.	4-8
Figure 4-7.	Example completed DA Form 7461-R.	4-12
Figure 4-8.	Helicopter day landing site, staggered trail-right formation.	4-16
Figure 4-9.	Helicopter day landing site, echelon right formation.	4-17
Figure 4-10.	Day or night slingload operation site.	4-18
Figure 4-11.	Day or night cargo landing site, "V" formation.	4-19
Figure 4-12.	Night landing site with landing points for aircraft and slingloads.	4-20
Figure 4-13.	Utility helicopter night landing site, diamond formations.	4-21
Figure 4-14.	Lighted night landing symbols as the pilot would see them from different approach angles.	4-22
Figure 4-15.	Intercept heading technique.	4-23
Figure 4-16.	Terrain flight modes.	4-24
Figure 4-17.	Placement of the inverted "Y" or NATO "T" at the number one touchdown point.	4-26
Figure 4-18.	Placement of additional touchdown point markings for night use.	4-26
Figure 4-19.	Placement of fifth light using inverted "Y," when coordinated.	4-27
Figure 4-20.	Emergency night lighting by vehicle headlights.	4-27
Figure 4-21.	Lessening the effects of loose snow on the ground.	4-30
Figure 6-1.	Recommended safety zones for high-tension lines.	6-8
Figure 6-2.	Example application of D=RT formula.	6-12
Figure 6-3.	Example application of T=D/R formula.	6-13
Figure 6-4.	Example application of D=KAV formula.	6-14
Figure 6-5.	Raised-angle marker.	6-21
Figure 6-6.	Drop zone coordination checklist.	6-24
Figure 6-7.	Drop zone cancellation and closing markers.	6-30
Figure 6-8.	Release point location.	6-31
Figure 6-9.	Panel emplacement.	6-33
Figure 6-10.	Horizontal clearance and marker construction.	6-36
Figure 6-11.	The 15-to-1 mask clearance ratio.	6-37

Contents

Figure 6-12. Example Army VIRS offset. 6-38
Figure 6-13. Wind streamer vector count. 6-39
Figure 6-14. Example USAF VIRS transmission. 6-40
Figure 6-15. Drop zone placement (day). 6-41
Figure 6-16. Code letters. 6-42
Figure 6-17. Drop zone placement (night). 6-43
Figure 6-18. Area drop zone. 6-44
Figure 6-19. Computation of circular drop zone. 6-45
Figure 6-20A. Example completed AF IMT 3823 (front). 6-51
Figure 6-20B. Example completed AF IMT 3823 (back). 6-52
Figure 6-21. Example completed AF IMT 4304. 6-56
Figure C-1. OH-58D Kiowa. C-3
Figure C-2. AH 64A Apache. C-5
Figure C-3. AH 64D Apache. C-7
Figure C-4. UH-1H Iroquois. C-9
Figure C-5. UH-60A/L Blackhawk. C-11

Tables

Table 2-1.	Air liaison officer's and ground unit commander's coordination of air movement table.	2-2
Table 3-1.	Numbers transmitted by units or digits.	3-3
Table 3-2.	Phrases.	3-4
Table 3-3.	Terms.	3-5
Table 3-4.	Traffic pattern legs.	3-8
Table 3-5.	A 360-degree turnout.	3-9
Table 3-6.	Light signals on or near a landing zone.	3-13
Table 3-7.	Information included in advisories.	3-15
Table 4-1.	Landing point uses.	4-3
Table 4-2.	Length of minimum width area.	4-9
Table 5-1.	Aerial delivery specifications for the Type XXVI sling.	5-3
Table 5-2.	Safe working loads (lift capacities) of polyester roundslings.	5-9
Table 5-3.	Large-capacity sling sets.	5-12
Table 5-4.	POL for external loads only.	5-18
Table 5-5.	Standard vehicle weights.	5-19
Table 5-6.	Standard artillery weights.	5-19
Table 6-1.	Airspeeds for rotary-wing aircraft.	6-1
Table 6-2.	Airspeeds for fixed-wing aircraft.	6-2
Table 6-3.	Example calculation of drop altitude in feet indicated.	6-2
Table 6-4.	Airdrop altitudes for rotary- and fixed-wing aircraft.	6-3
Table 6-5.	Minimum aerial delivery altitudes.	6-4
Table 6-6.	Size criteria for tactical airlift drop zones, personnel, and heavy equipment.	6-9
Table 6-7.	Size criteria for tactical airlift drop zones, Container Delivery System.	6-10
Table 6-8A.	Conversion chart for 10-gram helium (pilot) balloons.	6-16
Table 6-8B.	Conversion chart for 30-gram helium (pilot) balloons.	6-17
Table 6-9.	Forward throw distances for fixed-wing aircraft.	6-17
Table 6-10.	Surface wind limits for airdrops.	6-28
Table 6-11.	Favorable conditions for airdrops on tactically assessed DZs.	6-47
Table A-1.	CAS theater aircraft.	A-2
Table A-2.	Risk estimated distances.	A-5
Table A-3.	Target to weapons.	A-5
Table C-1.	Specifications for the OH-58D Kiowa.	C-2
Table C-2.	Specifications for the AH 64A Apache.	C-4
Table C-3.	Specifications for the AH 64D Apache.	C-6
Table C-4.	Specifications for the UH-1H Iroquois.	C-8
Table C-5.	Specifications for the UH-60A Blackhawk.	C-10
Table C-6.	Specifications for the CH-47 D Chinook.	C-12

Contents

Table E-1. Airdrop airspeeds. E-1
Table E-2. Standard drop zone size criteria. E-2
Table E-3. Ground marked release system load drift constants (K). E-3
Table E-4. Ground marked release system forward throw distance. E-4
Table E-5. Standard point-of-impact placement. E-4

Preface

This publication provides a foundation for training and employing pathfinder and terminal guidance personnel. The tactics, techniques, and procedures that describe the conduct of the various missions are guides. The pathfinder leader can modify them to suit the particular air assault operation.

This publication applies to the Active Army, the Army National Guard (ARNG), the Army National Guard of the United States (ARNGUS), and the United States Army Reserve (USAR) unless otherwise stated.

The manual includes an extensive glossary of acronyms and terminology peculiar to air assault operations, pathfinder operations, and Army-Air Force air traffic control. Using this glossary will help the reader understand the text.

This publication prescribes DA Form 7461-R, *Internal Net Record*, and implements the following international agreements:

- QSTAG 585, *Marshaling Helicopters in Multinational Land Operations*, 23 Apr 81 (*see* Chapter 4).

- STANAG 2863, *Navigational and Communication Capabilities for Helicopters in Multinational Land Operations*, 26 Sep 88 (*see* Chapters 2 and 3).

- STANAG 3117, *Aircraft Marshaling Signals*, 17 Oct 85 (*see* Chapters 1 and 2).

- STANAG 3281, *Personnel Locator Beacons*, 3 Apr 78 (*see* Chapters 1, 3, and 4).

- STANAG 3570, *Drop Zones and Extraction Zones--Criteria and Markings*, 26 Mar 86 (*see* Chapters 2 and 6).

- STANAG 3619, *Helipad Marking*, 10 Jul 80 (*see* Chapter 4).

The proponent for this publication is the United States Army Training and Doctrine Command. The preparing agency is the U.S. Army Infantry School. You may send comments and recommendations by any means, US mail, e-mail, fax, or telephone, as long as you use or follow the format of DA Form 2028, *Recommended Changes to Publications and Blank Forms*. You may also phone for more information.

E-mail	george.moore2@benning.army.mil
Phone	COM 706-545-3458 or DSN 835-3458
Fax	COM 706-545-6489 or DSN 835-6489
US Mail	Commandant, USAIS
	ATTN: ATSH-TPP-H /Bldg 2767
	Fort Benning, GA 31905-5593

Unless this publication states otherwise, masculine nouns and pronouns do not refer exclusively to the male gender.

> THIS CHAPTER IMPLEMENTS STANAGs 3117 AND 3281.

Chapter 1
Introduction

Army pathfinders mainly provide navigational aid and advisory services to military aircraft in areas designated by supported unit commanders. The pathfinders' secondary missions include providing advice and limited aid to units planning air assault or airdrop operations.

EMPLOYMENT

1-1. The pathfinders provide navigational aid and air traffic advisories for Army aircraft. This occurs at any phase of an air assault or ground operation that requires sustained support by Army aircraft. The commander employs pathfinders on a short-term basis for some missions. He can redeploy the pathfinders after they complete a major troop lift or airdrop.

PRIMARY

1-2. Ideally, the commander assigns a pathfinder team to each combat aviation battalion. This enhances the relationship between aviators and pathfinders, who have to work well together and understand each other to complete a mission successfully. Aviators and pathfinders must maintain a good working relationship, despite the limited number of pathfinder units and the assignment of pathfinder-coded positions to ground units.

1-3. Many units might have no trained pathfinder assets. In this case, higher headquarters must temporarily assign pathfinder assets from an external source to train supported unit personnel and oversee the conduct of pathfinder operations.

1-4. Non-pathfinder-qualified Soldiers receive training from the pathfinders and form a company-level pathfinder team. Once trained, the team provides navigational aid, air traffic advisories, and any other relevant information. Around the clock, the pathfinder team supports any type of air movement or resupply operation conducted by or for the ground unit and supported by an aviation unit.

1-5. Trained, equipped pathfinders select, mark, improve, and control landing sites. Engineers in direct support (DS) of lifted ground units may help pathfinders improve landing zones (LZs). In most situations, pathfinders perform two or more of these jobs at the same time. In each case, they start out by setting up ground-to-air radio communications. Combat lifesaver-qualified and emergency medical technician (EMT)-qualified pathfinders also supplement internal medical support.

SECONDARY

1-6. When not performing duties for supported units, pathfinders remain with their equipment, near and in communication with the supported ground unit command post (CP). While pathfinders await further missions, the parent or supported CP may task them to help control the aviation unit base airfield; to perform minor demolition work; or, in staff sections, to perform map and aerial photographic work. However, before the pathfinders perform secondary missions, they must train and perform routine maintenance on their equipment.

CAPABILITIES

1-7. Appropriately equipped and trained pathfinders—

- Reconnoiter areas selected by supported unit commanders.
- Select helicopter land zones (HLZs) and drop zones (DZs).
- Infiltrate areas of operation by foot, vehicle, watercraft, or air.
- Rappel, fast rope, or parachute from aircraft.
- Prepare HLZs and DZs.
- Establish and operate visual and electronic navigation aids.
- Remove minor obstacles.
- Use ground-to-air (GTA) radio communications to guide pilots and advise them of air traffic within the area of operations (AO).
- Coordinate directly with fire support units and keep pilots informed about friendly mortar and artillery fires.
- Provide technical assistance in assembling supplies, equipment, and troops before loading the aircraft for deployment to HLZs and DZs.
- Advise and provide limited physical assistance in preparing and positioning supplies, equipment, and troops for air movement.
- Conduct limited chemical, biological, radiological, or nuclear (CBRN) monitoring and surveying of designated areas.
- Provide limited weather observations, to include wind velocity and direction, cloud cover, visibility, and approximate cloud ceiling.
- In the absence of a special tactics team (STT), by agreement with the United States Air Force (USAF), operate DZs and airfields for USAF aircraft.
- Survey DZs for use by USAF and Army aircraft. In this situation, pathfinders might require USAF-compatible ultra high frequency (UHF) or very high frequency (VHF) radios. Aviators and pathfinders coordinate to make sure everyone knows the ground marking and radio procedures.

LIMITATIONS

1-8. Pathfinders require augmentation when they guide aircraft or perform other, related primary tasks such as the following:

- Provide security.
- Remove major obstacles.
- Recover and assemble equipment and supplies.
- Operate additional radio nets and telephones.
- Transport equipment.
- Conduct detailed CBRN monitoring and surveying.

EQUIPMENT

1-9. Pathfinders use a variety of equipment. Though the aviation unit standing operating procedures (SOP) may specify the type of equipment pathfinders will use, the mission dictates what specific items of equipment the pathfinders will take on the operation.

NAVIGATION AIDS

1-10. Pathfinders use navigation aids to help aviators find and identify an exact area.

Electronic

1-11. With these aids, pathfinders can signal farther than they can with visual navigation aids. Electronic navigation aids include—

- Homing beacons.
- Transponders.
- Radios.
- Any other electronic devices that can aid in aircraft navigation.

Visual

1-12. With these aids, pathfinders can designate specific areas or points on LZs and DZs. They use them as GTA signals. Unfortunately, because visual aids are visible, the enemy can also see them.

Day

1-13. Visual navigation aids that can be used during the day include—

- Panels.
- Smoke.
- Signal mirrors.
- Colored gloves and vests for signalmen.

Night

1-14. Visual navigation aids that can be used during the night include—

- Light beacons.
- Lanterns.
- Baton flashlights.
- Strobe lights.
- Pyrotechnics.
- Chem-lights.

Day or Night

1-15. Pathfinders can make field-expedient visual aids for day or night.

Infrared

1-16. At night, pathfinders can use any infrared navigation aids that are compatible with their night vision goggles (NVG).

COMMUNICATIONS

1-17. Pathfinders use FM radios with secure capability and limited wire equipment. These radios allow pathfinders to communicate with aircraft, other pathfinder elements, and supported units. Incorporated homing capabilities in these radios allow pathfinders to provide navigational aid to aircraft.

ASSEMBLY AIDS

1-18. Pathfinders use assembly aids to designate troop and supply assembly areas. Assembly aids include electronic, visual, and infrared devices. The pathfinders can also use or make field-expedient

Chapter 1

devices to aid in assembly. Because assembly aids can attract the enemy's attention, pathfinders must carefully avoid compromise.

Electronic

1-19. These include radios and homing devices that work by radio signal. Enemy direction-finding equipment detects electronic signals.

Visual

1-20. These simple-to-use aids allow positive identification of assembly areas. The enemy can also see them. To ensure understanding, pathfinders must closely coordinate the use of visual assembly aids. (See TM 9-1370-206-10, FM 21-60, and STANAGs 3117 and 3281.) Visual assembly aids include the following:

Day

1-21. Visual assembly aids that can be used during the day, which include—

- Panels.
- Smoke.
- Armbands.

Night

1-22. Visual assembly aids that can be used during the night, which include—

- Lanterns.
- Flashlights.
- Light beacons.
- Strobe lights.
- Chem-lights.
- Pyrotechnics.

Infrared

1-23. Pathfinders can use infrared light sources as assembly aids, but if they do so, both the pathfinders and the pilots must use night vision devices (NVDs).

MISCELLANEOUS

1-24. Pathfinder equipment also includes—

- Vehicles.
- Binoculars.
- Night vision devices.
- Nonelectric demolition kits.
- Wind-measurement equipment.
- Parachutes.
- Equipment for detecting CBRN.
- Thermal sights.

COMMUNICATIONS SECURITY

1-25. Pathfinders and terminal guidance personnel must know about any hostile data collection and exploitation activities. Such activities seek to disrupt, deceive, harass, or otherwise interfere with the command and control of pathfinder operations.

ENEMY INTERCEPTION

1-26. The enemy can intercept, analyze, determine the direction of, and exploit electromagnetic energy radiating from any signal equipment such as radios, radar, and more. He uses this intelligence for fire and maneuver and for electronic countermeasures.

1-27. The enemy may collect pathfinder emissions data for immediate or later use. He may use jamming or deception, or he may continue to monitor and analyze the data for later use.

1-28. Time-distance factors limit the enemy's ability to exploit signal intelligence in support of his ground operations. He may use a reaction force, or he may find the source of the signal using direction finding (DF) equipment. If he uses DF equipment, he can also use electronic countermeasures (ECM) to jam and deceive the pathfinder's electronic aids.

PATHFINDER AWARENESS

1-29. Pathfinders must plan for the enemy's DF capabilities. Automated DF systems determine line bearings for each signal detected. The enemy continuously processes and compares line bearings and plots fixes for pathfinder signals. Depending on the size of the DF base and the number of DF systems available, the enemy may accurately locate a friendly position with little difficulty.

1-30. What the enemy does to gain signals intelligence (SIGINT) reveals his intent. In combating enemy DF systems, pathfinders consider the following:

- The high priority of aviation-related missions.
- The length of time the pathfinders remain on the air.
- The number of pathfinder transmitters.
- The distance of friendly forces from enemy DF systems, enemy fire and maneuver elements, and enemy collection and jamming resources.
- Friendly actions to mask pathfinder operations.

1-31. Strict signal security practices, to include electronic warfare (EW), greatly reduce the vulnerability of signal devices to enemy exploitation. (FM 24-18 provides more information on communications.)

TRAINING

1-32. Personnel qualify as pathfinders only by completing the pathfinder course at the US Army Infantry School, Fort Benning, Georgia.

GOALS

1-33. The pathfinder training program stresses—

- The development of individual proficiency in air traffic control procedures.
- That pathfinders learn and know the SOP of the aviation and ground units they support.
- Proficiency in slingload operations.
- Establishment of helicopter landing zones and drop zones.

- Drop zone support team leader (DZSTL) and drop zone safety officer (DZSO) operations.
- Expertise in all aspects of long- and short-range communication (both of which are conducted at unit level).

COMMANDER'S RESPONSIBILITIES

1-34. Major unit commanders who use pathfinders bear the responsibility for sustaining the pathfinders' training and proficiency. Pathfinder training works best when integrated with the training of supported aviation and ground units.

PATHFINDER'S RESPONSIBILITIES

1-35. The assigned, qualified, and trained pathfinder must ensure that any nonqualified Soldiers assigned to his unit team receive adequate pathfinder training before going on a mission.

THIS CHAPTER IMPLEMENTS STANAGs 2863, 3117, AND 3570.

Chapter 2
Plans, Organization, Conduct, and Threat

Pathfinders conduct many different missions. Several of these supplement the ground unit's operation.

SECTION I. PLANS

To ensure success of the ground mission, pathfinders plan their own missions in detail. The more time they have to make plans, the more detailed plans they can make.

WARNING ORDER

2-1. As soon as he receives word of a pending operation, the senior pathfinder issues a mission alert. He immediately follows with a warning order. He includes just enough information to allow the other pathfinders to start preparing for the operation. This includes—

- Roll call.
- Enemy and friendly situations (in brief).
- Mission.
- Chain of command and task organization.
- Individual uniform and equipment (if not discussed in the SOP).
- Required equipment.
- Work priorities (who does what, when, and where).
- Specific instructions.
- Attached personnel.
- Coordination times.

INITIAL PREPARATIONS

2-2. On receiving the alert or warning order, pathfinders inspect and, as needed, augment personnel and equipment. Pathfinders prepare equipment in the following order, from the most to the least important:

- Radios.
- Navigation aids (electronic and visual).
- Weapons.
- Essential individual equipment.
- Assembly aids.
- Other items as needed.

2-3. The pathfinder element leader (or his representative) and the air mission commander begin coordinating with the supported aviation unit(s), ground unit(s), or both.

2-4. As the pathfinders receive more information, they reorganize personnel and equipment to accomplish the mission better. If time permits, they rehearse. Rehearsals are the time to make sure the members on the pathfinder team are completely aware of their duties for that specific mission. They use available briefing aids, and they rehearse on terrain that most nearly resembles the AO.

Chapter 2

2-5. To succeed, an operation must have security. So, each person receives only the information he must have to complete each phase of the operation. For example, the commander isolates any Soldiers who know the details of the operation. The situation dictates the extent of security requirements.

COORDINATION

2-6. Ground and aviation commanders work together to coordinate and plan the details of operations for which they require pathfinder assistance.

2-7. In any type of operation (combat assault, reinforcement, artillery displacement, resupply, or evacuation), the pathfinders might have to recommend—

- Exact locations for DZs or LZs.
- A time schedule.
- Landing formations.
- Employment techniques.

2-8. Before selecting a DZ or LZ, the supported unit commander considers the factors of METT-TC (mission, enemy, terrain and weather, troops, time, and civil considerations). He also considers what the pathfinder and aviation commanders (or their representatives) suggest.

2-9. While preparing for an operation, air liaison officers (ALOs) and ground unit commanders (GUCs) coordinate with pathfinders to make an air movement table. Table 2-1 shows who coordinates what.

Sequence	ALO	GUC	Coordinate with Pathfinders
1	X	X	Operational location (coordinates).
2	X		Locations of the primary and alternate communications checkpoints (coordinates).
3	X		Location of release point. • Coordinates. • Whether manned or unmanned.
4	X	X	Time the site can begin operating.
5	X		Aircraft information. • Formation. • Time interval. • Time of flight. • Drop speed. • Drop altitude.
6	X		Pathfinder transportation and time available for briefing.
7	X		Pathfinder transportation station time.
8	X	X	Routes into the objective area.

Table 2-1. Air liaison officer's and ground unit commander's coordination of air movement table.

Plans, Organization, Conduct, and Threat

Sequence	ALO	GUC	Coordinate with Pathfinders
9	X	X	Call signs. • Aircraft. • Pathfinders. • Supported units. • Other friendly units.
10	X	X	Primary and alternate frequencies. • Aircraft. • Pathfinders. • Supported units. • Other friendly units. • Homing beacon.
11	X	X	Fire support. • Artillery. • Tactical air support.
12	X		Weather forecast. • Ceiling. • Visibility. • Temperatures (high and low).
13.	X	X	Logistical support, including locations of— • Medical aid station. • Prisoner collection point. • Fuel. • Ammunition. • Rations.
14	X	X	Alternate plans (ALO and GUC). • Evacuation plan. • Escape and evasion.
15	X	X	Friendly unit locations.
16	X	X	Authority to implement mission change.
17		X	Support personnel required.
18	X		No-land or no-drop signals (day and night).
19			Markings for obstacles (only on request of flight commander).
20	X		Marking of objective site for identification from the air.
21	X	X	Time allowed for approval.

Table 2-1. Air liaison officer's and ground unit commander's coordination of air movement table (continued).

2-10. The pathfinder needs this information because he helps coordinate planning. He uses the information to make final plans for the pathfinder phase of the operation. To make sure that he can safely and efficiently control all aircraft in and around the DZs or LZs, he must know all about the operation's air movement phase. Aviation and ground commanders inform pathfinders of all changes to plans and landing sites, and about any emergencies. The pathfinder coordinates all activities with every agency or unit involved, and then gives the information to all of the pathfinders involved in the operation.

2-11. When the pathfinder reaches the objective site, he may find it unsuitable. He evaluates the coordinated landing formation, heading, drop altitude, and the ground site itself. Then he coordinates with the ground commander, aviation commander(s), or both to see whether any of the original requirements have changed. Depending on the mission, enemy, terrain, troops, time, and civil considerations (METT-TC), the commander(s) determines what, if any, changes to make to accomplish the mission. If for any reason he cannot contact the GUC or aviation commander, the pathfinder can also coordinate for authority to change requirements.

2-12.   The pathfinder limits augmentation to that appropriate to the amount and type of transport. The reinforced pathfinder team remains under the command of the pathfinder leader, who is responsible for team functions. Based on the coordinated plans for the operation, the pathfinder requests augmentation in personnel and equipment. He considers—

- Mission.
- Use of personnel and equipment for security.
- Requirement to help assemble the supported units' personnel, supplies, and equipment.
- Need for assistance in removing obstacles.
- Assistance required to transport and operate navigation aids under pathfinder direction.

LINKUP WITH SUPPORTED UNIT

2-13.   Pathfinders join the supported unit early enough to allow final coordination between pathfinder, aviation, and lifted ground unit representatives. Pathfinders designated to accompany and provide continuous support to a ground unit can enter a DZ or LZ ahead of the assault echelon. After the initial phase of the air movement, they link up with the supported unit.

FINAL PREPARATIONS

2-14.   The pathfinder leader issues his operation order (OPORD). If he issues it before linking up with the supported unit, he issues any changes as a fragmentary order (FRAGO). The order describes any member's duties not covered in the unit SOP. Team members must have a chance to study maps, aerial photos, and terrain models of the area. The order provides details about the location and operation of proposed air delivery facilities, flight routes, flight formations, time schedules, release points (RPs), and communication checkpoints (CCPs).

2-15.   The pathfinder conducts a final, thorough check of equipment. The commander decides exactly how to transport the equipment into the objective area. Then the pathfinders prepare all of the equipment for rapid displacement.

2-16.   Just before departure, at a final weather and operational briefing, the pathfinders and supported units conduct final coordination.

SECTION II. ORGANIZATION FOR COMBAT

The pathfinder mission itself determines the specific requirements of the mission. In most operations, three to six Soldiers comprise the pathfinder element supporting a DZ or an LZ or continuously supporting an Infantry battalion. Seldom does a pathfinder section deploy as a unit from a single location. The pathfinder leader plans for his elements to operate widely separated and disconnected.

INSERTION

2-17.   Pathfinders can insert by a variety of air, sea, or land transportation modes.

HELICOPTER DELIVERY

2-18.   Helicopters can deliver more personnel and equipment in a better state of operational readiness than any other means. Even in marginal weather, helicopters allow more precise, flexible deliveries than parachutes do. Some terrain does not allow helicopter landings. In these cases, trained Soldiers rappel or fast rope from helicopters while the helicopters hover over the unsuitable landing areas. Personnel can insert or withdraw by ladders suspended from hovering helicopters, or extract using special patrol insertion-extraction system (SPIES) techniques. Helicopters can also—

- Rapidly shift or evacuate pathfinders.
- Carry nonparachutists to support pathfinders.
- Deliver when rain or low ceilings prohibit parachuting.
- Rapidly change insertion locations.

PARACHUTE DELIVERY

2-19. Parachute delivery by fixed-wing aircraft normally affords greater range and speed of movement than landing by helicopter. In a short-distance operation, helicopters can serve as the jump aircraft.

2-20. Depending on wind conditions, pathfinders should compute their desired parachute RPs before arriving over the DZ. For accuracy and security, the pathfinders jump at the lowest practical altitude. Aircraft SOPs prescribe jump altitudes and personnel procedures. Such procedures vary in accordance with (IAW) peacetime and wartime restrictions.

2-21. As highly trained parachutists, pathfinders can insert into unimproved and marginal DZs. They know how to control the canopy of a maneuverable parachute, and they know how to make emergency landings. They also know how to parachute into rough-terrain DZs. These skills give them some flexibility in planning parachute delivery.

> **CAUTION**
> During preparation for the operation, pathfinders carefully arrange and pad all essential items of operational equipment into appropriate containers. Carrying this equipment with them when they insert ensures they have it as soon as they land.

2-22. The best time to insert by parachute is during nonilluminated, nonsupported night operations that emphasize secrecy.

2-23. Because fixed-wing aircraft need large, secure, obstacle-free landing areas, they seldom deliver pathfinders.

WATER AND LAND DELIVERY

2-24. Delivering pathfinders by watercraft offers security only up to the point of debarkation from the craft. The pathfinders still must move from the landing point (debarkation) to their final destination. To do this, they infiltrate by land.

OVERLAND MOVEMENT

2-25. Because it limits small elements to short movements, infiltrating by land is the worst way to insert pathfinders.

2-26. A well-organized, stable, close-knit enemy defense in depth can prohibit land infiltration. When time allows, the pathfinders can increase infiltration security by combining overland infiltration with parachute or airland infiltration.

2-27. Pathfinders infiltrate overland when the following conditions exist:

- Limited visibility over difficult terrain.
- Overextended enemy lines.
- Fluid combat zone.
- Unsecured portions of enemy boundaries.

STAY-BEHIND OPERATION

2-28. In a stay-behind operation, pathfinder elements remain in the operational area while another friendly force withdraws from the area. The commander can use stay-behind operations for the following reasons:

- To lure enemy forces into a vulnerable position.
- To hold an area for reoccupation. If the commander plans to reoccupy a friendly area he knows the enemy could overrun, he leaves a stay-behind force to hold it. If he leaves the stay-behind force for this reason, then he must also plan an air assault to regain the area, if needed.

SECTION III. CONDUCT OF OPERATIONS

Pathfinders provide air traffic advisories and navigational aid for airplanes and helicopters. They also perform limited physical improvement and CBRN monitoring and surveying within DZs or LZs. Pathfinder availability, the tactical plan, the complexity of the operation, the terrain, and the air assault proficiency of the supported ground unit dictate pathfinder support. However, every air assault operation requires positive aircraft control. During an air-assault operation, pathfinders cross load before entering an LZ with the initial assault elements.

DAYLIGHT ASSAULT

2-29. In daylight operations, pathfinders insert into an LZ before the initial assault echelon only if the LZ requires extensive improvement or if planners expect unusual control problems. Either way, the pathfinders start setting up at once so they can provide air traffic control and other aid to all subsequent lifts of troops, supplies, and equipment. They may have a few minutes or several hours to do this before the other elements arrive. The tactical plan spells out exactly when and how the pathfinders will enter the area, whether they will go in alone or not, and what time the next element will arrive.

NIGHT ASSAULT

2-30. Security and operational requirements determine the method of delivering pathfinders at night. Pathfinders can move cross-country on foot, airdrop onto or near objective areas, airland in total blackout, or airland with minimum natural illumination. When they do insert this way, they sometimes arrive before the main body does. As soon as they arrive, the pathfinders reconnoiter the LZ, install visual and electronic aids, and establish air traffic control. Soldiers from the supported ground unit sometimes accompany the pathfinders. These additional Soldiers provide security and help clear obstacles. The on-site pathfinder element remains concealed and observes the objective. Pathfinders analyze the planned landing formation, heading, and assembly area. To avoid compromising the mission, no one on the DZ or LZ moves until an incoming aircraft reaches the CCP.

EXTRACTION

2-31. As the ground force at the LZ shrinks, vulnerability to attack increases. Therefore, the commander has pathfinders speed up the air assault extraction operations.

2-32. Planned artillery fires and air strikes as well as the need to maintain ground security to the last minute require that ground controllers control supporting aircraft throughout the extraction. This means they make sure aircraft land at specific points within the extraction site where ground security can cover them. This speeds the operation and helps ensure the safe withdrawal of personnel, equipment, and aircraft from the area.

2-33. Unless they land with the lifted unit, pathfinders must arrive at the extraction site in time to reconnoiter thoroughly and coordinate with the lifted unit.

2-34. During the planning stage, the pathfinder team leader designates near and far rally points for use in case the DZ or LZ becomes unusable. Pathfinders may have to fight their way to these rally points and reorganize. To increase the chance of survival, evasion, resistance, and escape, the team leader designates far rally points several kilometers from the DZ or LZ.

STAGING AREAS

2-35. In staging areas, in the absence of air traffic control (ATC) units, pathfinders can provide air traffic advisories. They may also act as liaison between the aviation and ground units and help the ground unit commander prepare and position troops, supplies, and equipment for air movement. When pathfinders must set up a temporary staging area to support an operation of short duration, they move into the area before the operation begins. This gives them enough time to reconnoiter, mark the site, coordinate, and set up positive ATC. Safe, efficient, and rapid movement of helicopters or airplanes requires positive ATC in staging areas. The need for positive ATC increases when the weather deteriorates, when the number of aircraft increases, or when changes in the situation or plans require it.

ARTILLERY DISPLACEMENT

2-36. Pathfinders should help safely and rapidly displace artillery, day or night. Coordinating with ground and aviation unit commanders and understanding their SOPs ensure pathfinders accurately and efficiently deliver equipment, personnel, and ammunition.

SUPPORT OF GROUND OPERATIONS

2-37. During ground operations that require sustained Army aviation support, pathfinders might continuously aid and control aircraft. The commander can attach pathfinders he has already attached to Infantry battalions to companies as well. The pathfinders provide support consistent with the availability of personnel and equipment. Continuous support improves operational efficiency and aviation safety during all types of air assault operations. However, aviation units with limited pathfinder resources cannot provide continuous support. In such cases, commanders usually employ pathfinders on a short-term, priority basis wherever the pathfinders can help accomplish major unit missions. In the absence of pathfinders, selected personnel in the ground units must receive enough training and preparation to allow them to provide minimum aid to supporting aircraft.

SUPPORT OF AIR FORCE

2-38. By joint US Army and USAF agreement, in the absence of USAF STTs, Army pathfinders can provide day or night control for USAF aircraft on airfields, DZs, and LZs. However, the pathfinders may need UHF and VHF communications equipment that is compatible with USAF aircraft.

MIXED OPERATIONS

2-39. Some situations could require the simultaneous control of mixed air traffic at the same location, such as resupply parachute drops into forward helicopter LZs. Fixed-wing airfields can expect helicopter traffic. Mixed air traffic often presents difficult control problems, so controllers must apply strict control measures. To ensure control, they designate, coordinate, and clearly identify landing, parking, loading, unloading, refueling, and rearming areas.

RADIO COMMUNICATIONS

2-40. For success, a pathfinder requires the essential element of communication by GTA voice radio. The pathfinders place this into operation first at a DZ or LZ, and they take it out of operation last.

2-41. Pathfinders must thoroughly understand radio procedures. This includes the phraseology unique to ATC (Chapter 3). They must send clear, concise, applicable, accurate, and correctly-timed communications. To achieve speed and clarity of transmission, pathfinders and aviators practice radio discipline. They transmit only necessary messages. Also, except in emergencies, they use pathfinder ATC frequencies only for ATC (Figure 2-1).

2-42. Because they exchange a lot of vital information, aircraft crews normally record the important parts of GTA messages. This helps them to make sure they understand and can follow instructions.

2-43. Pathfinders use electronic homing beacons, visual aids, and arm-and-hand signals to complement voice communications. Pilots and transported troops must know the purpose and meaning of the aids used and the techniques for using them (see STANAG 3570). (FM 21-60 discusses arm-and-hand signals and visual aids.)

2-44. When possible, to keep informed about changing situations that could influence their operations, pathfinders monitor supported unit command radio nets.

2-45. Pathfinders set up positive communications between pathfinder ATC facilities and collocated fire support elements. This ensures aircraft receive timely and accurate information about friendly fires.

2-46. Pathfinder operations require the constant use of radios. This gives the enemy force many chances to intercept, analyze, and exploit friendly transmissions. They try to gain intelligence and conduct electronic jamming and deception. Defeating enemy jamming or imitative deception methods falls mostly to the radio operator. He must know how to recognize and report this deliberate interference. To plan and execute a tactical mission, he must know how to—

- Defend against and beat ECM using electronic counter-countermeasures (ECCM).
- Secure transmissions.
- Communicate using other means.

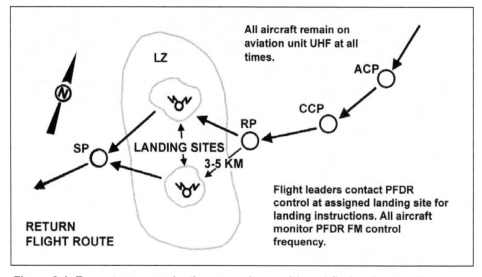

Figure 2-1. En route communication procedures with pathfinders in a landing zone.

TERMINAL GUIDANCE BY SUPPORTED UNITS

2-47. Terminal guidance refers to information and minimal guidance given to pilots by anyone in a ground unit other than a qualified pathfinder. Selected personnel normally furnish terminal guidance within the supported unit. To do so, they use both organic and improvised equipment.

2-48. When pathfinders accompany ground units, aviation unit SOP may direct that terminal guidance personnel augment pathfinder elements.

2-49. Terminal guidance personnel should know the following:

- The supporting aviation unit SOP.
- How to operate electronic and visual navigation aids to help aircraft find DZs or LZs.
- To provide essential information through GTA radio to guide and control Army aircraft.
- To reconnoiter and recommend suitable DZs or LZs.
- To determine, recommend, or perform ground-clearing pioneer work to prepare DZs or LZs.

SECTION IV. HIGH-THREAT ENVIRONMENT

The threat comes in many forms. To ensure mission success, aviation and ground commanders must consider all possibilities. They must consider a threat anything that could disrupt or delay the mission, or that could otherwise cause the mission to fail.

CONTROL AND NAVIGATION

2-50. Pathfinders have limited voice control of aircraft. Thus, the ground unit commander and the air mission commander must coordinate closely. Navigation presents special problems—aviators must fly low to avoid detection. In a high-threat environment, critical factors include time, distance, routes, and tactical instruments.

2-51. For example, two pathfinders with beacons could emplace along a route in advance of the initial flight. They provide pilots with air control points. If the pilot needs the beacon turned on due to navigational error, he can transmit a prearranged signal or code word.

2-52. Pathfinders might discover a threat, such as an antiaircraft weapon, along the primary route. If so, they can alert pilots by prearranged code word or signal to change to an alternate route.

TACTICAL INSTRUMENT FLIGHTS

2-53. Flying under instrument meteorological conditions poses special problems in a high-threat environment. This threat overrides the controlled instrument flight rules in the aviation-series manuals. It forces aircraft to fly at altitudes well below the minimums for normal instrument flight.

2-54. Weather variances can create a tactical emergency. If so, the commander might have to use aviation assets under instrument conditions and well below the altitudes specified by standard instrument flight rules. The commander will only send aircraft on a mission in a high-threat environment under these conditions when the situation meets the following criteria:

- The aviation and ground commanders cannot postpone the mission to wait for better weather.
- The pathfinders must conduct the mission in a high-threat environment.
- Low visibility en route precludes nap-of-the-earth flight.

2-55. Aviation and ground commanders employ tactical instrument flight whenever weather or time and distance considerations prevent mission completion in other flight modes. Therefore, they must often use tactical instrument flight during round-the-clock operations on the high-threat battlefield. Aircrews and pathfinders must rehearse tactical instrument flight until they achieve proficiency.

2-56. Pilots fly in one of two altitude modes.

MODE 1

2-57. When the air defense threat keeps flight altitudes below those established by AR 95-1 (for standard instrument flight), then pilots can fly at least 1,000 feet over mountainous terrain, and 500 feet over flat terrain.

MODE 2

2-58. When the threat limits flight altitudes to the least possible clearances, pilots can fly as low as 50 to 500 feet above the ground, regardless of terrain.

AIR ROUTES

2-59. Aircraft traffic management personnel (and pathfinders) can expect to move their equipment as often as every four hours, depending on the threat. Terrain, weather, and, most importantly, whether the enemy could intercept friendly aircraft from that location, determine when to move.

THREAT AND TERRAIN

2-60. In many instances, the threat and terrain prohibit a straight-line flight between the takeoff (liftoff) point and the destination (Figure 2-2). This applies to both Modes 1 and 2.

FLIGHT MONITORING AND LANDING ZONE APPROACH

2-61. Enemy presence keeps the pathfinders from using nondirectional beacons. However, for pilots to approach and land on the LZ visually, they need good visibility. Using radio homing signals for directional guidance presents a dubious option. Whether or not aircraft traffic-management personnel decide to use this electronic device, they should try to orient its signal away from the FEBA. This reduces the chance of detection.

Plans, Organization, Conduct, and Threat

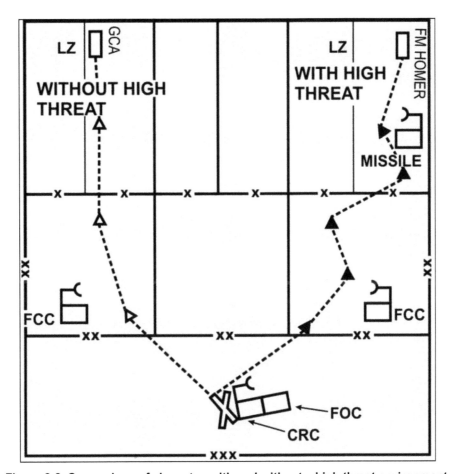

Figure 2-2. Comparison of air routes with and without a high-threat environment.

THIS CHAPTER IMPLEMENTS STANAGs 2863 and 3281.

Chapter 3
Air Traffic Control

This chapter discusses the pathfinder air traffic controller, not the regular air traffic controller. The latter has radar and other sophisticated tools to monitor weather and guide aircraft. The pathfinder has only his training, so he can only advise and inform the pilot. Based on what the pathfinder tells him and on his own observations, the pilot must then decide whether to land, take off, or drop equipment or personnel.

Unless clearly stated otherwise, "air traffic controller" refers to the *pathfinder* air traffic controller. This chapter also includes other terms peculiar to air traffic control (ATC) tasks.

SECTION I. PATHFINDER AIR TRAFFIC

The pathfinder air traffic controller uses radio or directional light signals to provide flight information, expedite traffic, and prevent collisions.

SAFETY

3-1. Pathfinders issue specific commands regulating vehicles, equipment, or personnel in the movement area. They help with search-and-rescue operations (STANAGs 2863 and 3281). They also promote the safe, efficient flow of air traffic by issuing clearances, instructions, and information.

3-2. Pathfinders survey all visible air traffic operating within and around the airspace of the LZ, DZ, or airfield. They also bear the responsibility for all aircraft, vehicles, and personnel in the movement area of the LZ, DZ, or airfield.

3-3. Pathfinders acting as air traffic controllers provide control service by observing or knowing of traffic and airfield conditions that might constitute a hazard. These include—

- Surface conditions.
- Parachutists within control zones.
- Vehicular traffic.
- Temporary obstructions on or near the LZ, DZ, or airfield.
- Other aircraft.
- Enemy or friendly activities.

3-4. Because of their communication capability and expertise, pathfinders might have to transmit medical evacuation (MEDEVAC) requests for the ground unit, the aviation unit, or even themselves. Therefore, they must be thoroughly familiar with request procedures and the capabilities of MEDEVAC aircraft.

VOICE CONTROL

3-5. To communicate vocally, pathfinders and pilots must speak clearly and listen to each other. A clear, decisive tone of voice indicates control of the situation. Pilots might mistrust instructions delivered

Chapter 3

in a vague or hesitant voice. To ensure that traffic flows safely and smoothly, the pathfinder must speak firmly and confidently, using standard words and phrases. Pathfinders use the phonetic alphabet to indicate single letters or initials, or to spell words, whenever similar sounds or difficulties in communication require them to do so.

3-6. Voice transmission offers a brief, concise, uniform flow of communication. The pathfinder controller must speak distinctly and pay special attention to numbers. When the accuracy of a message is doubtful, he repeats the complete message or essential parts. Radio operators use the following techniques to ensure clear understanding:

- Speak directly into the microphone.
- Speak in a normal, conversational tone.
- Vary your pitch—avoid speaking in a monotone.
- Speak at a comfortable speed—avoid speaking too slow or too fast.
- Keep your tone clear, professional, and firm. Avoid showing fear, indecision, anger, or other negative emotions in your tone of voice.
- Speak with confidence, especially in emergencies.

3-7. The pathfinder ATC must transmit messages only as necessary for control or to help ensure safety. Specific procedures and control techniques vary, but the following rules apply regardless of the techniques used:

- The pathfinder issues instructions and information about all known traffic conditions.
- The pilot uses at lease one component of a standard traffic pattern (final approach), consistent with the pathfinder's instructions.
- The pilot has the final authority about whether to accept clearances issued by a controller.

FORMATS

3-8. A pathfinder controller uses the following formats and sequences for ground-to-air radio communication:

- To initially call up an aircraft, he--
  - Identifies the aircraft he wishes to call.
  - Says, "THIS IS."
  - Identifies the calling unit.
  - Identifies the type of message to follow (when this will help the pilot).
  - Says, "OVER."

  Example: TANGO TWO SIERRA TWO SIX (T2S26), THIS IS CHARLIE THREE DELTA THREE SIX (C3D36) (short pause), OVER.

- To reply to an aircraft's initial call-up, he--
  - Identifies the aircraft initiating the call-up.
  - Says, "THIS IS."
  - Identifies the pathfinder control unit.
  - Says, "OVER." After establishing communications with an aircraft, shortens the transmission by using only the last three numbers (or letters) of each party's (his and the aircraft's) identification.

  Example: SIERRA TWO SIX, THIS IS DELTA THREE SIX, OVER.

3-9. The controller always starts a clearance (instruction) intended for a specific aircraft by identifying that aircraft. If he thinks that using the shortened identification could cause or is causing confusion, he can go back to using the full identification.

Example: SIERRA TWO SIX, WIND CALM, CLEAR TO LAND, OVER.

3-10. The controller can omit "THIS IS" from the reply.

Example: SIERRA TWO SIX, DELTA THREE SIX, OVER.

3-11. The controller can omit the facility identification.

Example: SIERRA TWO SIX, TURN TO HEADING ZERO FOUR FIVE, OVER.

3-12. Right after call-up, without waiting for the aircraft to reply, the controller can send a short message that he expects the aircraft to receive.

Example: SIERRA TWO SIX, EXTEND DOWNWIND, OVER.

3-13. If the message obviously requires a reply, he can omit "OVER."

Example: SIERRA TWO SIX, WHAT IS YOUR LOCATION?

3-14. To distinguish between similar aircraft identifications, he might emphasize appropriate numbers, letters, or words. The controller never transmits to an aircraft during the final approach, touchdown, landing roll (touchdown), takeoff (liftoff), initial climb, or turnaway from the field. At these times, the pilot must concentrate on flying the aircraft. However, he transmits at once any condition or information that could affect the safety of the aircraft. Under no circumstances does the controller withhold from the pilot of an approaching aircraft any information about hazardous runways, fields, weather, or traffic conditions.

NUMBERS

3-15. A pathfinder controller transmits numbers by units or digits (Table 3-1).

To Transmit	Say
CEILING HEIGHTS and FLIGHT ALTITUDES	"CEILING FIVE HUNDRED" (one unit) or "CEILING FIVE-ZERO-ZERO" (digits for emphasis).
	"ALTITUDE ONE THOUSAND THREE HUNDRED" (two units) or "ALTITUDE ONE-THREE-ZERO-ZERO" (in digits).
TIME	Use the word TIME followed by the number. For example, "0115 HOURS TIME, ZERO-ONE-ONE-FIVE" or "1315 HOURS TIME, ONE-THREE-ONE-FIVE."
ELEVATION NUMBERS	Use the words FIELD ELEVATION and the number. For example, for a 17-foot elevation, say, "FIELD ELEVATION SEVENTEEN." For a 50-foot elevation, say, "FIELD ELEVATION FIFTY."
WIND SPEED	Use the word WIND followed by compass direction and velocity (knots). For example, "WIND TWO-SEVEN-ZERO AT FIVE."
HEADING	Use the word HEADING followed by compass numbers (degrees); omit the word DEGREES. For example, "HEADING ONE TWO ZERO," "HEADING ZERO-ZERO-FIVE," or "HEADING THREE-SIX-ZERO." (The latter indicates a North [direction] heading.)

Table 3-1. Numbers transmitted by units or digits.

Chapter 3

PHRASES AND TERMS

3-16. A pathfinder controller uses particular phrases (Table 3-2) and terms (Table 3-3) to control and communicate with aircraft. He must know these phrases and how to use them.

Intent	Example
Issue takeoff, liftoff, or departure clearance when delay is undesirable.	SIERRA TWO SIX, CLEARED FOR IMMEDIATE TAKEOFF (or DEPARTURE), OVER.
Issue takeoff (liftoff) clearance when aircraft is delaying on the runway.	SIERRA TWO SIX, TAKE OFF (or DEPART) IMMEDIATELY OR TAXI OFF THE RUNWAY, OVER.
Authorize a requested straight-in approach after issuing landing instructions.	SIERRA TWO SIX, STRAIGHT-IN APPROACH (to landing strip or LZ) APPROVED, OVER.
Authorize a right-hand traffic pattern.	SIERRA TWO SIX, RIGHT TRAFFIC APPROVED, OVER.
Issue the landing sequence.	SIERRA TWO SIX, YOU ARE NUMBER THREE TO LAND; FOLLOW THREE EIGHT FIVE (aircraft identification number) ON DOWNWIND, OVER.
Instruct pilot to extend downwind leg to obtain necessary aircraft separation.	SIERRA TWO SIX, EXTEND DOWNWIND FOR TRAFFIC SPACING, OVER.
Advise pilot of information not included in landing instructions, but important to aircraft safety.	SIERRA TWO SIX, BE ADVISED WE ARE RECEIVING AUTOMATIC FIRE FROM THE EAST, OVER.
Try to establish communication with and learn the identification of an aircraft in the area.	UNIFORM HOTEL ONE, TWO MILES WEST OF BLUE STRIP, STATE CALL SIGN, OVER.
Instruct pilot to circle the LZ or landing strip.	SIERRA TWO SIX, MAINTAIN LEFT (RIGHT) CLOSED TRAFFIC, OVER.
Issue clearance to land.	SIERRA TWO SIX, CLEAR TO LAND, OVER.
Instruct a pilot on his final landing approach that his clearance to land has been cancelled.	SIERRA TWO SIX, CONDUCT GO-AROUND, OVER.
Inform pilot to continue his approach to the landing area.	SIERRA TWO SIX, CONTINUE APPROACH, OVER.
Inform pilot of observed aircraft condition upon request or when necessary.	SIERRA TWO SIX, LANDING GEAR APPEARS DOWN AND IN PLACE, OVER.
Describe vehicles, equipment, or personnel in the movement area in a way that will help pilots see or recognize them.	SIERRA TWO SIX, AIRCRAFT TO LEFT OF RUNWAY, OVER. SIERRA TWO SIX, VEHICLES ON TAXIWAY, OVER.
Describe military traffic as appropriate.	SIERRA TWO SIX, BE ADVISED HELICOPTER ON DEPARTURE END, OVER. SIERRA TWO SIX, BE ADVISED, CHARLIE HOTEL FOUR SEVEN (CH-47) ON RIGHT SIDE OF RUNWAY, OVER.
Describe the relative positions of traffic using the clock direction-and-distance method.	SIERRA TWO SIX, UNIFORM SIX, YOUR THREE O'CLOCK, FIVE HUNDRED METERS, OVER.

Table 3-2. Phrases.

Term	Meaning
ABORT	Do not complete landing or takeoff (liftoff).
ACKNOWLEDGE	Did you receive and understand the message?
AFFIRMATIVE	Yes.
BE ADVISED	Indicates additional information is forthcoming, such as an unusual condition or hazard to flight.
BREAK	That is the end of my transmission to you. The following message is for another aircraft. OR, that is the end of this part of the message. The next portion follows.
CONDUCT GO-AROUND	Do not land. Circle the landing area, and begin another approach.
CORRECTION	I gave you some incorrect information. The correct information follows.
EXECUTE	Drop personnel or equipment.
FORM YOUR OWN APPROACH.	You might enter the traffic pattern at your discretion. (Most suitable for aircraft with a slingload or for aircraft flights.)
GO AHEAD	Proceed with your message.
I SAY AGAIN	I am about to repeat my previous message.
LAST CALLING STATION	I do not know the identity of the station trying to establish communication.
MAYDAY	This is an emergency—clear the airways.
NEGATIVE	No.
NO DROP	Do not drop personnel or equipment.
OUT	That is the end of my transmission; you need not respond.
OVER	That is the end of my transmission; please respond.
READ BACK	Repeat message.
REPORT	Contact the control facility when you reach the location (or distance from the control station) that I am about to designate.
ROGER	I received and understand your transmission.
SAY AGAIN	Repeat your message.
STAND BY	Pause for a few seconds. OR, prepare to drop personnel or equipment.
STATE CALL SIGN	Identify your aircraft.
STATE INTENTIONS	Tell me your plans.
STATE LOCATION	Tell me your exact location.
UNABLE TO APPROVE	I must refuse your request.
VERIFY	Check with the originator.
WILCO	I understand and will comply.
WORDS TWICE	Communication is difficult; transmit each phrase twice.
YOU ARE UNREADABLE (BROKEN OR GARBLED)	I do not understand the transmission.

Table 3-3. Terms.

Chapter 3

SECTION II. LANDINGS

The safe landing of aircraft requires control of the airspace and grounds around the site. Managing air traffic involves using traffic patterns and maintaining separation of aircraft.

TRAFFIC PATTERNS

3-17. The pathfinder uses a traffic pattern to help manage airspace over his location, that is, in and around a landing site, airfield, LZ, or DZ (Figure 3-1). A traffic pattern normally extends out 1 statute mile from the final approach of the landing area in all directions, depending on the type of aircraft or size of the facility.

3-18. In a normal (left) traffic pattern, the aircraft makes only left turns. The pilot keeps the airfield, landing site, LZ, or DZ to his left. In a right traffic pattern, the aircraft makes all right turns. The pilot keeps everything to his right.

3-19. The controller uses traffic patterns to manage aircraft separation around a no-threat landing site. Rotary-wing aircraft can enter the pattern from any direction as long as they meet safety requirements. The height of the obstacles or aircraft requirements determines the altitude, which the controller can adjust as needed.

3-20. While in the traffic pattern, the aircraft flies between 1,000 and 1,200 feet (known as *civil altitude*), though this might vary depending on the nature and requirements of the mission.

METHODS OF ENTRY

3-21. An aircraft might enter the traffic pattern from any point and direction within the area around the landing strip or zone, consistent with safety requirements.

3-22. Fixed wing aircraft normally enter the traffic pattern in the first one-third of the closest leg, at a 45-degree angle or less. Rotary wing aircraft might enter at any point in a leg, normally at a 45-degree angle or less.

3-23. A straight-in approach might work best if it falls within safety requirements. On a straight-in approach, the aircraft must remain within 30 degrees to either side of the land heading.

3-24. When circling to approach from any direction, the aircraft overflies the landing site then circles to the direction of landing. Normally, the pathfinder advises the pilot which direction to circle. This saves time and helps the aircraft avoid other traffic in the same airspace. The pathfinder most often encounters this type approach.

3-25. Departing aircraft normally leave on the same heading as landing aircraft, or as close to the same heading as they can, up to 45 degrees left or right of the land heading, depending on the wind direction. When the destination does not fall in the same direction as the departure, the aircraft might fly a portion of the traffic pattern. The pathfinder ensures that arriving and departing traffic do not conflict.

3-26. The controller commands GO-AROUND if for some reason the aircraft does not land after the pilot reaches the final approach leg of the traffic pattern.

3-27. The pathfinder uses closed traffic in either of two cases:

- When an aircraft fails to land on the first approach.
- During DZ operations, when an aircraft must make more than one pass over the DZ.

Air Traffic Control

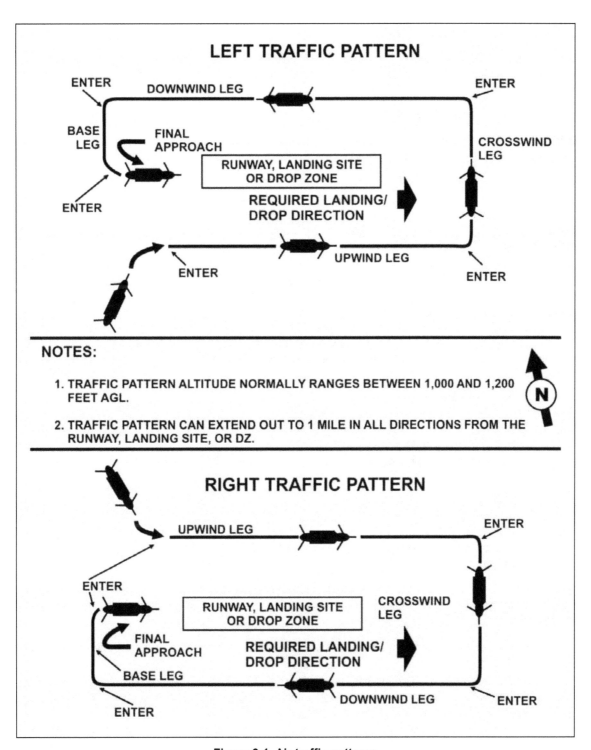

Figure 3-1. Air traffic patterns.

Chapter 3

TRAFFIC PATTERN LEGS

3-28. The traffic pattern has five possible legs. The pathfinder does not use them all at once. The pilot must at least fly the final approach leg, regardless of the type of approach (Table 3-4).

Leg	Flight Course	Direction
UPWIND	Parallel to land heading	Landing direction
CROSSWIND	Right angle to land heading	Landing direction
DOWNWIND	Parallel to land heading	Direction opposite of landing direction
BASE	Right angle to landing runway	Extends from downwind leg to intersection of runway centerline (extended)
FINAL (APPROACH)	Along runway centerline	Landing direction; extends from base leg down to the runway

Table 3-4. Traffic pattern legs.

ADVISORY SERVICE

3-29. The pathfinder controller issues advisories for the safe operation of aircraft in his area of responsibility. He might include such information as the temporary or permanent conditions on the landing field.

3-30. Temporary conditions can include—

- Construction work on or immediately next to the movement area.
- Rough portions of the movement area.
- Degraded runway braking conditions due to ice, snow, mud, slush, or water.
- Parked aircraft on the movement area.

3-31. Permanent conditions can include—

- Excessive slope.
- Obstacles 18 inches high, wide, or deep on the HLZ.
- Elevation.

3-32. No two landing areas and situations are the same. Each location presents its own problems with respect to environmental conditions, peculiar weather, preferred landing directions, and so forth. For example—

- The final approach to a particular runway or HLZ might require a higher-than-normal glide slope angle.
- Under certain wind conditions, unusual terrain features near the airfield or HLZ can cause turbulence. This could threaten nearby aircraft. Helicopters also can create turbulence that could result in harm to light aircraft.
- Prohibited areas, trees, mountains, or other obstacles and hazards directly in line with the end of the runway or around the HLZ can require the pilot to turn or maneuver the aircraft abruptly right after takeoff (liftoff).
- If friendly forces fire either artillery or mortars within the control zone, the pathfinder might need to tell the pilot the origin, range, direction, and maximum ordinate of the firing. He also tells the pilot about any air strikes in the control zone, especially those by high-performance aircraft. He also gives the pilot any available information about the enemy situation.

SPACING TECHNIQUES

3-33. Spacing provides more separation between aircraft in the traffic pattern. This relieves traffic congestion. The pathfinder controller uses two methods to obtain the required separation: the 360-degree turnout and the traffic pattern extension.

360-Degree Turnout

3-34. Except on the final approach, the pathfinder can issue instructions for the 360-degree turnout (a two-minute maneuver) at any point in the traffic pattern. When a pilot receives instructions to begin a 360-degree turnout, he turns away from the center of the landing site, makes a wide circle, and reenters the traffic pattern at about the same point where he left it (Figure 3-2 and Table 3-5). If the first turnout does not give him enough room, he might have to make more turnouts.

Pathfinder:	DELTA THREE SIX, BEGIN THREE SIX ZERO DEGREE TURNOUT FOR SPACING, AND REPORT REENTRY.
Pilot:	ROGER. (After completing turnout) LIMA ONE SIX, DELTA THREE SIX HAS REENTERED.
Pathfinder:	DELTA THREE SIX, ROGER, REPORT BASE.
Pilot:	ROGER.

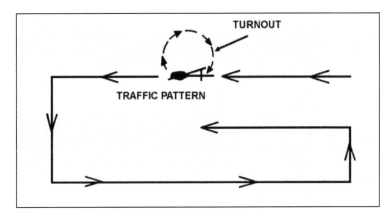

Figure 3-2. 360-degree turnout.

Situation	Reporting Point
AIRCRAFT IN TRAFFIC	BASE LEG OF TRAFFIC PATTERN
STRAIGHT-IN APPROACH	FINAL
AIRCRAFT AUTHORIZED TO FORM OWN APPROACH	FINAL

Table 3-5. A 360-degree turnout.

Chapter 3

THREE LEGS OF TRAFFIC PATTERN

3-35. The pathfinder can only extend the traffic pattern on three legs: upwind, crosswind, and downwind (Figure 3-3). He can only extend one leg at a time. He cannot extend the base leg or the final approach, because they run back into the traffic pattern itself. When giving instructions to extend the traffic pattern, the pathfinder includes the length of the extension. The extension normally measures twice the original length of that leg (1 statute mile). The pathfinder takes care to ensure that he does not extend the leg so far that he loses visual contact with the aircraft.

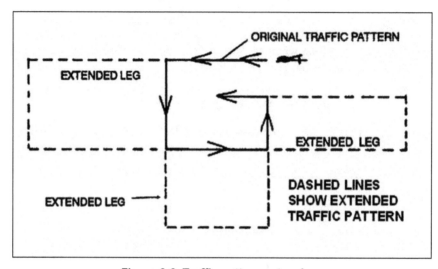

Figure 3-3. Traffic pattern extension.

FINAL LANDING INSTRUCTIONS

3-36. Final landing instructions consist of a current wind reading (direction and velocity) and clearance to land. The pathfinder includes any change to the situation in the final landing instructions, which he issues as soon as the pilot reports from the designated point. As a rule, once the pathfinder clears an aircraft to land, he can only rescind that clearance in extreme situations.

3-37. The best reporting points vary with the situation.

3-38. Aircraft flying in formation, except those flying in trail, and aircraft with a slingload, usually form their own approach.

3-39. If two or more missions arrive at the same time, the controller gives first landing priority to in-flight emergencies, followed by MEDEVAC aircraft. His next priority is coded aircraft, multiple aircraft in formation, and aircraft with slingloads. His last priority is single aircraft.

TAXIING AIRCRAFT

3-40. When issuing taxiing instructions, the pathfinder includes a route for the aircraft to follow in the movement area. He also includes instructions for the pilot to hold the aircraft at a specific point, if needed. The pilot moves the aircraft in the loading, maintenance, dispersal, or parking areas without the pathfinder's help but sometimes aided by signalmen. The controller holds a taxiing aircraft short of an active runway by at least two airplane lengths. This ensures that landing aircraft have sufficient clearance. The controller issues concise, easy-to-understand information.

Example: SIERRA TWO SIX, TURN RIGHT AT SIGNALMAN.
TANGO THREE SIX, TURN LEFT AT END OF RUNWAY, OVER.

MINIMUM AIRCRAFT SEPARATION REQUIREMENTS

3-41.   During normal operations, pathfinders ensure pilots follow minimum separation criteria. Combat situations might dictate less separation (Figure 3-4).

ARRIVING AIRCRAFT

3-42.   The preceding aircraft (1) taxis off the landing strip before the arriving aircraft (2) crosses the approach end on its final glide (A, Figure 3-4).

DEPARTING AIRCRAFT

3-43.   The preceding aircraft either crosses (1) the opposite end of the runway or turns away from the projected path of the departing aircraft (2) before the latter begins its takeoff run (B, Figure 3-4).

DEPARTING AND ARRIVING AIRCRAFT

3-44.   The departing aircraft (1) crosses the opposite end of the runway before the arriving aircraft (2) crosses the approach end on its final glide path (C, Figure 3-4).

DEPARTING, PRECEDING, AND ARRIVING AIRCRAFT

3-45.   The preceding aircraft (1) and the arriving aircraft (2) both taxi off the runway before the departing aircraft (3) begins the takeoff run (D, Figure 3-4).

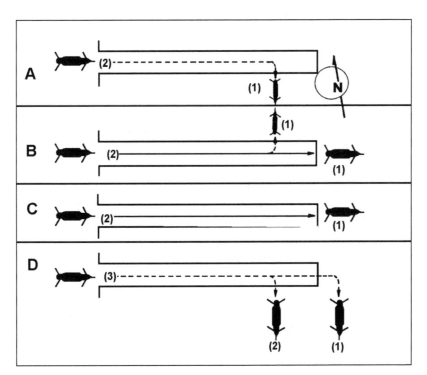

Figure 3-4. Minimum separation requirements.

Chapter 3

> **DANGER**
> Arriving and departing aircraft with slingloaded cargo must *never* fly over personnel, equipment, or other aircraft.

SECTION III. GROUND-TO-AIR COMMUNICATIONS

Air traffic control requires a rapid and efficient means of communication between aircraft and ground stations. Two-way radio offers the most efficient means because it allows clear and rapid exchange of information. Not all aircraft have radios that work. A system of visual signals serves as a backup or standby means of communication when the control center or aircraft radio does not work, or if the aircraft does not have the control frequency (Table 3-6). Pathfinders might also use colored smoke signals but must coordinate with the aviation unit so that the pilots will know what each color means.

ELECTRONIC WARFARE ENVIRONMENT

3-46. The pathfinder should expect an active EW environment for all operations. He should make sure he knows the proper ECCM. These include prowords that signal a switch to an alternate radio frequency, transmission authentication procedures, brevity codes, and required reports when he suspects enemy interference. The pathfinder uses proper communications procedures and signal operating instructions (SOI) during all operations.

3-47. To limit the possibility of compromise, the pathfinder reduces the electronic signature at the LZ or DZ. For this, he depends on thorough mission planning and coordination. He plans control procedures that enable him to execute the mission under radio listening silence. All pathfinder missions seek to achieve this goal.

3-48. Sometimes, the pathfinder has little time to plan the mission. At other times, tactical or meteorological conditions can affect the operation. In either case, the pathfinder might have to use GTA communications to resolve possible conflicts between friendly airspace users and to advise them of previously-unknown restrictive landing conditions. These conditions could include wind gusts, hazardous slopes, obstacles, soft landing surfaces, or a limited number of landing points. Training and close liaison with aviation aircrews enable the pathfinder to develop an understanding of what information pertains to the situation. This reduces transmission time.

3-49. The pathfinder manages any variation due to unknown influences just as he would manage any other exception to set procedure. The landing site is the variable most subject to change. Many conditions could require its relocation. For example, ground fog could cause a delay while the pathfinders move the site to a higher elevation.

3-50. Before they know whether a site will support sufficient landing points or an assembly area for the ground unit, the pathfinders must first secure the site, and then conduct air and ground reconnaissance and surveillance.

3-51. If the mission is to reinforce or resupply a ground unit in contact, a change in the tactical situation could render the proposed location unsuitable. If the pathfinders locate the proposed site near enemy activity, they will most likely have to move it sometime between planning and execution to ensure that it continues to meet mission requirements.

3-52. Maintaining radio silence within the LZ is important. Because of this, most air movements require the establishment of a CCP. This ensures a common point where the pathfinders and the aircraft can refer their relative positions and give each other time to adjust to other changes.

3-53. The GTA net is reserved for communications, but the pathfinder cannot assume that all transmissions originate from aircraft. The headquarters in charge of flight plans logs all arrivals. They will know if an aircraft fails to arrive at its destination on time. When this happens, they contact intermediate stop points to identify the last known location, and to aid in search-and-rescue operations.

Color And Type of Signal Lights	What This Means to an Aircraft on the Ground	What This Means to an Aircraft in Flight
Steady green	Cleared for takeoff (or liftoff)	Cleared to land
Flashing green	Cleared to taxi	Return for landing (followed by a steady green light at the proper time)
Steady red	Stop	Give way to other aircraft and continue circling
Flashing red	Taxi clear of landing area of runway in use	Airport unsafe—*do not land*
Flashing white	Return to starting point (on airfield)	NA
Alternating red and green (general warning signal)	Use extreme caution	Use extreme caution
Red pyrotechnic (red flare)	NA	Do not land for the time being, despite previous instructions.

Table 3-6. Light signals on or near a landing zone.

GROUND-TO-AIR TRANSMISSIONS

3-54. The pathfinder might encounter endless situations while using GTA. If he can master the following four most common ones, he can handle most situations:

SITUATION 1, KNOWN AIRCRAFT LOCATION

3-55. Known aircraft location is the simplest of the GTA transmissions.

Chapter 3

Initial Contact

3-56. The pilot radios transmissions at coordinated time and location. After establishing two-way communications, the controller can abbreviate call signs. With multiple flights, instructions issued by pathfinder GTA communications should identify the particular situation by including that station's call sign at the beginning of the transmission, for example--

Pilot:	*ALPHA ONE LIMA ONE SIX (A1L16), THIS IS ROMEO TWO BRAVO TWO SEVEN (R2B27), OVER.*
Pathfinder:	ROMEO TWO BRAVO TWO SEVEN, THIS IS ALPHA ONE LIMA ONE SIX, OVER.
Pilot:	*THIS IS BRAVO TWO SEVEN, CCP INBOUND, OVER.*
Pathfinder:	THIS IS LIMA ONE SIX, STATE TYPE, NUMBER, AND INTENTIONS, OVER.
Pilot:	*THIS IS BRAVO TWO SEVEN, FOUR UNIFORM HOTEL SIXTIES (UH-60s), TROOP DROP-OFF AND SLINGLOAD, FOR YOUR SITE, OVER.*
Pathfinder:	THIS IS LIMA ONE SIX, ROGER, HEADING THREE-TWO-FIVE (325), THREE THOUSAND (3,000) METERS. LAND THREE TWO FIVE, SIGNAL ON CALL, LAND ECHELON RIGHT, SLINGLOAD AIRCRAFT USE NUMBER FOUR LANDING POINT, CONTINUE APPROACH FOR VISUAL CONTACT, OVER.

Air Traffic Control Information

3-57. An example of what the air traffic controller might say follows:

Example: HEADING THREE TWO FIVE, (distance) THREE THOUSAND METERS, OVER. LAND THREE TWO FIVE, OVER.

Pertinent Information

3-58. The air traffic controller also gives any other pertinent information, for example--

Example: SIGNAL ON CALL (prepare to establish positive visual contact).

FOUR UNIFORM HOTEL SIXTIES (UH-60s) IN ECHELON RIGHT (advises pilot of the size of landing site).

SLINGLOAD POINT ON NUMBER FOUR TOUCHDOWN POINT (night only).

FIELD ELEVATION, FOUR TWO FIVE FEET (actual field elevation).

Advisory Information

3-59. See Table 3-7.

Type of Advisory	Information Included
FLIGHT	The enemy situation, if it presents a threat to the aircraft.
LANDING	Surface conditions on the landing site such as the presence of sand, mud, or blowing snow.
DEPARTURE	Obstacles in the path of aircraft leaving the site (obstacles above the obstacle departure lights).

Table 3-7. Information included in advisories.

Aircraft in Sight

3-60. The following shows what the pilot and pathfinder say when an aircraft is in sight of the runway:

Pathfinder: BRAVO TWO SEVEN, THIS IS LIMA ONE SIX, I AM AT YOUR TWELVE O'CLOCK, FIVE HUNDRED METERS, IDENTIFY SIGNAL, OVER.

Pilot: *THIS IS BRAVO TWO SEVEN, I IDENTIFY GREEN SMOKE, OVER.*

3-61. At night, during specialized activities such as external load drop-off or pickup, or when unsafe surface conditions require pathfinders to mark specific landing points, the flight leader must know all arrangements. This allows him to organize the flight for landing. Pathfinders identify the site by flashing a visible or infrared light source in a dot-dash sequence.

Pathfinder: THIS IS LIMA ONE SIX, VISUAL CONTACT (and, once the pilot identifies the site), WIND THREE TWO FIVE AT EIGHT, CLEAR TO LAND, OVER.

3-62. Once the pilot identifies the site, the pathfinder issues final landing instructions. If the controller already has other aircraft flying in a traffic pattern, he places the incoming aircraft into the traffic pattern at a safe and convenient location. Then, he instructs the pilot to report base. When the pilot reports base, the pathfinder issues final landing instructions. For special situations, instead of placing the aircraft in the traffic pattern, the controller might tell the pilot to circle left or right. Then the controller will issue final landing instructions.

Departure Instructions

3-63. If the departure heading differs from the land heading, the controller gives the departure heading as the first element of the departure instructions.

Pilot: *LIMA ONE SIX, THIS IS BRAVO TWO SEVEN, READY FOR DEPARTURE, OVER.*

Pathfinder: THIS IS LIMA ONE SIX, WIND THREE TWO FIVE AT EIGHT, CLEAR TO DEPART, STATE INTENTIONS, REPORT CLEAR OF LANDING ZONE, OVER.

Pilot: *THIS IS BRAVO TWO SEVEN, RIGHT BREAK, AFTER DEPARTURE, OVER.*

Pathfinder: THIS IS LIMA ONE SIX, ROGER, OVER.

Pilot: *THIS IS BRAVO TWO SEVEN, CLEAR TO THE WEST, OVER.*

Pathfinder: THIS IS ALPHA ONE LIMA ONE SIX, ROGER, OUT.

SITUATION 2, AIRCRAFT REPORTING FROM A CARDINAL DIRECTION AND DISTANCE

3-64. Often, units conduct mutually-supporting helicopter operations to increase the security of an LZ operation. For example, a team of observation and attack helicopters might screen the LZ

3-65. Because no aircraft plan to land there, and because the utility or lift aircraft know the LZ and screen team's location from communications over internal UHF or VHF radio nets, the screening helicopters need not contact the pathfinder. However, if they learn an aircraft does need to land at the LZ, the screening helicopter team responds differently to initial contact.

3-66. Due to a possible conflict with aircraft departing the landing site in the same direction, the pathfinder must track the inbound aircraft's course and advise mission aircraft of the unexpected arrival. To accurately track the aircraft and control the situation, the pathfinder uses a commonly known point in the direction of the aircraft. He can use a prominent terrain feature, a checkpoint, or an aerial control point previously established by the ground unit for maneuver control. This situation matches Situation 1 exactly, except that the controller does not give the aircraft's heading and distance.

SITUATION 3, AIRCRAFT WITH IN-FLIGHT EMERGENCY

3-67. An in-flight emergency occurs when an aircraft develops a mechanical problem that challenges the pilot's ability to maintain control. Because the pilot must focus on the problem with the aircraft, the pathfinder helps by moving other air traffic away from the one having the problem, which has first priority. If the emergency develops before initial contact, OPSEC requires a full information exchange, just like in a standard transmission. After the pilot declares the emergency, the situation continues as follows:

Pilot:	*ALPHA ONE LIMA ONE SIX (A1L16), THIS IS CHARLIE ZERO WHISKEY ZERO TWO (C0W02), IN-FLIGHT EMERGENCY (MAYDAY), OVER.*
Pathfinder:	THIS IS LIMA ONE SIX, WIND ZERO THREE FIVE AT SIX, CLEAR TO LAND, STATE INBOUND HEADING, OVER.
Pilot:	*THIS IS WHISKEY ZERO TWO, HEADING TWO SIX ZERO, OVER.*
Pathfinder:	ALL STATIONS, THIS IS ALPHA ONE LIMA ONE SIX, BE ADVISED, IN-FLIGHT EMERGENCY APPROACHING FROM THE EAST, REMAIN CLEAR OF LANDING SITE AND MAINTAIN RADIO SILENCE UNTIL EMERGENCY HAS BEEN TERMINATED - BREAK - WHISKEY ZERO TWO, CAN I BE OF FURTHER ASSISTANCE, OVER.
Pilot:	*THIS IS WHISKEY ZERO TWO, NEGATIVE, OVER.*
Pathfinder:	THIS IS LIMA ONE SIX, ROGER, OVER.

3-68. The controller tells the emergency aircraft of any aircraft that remain on the landing site.

Pathfinder:	WHISKEY ZERO TWO, BE ADVISED, TWO UNIFORM HOTEL ONES ON NORTH END OF SITE.

3-69.   Only the pilot who originally declared the emergency can terminate that same emergency. Once the pilot does so, the pathfinder transmits a net call to inform all stations that normal operations can continue.

> Pathfinder: ALL STATIONS, THIS IS ALPHA ONE LIMA ONE SIX, EMERGENCY HAS TERMINATED, I CAN ACCEPT TRAFFIC, OVER.

3-70.   Departure instructions are the same as those given for Situation 1.

SITUATION 4, DISORIENTED AIRCRAFT

3-71.   During limited visibility, adverse weather, in-flight emergencies or, when he has no map, a pilot might not know the location of the LZ. Also, he might not see any easily-identifiable land point.

3-72.   In such cases, the pathfinder can help the pilot by directing him either to a known location or to the LZ. At terrain flight altitudes, and in some environments, the pilot might experience disorientation of as little as 200 meters. The pathfinder might hear but not see the aircraft. Pilots who have FM homing equipment onboard might use that to orient themselves during the initial contact, without having to ask for a long or short count. Because it requires the ground station to increase transmissions, FM homing risks loss of signal security (SIGSEC).

3-73.   In this example, an aircraft at the CCP cannot establish voice communication with the pathfinder due to low altitude or radio interference. Knowing the LZ location, but unsure of the exact location of the landing site, the pilot continues his flight closer to the center of the zone.

> Pilot: *ALPHA ONE LIMA ONE SIX (A1L16), THIS IS CHARLIE TWO ECHO THREE FOUR (C2E34), OVER.*
>
> Pathfinder: CHARLIE TWO ECHO THREE FOUR, THIS IS ALPHA ONE LIMA ONE SIX, OVER.
>
> Pilot: *THIS IS ECHO THREE FOUR, FOUR UNIFORM HOTEL ONES (UH-1s) ARE INBOUND FOR LANDING, REQUEST NAVIGATIONAL ASSISTANCE, OVER.*
>
> Pathfinder: THIS IS LIMA ONE SIX, DO YOU HAVE FM HOMING CAPABILITY?
>
> Pilot: *THIS IS ECHO THREE FOUR, AFFIRMATIVE, OVER.*
>
> Pathfinder: THIS IS LIMA ONE SIX, SHORT COUNT FOLLOWS: 1-2-3-4-5-5-4-3-2-1. END SHORT COUNT, STATE INBOUND HEADING, OVER.
>
> Pilot: *THIS IS ECHO THREE FOUR, SAY AGAIN, OVER.*
>
> Pathfinder: THIS IS LIMA ONE SIX, ROGER, ORBIT PRESENT LOCATION, DESCRIBE PROMINENT TERRAIN FEATURES, STATE LAST KNOWN LOCATION, HEADING, AND DISTANCE FLOWN, OVER.
>
> Pilot: *THIS IS ECHO THREE FOUR, CCP HEADING THREE SIX ZERO, TWO THOUSAND METERS, I SEE A THREE-ACRE POND WITH DAM ON THE SOUTH, ORIENTED EAST-WEST, OVER.*
>
> Pathfinder: (Plots the course correction and continues with the standard transmission.) THIS IS LIMA ONE SIX, HEADING TWO NINE ZERO, EIGHT HUNDRED METERS, (gives advisories if any), OVER.

3-74.   The standard ATC information continues as in Situation 1 and ends with—

> Pathfinder: DESCRIBE PROMINENT TERRAIN FEATURES EN ROUTE, OVER.

THIS CHAPTER IMPLEMENTS QSTAG 585 AND STANAGs 3281 AND 3619.

Chapter 4
Helicopter Landing Zones

Helicopter landing zones contain one or more helicopter landing sites. Each landing site has a control center and, in most cases, a manned or unmanned release point (STANAG 3619). Each landing site might have one or more specific landing points for individual aircraft to touch down.

SECTION I. SELECTION OF LANDING SITES

The ground unit commander coordinates with the supporting aviation unit to select helicopter landing zones that can support the ground tactical plan.

CONSIDERATIONS

4-1. Tactical considerations are those that pertain to the actual mission of the supported ground unit. These considerations are the responsibility of the ground unit commander and staff. The pathfinder must understand the ground tactical plan to best support the ground unit and facilitate mission accomplishment.

TACTICAL CONSIDERATIONS

4-2. These include—
- An estimate of the situation based on METT-TC.
- The location of the objective in relation to the tentative HLZ.
- The size and type of unit being supported.

TECHNICAL CONSIDERATIONS

4-3. These pertain to the technical aspect of the operation of a day or night HLZ. These are the responsibility of the pathfinder. The minimum landing space requirements and minimum distance between helicopters on the ground depend on many factors. If the aviation unit SOP fails to spell out these requirements, the aviation unit commander works with the pathfinder leader. The final decision about minimum landing requirements rests with the aviation unit commander. In selecting helicopter-landing sites from maps, aerial photographs, and actual ground or aerial reconnaissance, the pathfinder considers the following factors (Figure 4-1, page 4-2):

NUMBER AND TYPE(S) OF HELICOPTERS

4-4. To land a large number of helicopters at the same time, the commander can provide another landing site(s) nearby or he can have the helicopters land at the same site, but in successive lifts. A larger site might also be required for cargo aircraft with external loads as compared to several utility aircraft. The required size of the site is determined by the size and number of aircraft that will be required to land at a given time. A landing point, or touchdown point (TDP), is the specific point on the ground for a specific aircraft. The size of the landing point is determined by the aviation unit commander and is based on—
- Pilot or unit proficiency.
- Size and type of aircraft.
- Atmospheric conditions.

- Visibility (day/night).
- Type of mission (insertion, extraction, resupply, slingload drop-off, forward area arming and refuel point [FAARP], and so forth).

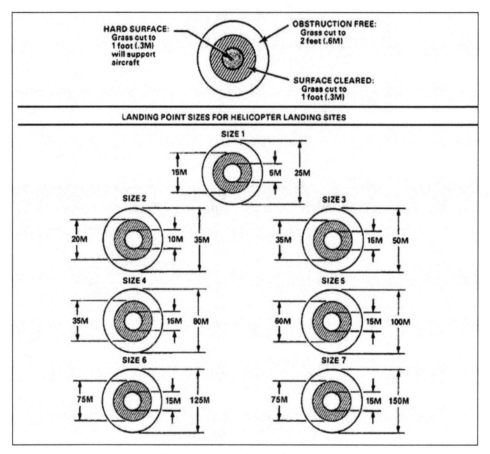

Figure 4-1. Landing point sizes.

4-5.   Standard landing point uses and types of aircraft are listed in Table 4-1. Standard landing point sizes are listed in Table 4-1.

4-6.   In a landing site, pathfinders measure the minimum distances between landing points, from center to center. When aircraft sizes vary, pathfinders separate landing points by the most generous measure, allowing 100 meters for size 5; 125 meters for size 6; 150 meters for size 7, measured center to center on the landing points.

4-7.   The aviation unit commander, during coordination, might have authorized pathfinders to reduce the TDP by one size. Reducing TDP is a last-resort means to make an HLZ suitable to accomplish the mission. TDP sizes are reduced in a deliberate manner after careful consideration of all factors. If mixed aircraft types will use the TDP, the size should be reduced for utility (lighter) aircraft before slingload aircraft.

Landing Point	Minimum Diameter Of Landing Point	Type Of Helicopter/Operation
Size 1	80 ft (25 m)	Light observation helicopters such as the OH-6 and OH-58D.
Size 2	125 ft (35 m)	Light utility and attack helicopters such as the UH-1H, H-65, and AH-1W.
Size 3	160 ft (50 m)	Medium utility and attack helicopters such as the UH-60, H-2, and AH-64.
Size 4	265 ft (80 m)	Cargo helicopters such as the CH-47, H-3 and CH-53, or with prior coordination
Size 5	328 ft (100 m)	Slingload helicopters and aircraft of an unknown origin.
Size 6	410 ft (125 m)	Slingload long-line operations.
Size 7	492 ft (1,505 m)	Slingload operations with night vision goggles (NVG).

Table 4-1. Landing point uses.

LANDING FORMATIONS

4-8. Helicopter pilots should try to match the landing formation to the flight formation. Pilots should have to modify their formations no more than necessary to accommodate the restrictions of a landing site (Figure 4-2, page 4-4), but it might be necessary to land in a restrictive area. TDPs are established in the same order as indicated in the formation.

SURFACE CONDITIONS

4-9. Pathfinders choose landing sites that have firm surfaces; are free of dust, sand, and debris that might create problems when disturbed by rotor wash; and are cleared of obstacles.

Choose a Hard Surface

4-10. Pathfinders choose a landing point with a hard surface to support the weight of the aircraft to prevent helicopters from becoming mired, creating excessive dust, or blowing snow. The surface of the landing point must allow a fully-loaded helicopter to land, restart, and leave again, all without sinking into the ground. If the surface does not meet these conditions, an advisory must be given and the aircraft must either terminate at a hover or touch down while under power. If the mission is one that requires the aircraft to firmly land, such as an FAARP or unload an internal load, a new site must be selected.

Clear to Ground Level

4-11. Pathfinders must clear the entire landing point of any loose material that the rotors could blow up. The term is "cleared to ground level." Unless a fire risk exists, they need not clear grass less than 0.3 meter (1 foot) high, as long as the field is level. They can cut down on dust by wetting down dry dirt. They can reduce snow to reveal hazards, and then pack it down firm, which will also reduce the amount blowing around. Rotor wash stirs up any loose dirt, sand (brownout), or snow (whiteout). This can obscure the ground and other aircraft, especially at night. If a site must be used with obscuring conditions, pathfinders note these conditions and provide advisories and radio guidance as required. Pathfinders also remove any debris from landing points because airborne debris could damage the rotor blades or turbine engine(s).

Chapter 4

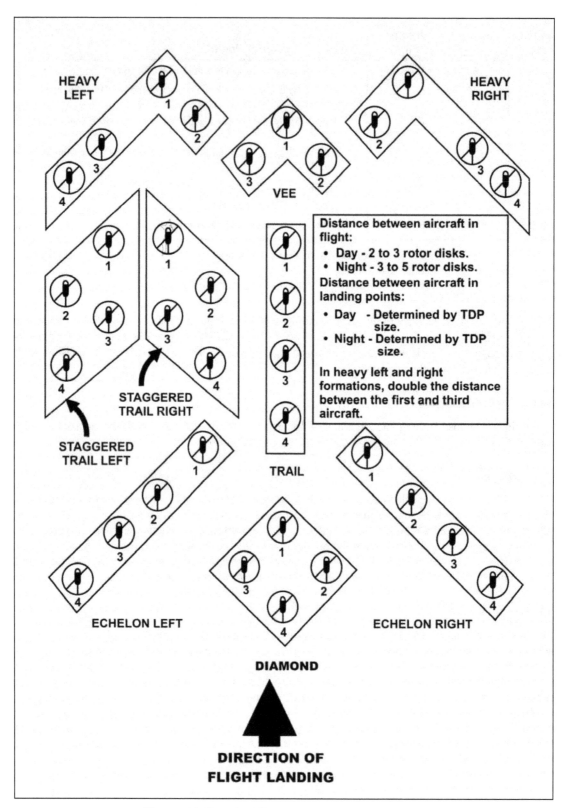

Figure 4-2. Standard flight and landing formations.

Clear Around Obstacles

4-12. Ground troops must do everything they can to improve landing point surfaces so aircraft can land. In general, an obstacle is a stump, rock, hole, or other object, 18 inches or larger, that might damage the aircraft or impede aircraft landing. No obstacles can be in a TDP in which an aircraft is going to land. Note, however, that even if pathfinders cannot clear ground obstructions, they can perform some helicopter operations without the helicopter landing. They must still clear and mark the area just as they would if the helicopter were going to land. Helicopters are given an advisory and hover above the ground obstructions that prevent them from landing.

GROUND SLOPE

4-13. Pathfinders choose landing sites with relatively level ground. For the helicopter to land safely, the slope should not exceed 7 degrees (Figure 4-3, page 4-6). Whenever possible, pilots should land upslope rather than downslope. All helicopters can land where ground slope measures 7 degrees or less and no advisory is required. When the slope exceeds 7 degrees, observation and utility helicopters that utilize skids for landing must terminate at a hover to load or off-load personnel or supplies. When the slope measures between 7 and 15 degrees, large utility and cargo helicopters that use wheels for landing are issued an advisory, and they land upslope. When the slope exceeds 15 degrees, all helicopters must be issued an advisory and terminate at a hover to load or off-load personnel or supplies.

Note: To determine slope in percentage or degrees, express all measurements in either feet or meters, but not both. If the map sheet expresses elevation in meters, multiply by three to convert into feet. If the map sheet expresses elevation in feet, divide by three to convert to meters.

CAUTION
Never land an aircraft facing downslope, if possible.

GROUND SLOPE EXPRESSED IN DEGREES

The approximate slope angle may be calculated by multiplying the gradient by 57.3. This method is reasonably accurate for slope angles under 20 degrees.

$$VD = B-A = 150$$
$$HD = 3{,}000$$
$$DEGREE\ OF\ SLOPE = \frac{150 \times 57.3}{3{,}000} = \frac{8{,}595}{3{,}000} = APPROXIMATELY\ 3°\ OF\ SLOPE$$

(SLOPE ANGLE: A = 550, B = 700, horizontal = 3,000')

GROUND SLOPE EXPRESSED AS PERCENTAGE

To determine the percent of ground slope, divide the vertical distance (VD) by the horizontal distance (HD) and multiply by 100.

$$PERCENT\ of\ SLOPE = \frac{VD}{HD} \times 100$$

Verticle distance is the difference in field elevation between the two ends of the landing site. Always round number up to the next whole number.

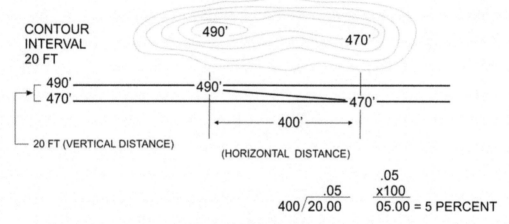

$$\frac{.05}{400\overline{)20.00}} \quad \begin{array}{r}.05 \\ \times 100 \\ \hline 05.00\end{array} = 5\ PERCENT$$

PATHFINDER SLOPE LANDING RULES

Do not land small utility and observation aircraft on slopes exceeding 7 degrees.
Give large utility and cargo aircraft an advisory if ground-slope is between 7 and 15 degrees.
Always advise pilot when landing wheeled aircraft on a sideslope.

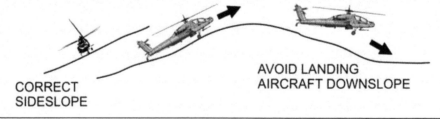

Figure 4-3. Determination of ground slope.

APPROACH AND DEPARTURE DIRECTIONS

4-14. Ideally, to land or take off, especially at night, the helicopter pilot generally chooses the approach or departure path facing into the wind, over the lowest obstacle, and along the long axis of the site. The departure heading must be within 45 degrees left or right of land heading.

Prevailing Wind

4-15. Always attempt to land a helicopter facing into the wind. Wind direction within 45 degrees left or right of land heading is considered a head wind. Depending on the helicopter's capabilities, if only one direction offers a good approach, or to make the most of available landing area, the pilot might be able to land with a crosswind of 0 to 9 knots or a tailwind of 0 to 5 knots. When wind speeds exceed 9 knots, the pilot must land into the wind. The same considerations apply to departures from landing sites. Except when the crosswind velocity exceeds 9 knots during a landing, the prevailing wind requires less attention than it does on the approach and departure routes. The wind affects smaller aircraft more than larger, more powerful ones.

Approach and Departure Obstacle Ratio

4-16. For HLZs that are bordered on the approach and departure ends by tall obstacles such as trees, power lines, or steep mountains, planners figure on an obstacle ratio of 10 to 1. That is, if a helicopter must approach or depart directly over a 10-foot tall tree, then the landing point must have 100 feet of horizontal clearance. If they have coordinated with the aviation unit commander, qualified pathfinders might have the authority to reduce the obstacle ratio to no less than 5 to 1. Reducing obstacle ratio is a last-resort means to make an HLZ suitable to accomplish the mission, second only to reduction of TDP size. Obstacle ratios are reduced in a deliberate manner after careful consideration of all factors, and only to the minimal reduction possible. The obstacle ratio should first be reduced over the route that the helicopters will be the lightest. For example, if the mission of the aviation unit is an insertion, they will be loaded on the approach and will require the most power to ingress and land, needing the longest glide path possible. After the unloading of troops and equipment, the aircraft will be lighter and will be able to use a shorter departure route. In this case, the pathfinder would reduce the obstacle ratio on the departure end and maintain a 10 to 1 or greater ratio on the approach end (Figure 4-4).

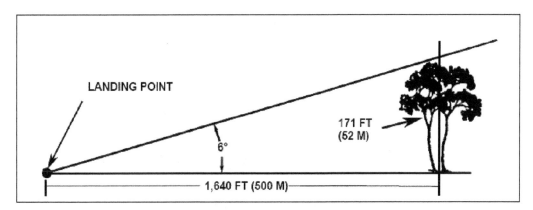

Figure 4-4. Maximum angle of approach (daylight).

Night Approach

4-17. Within the night approach and exit path, the maximum obstruction angle should not exceed 4 degrees measured from the center of the landing point to a distance of 3,000 meters (9,843 feet, Figure 4-5). The maximum obstacle height at 3,000 meters is 210 meters (689 feet). The field-expedient formula is that for every meter of vertical obstacle, you must have 14 meters from the center of the landing point to the obstacle. That is, a landing point must be 280 meters from a 20-meter tree if the helicopter must approach or exit directly over the tree. Another night operation planning consideration is the helicopter approach and exit path area and the maximum obstacle height within that area. These criteria apply to both the approach path to the landing point as well as the exit path from the landing point. First, we must define the area that is the approach and exit path.

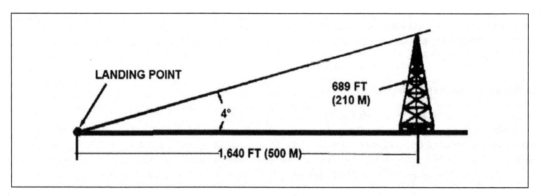

Figure 4-5. Maximum angle of approach (night).

APPROACH AND EXIT PATH

4-18. The approach and exit path is a 16-degree (277 mils) sector or arc extending outward and is measured from the center of the landing point (Figure 4-6). The "V"-shaped approach and exit path is shown by the dashed and dotted line in the illustration. The 4-degree maximum obstruction angle applies to the entire area within the approach and exit path (both the dark and light shaded area) measured from the landing point center to a distance of 3,000 meters.

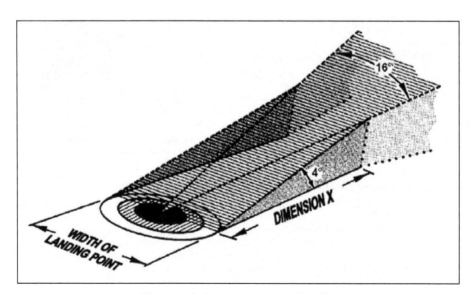

Figure 4-6. Approach and exit path.

Night Operations

4-19. During night operations, as the pilot gets closer to the landing point, he needs a wider area for a safe approach than just the 16-degree sector. Therefore, the minimum width of the approach and exit path, illustrated by the darker shaded area, must be equal to or wider than the width of the landing point that must be cleared to a maximum height of 2 feet (Figure 4-1). The length of the minimum width area, dimension X, will vary depending on the size of the landing point (Table 4-2). Follow along as we use a UH-60 Blackhawk as an example to help clarify the night approach and exit path criteria. Table 4-1 identified the UH-60 Blackhawk as a size 3 helicopter. Next, you must determine the landing point area that must be free from obstructions and grass cut to maximum height of 2 feet. Figure 4-2 shows 50 meters as the area needed for a size 3 landing point. Therefore, the minimum width of the night approach and exit path is 50 m. The minimum width distance intersects the 16-degree V-shaped arc (night approach and exit path) 180 meters from the center of the landing point. In other words, the night maximum obstruction angle applies to the complete approach and exit path; both the rectangular-shaped wedge (dark shaded area of the diagram) as well as the 16-degree "V"-shaped arc (light shaded area and dotted line).

Landing Point Size	Width of Landing Point (Meters)	Dimension X (Meters)
1	25	90
2	35	125
3	50	180
4	80	285
5	100	355
6	125	444
7	150	533

Table 4-2. Length of minimum width area.

Note: The aviation unit commander makes the final decision on minimum landing requirements. He bases his decision on the effects of air density, slope, and surface conditions. He explains these requirements verbally during early mission planning.

Along the Long Axis

4-20. Allows the pilot a better opportunity to identify the TDP and obstacles, select the best flight path, and prevent overflying the TDP. It also allows the pathfinder to maximize the space available in the site.

DENSITY ALTITUDE

4-21. Altitude, temperature, and humidity determine the density altitude. As each of these conditions increase, aircraft lift capabilities decrease. Planners should try to remember that as the density altitude increases, the size of the LZ also increases. This will also be a consideration for the aviation unit commander when determining the authority for Pathfinders to reduce TDP size or obstacle ratio.

LOADS

4-22. When fully loaded, most helicopters can neither climb nor descend vertically. They need a larger area and better approach or departure routes than when they carry lighter loads. Other load considerations are—

- Equipment or personnel.
- Internal or external load.

- Insertion or extraction mission.
- Weight.

OBSTACLES

4-23. These include any obstruction that might interfere with aircraft operation on the ground. Landing zones should have no tall trees, power lines, or similar obstructions on the landing site. Pathfinders must remove or reduce any obstacles within the landing site. This includes any rocks, stumps, holes, and thick grass or brush that might hinder safe landing over 0.45 meters (18 inches). Obstacles that cannot be removed or reduced must be marked (preferably in red) and an advisory given to the pilots. Marking will be done as follows:

- If the obstacle is on the approach route, both the near and far sides of the obstacle will be marked.
- If the obstacle is on the departure route, only the near side of the obstacle will be marked.
- If the obstacle protrudes into the LZ, but not on the flight route, the near side of the obstacle will be marked.
- Large obstacles on the flight route and on the LZ will be marked on all sides of the obstacle. At a minimum, one light is required on each of the four sides.

ALTERNATE SITES

4-24. Enemy action, unfavorable terrain, or changes in the tactical or logistical situation can require alternate landing sites. The ground unit commander usually selects these to support the tactical plan. He (or his representative) decides when to use them based on the recommendations of the aviation unit commander and the pathfinder on the site. The commander uses the fastest means to get instructions for using alternate sites to the pathfinders. Neither pathfinder nor aviation unit commanders can shift to an alternate LZ(s) unless the supported ground unit commander has delegated that authority to them.

SECTION II. ORGANIZATION AND DUTIES

The commander task organizes the pathfinder element to set up and operate the installations required by the supported unit's tactical plan. They might set these up within a single LZ or separate them widely throughout a large AO. The pathfinder leader normally stays at the most important site. To set up and operate one helicopter LZ, the commander task organizes the pathfinder element into two working parties: a reconnaissance party and a marking party. Each site requires its own landing site party. The control center party and the release point party provide the same function for LZs or DZs.

CONTROL CENTER

4-25. The control center (CC) coordinates aircraft in and around an LZ or DZ and promotes a safe, orderly, and speedy flow of air traffic. Upon arrival in the area, the pathfinder leader selects the exact location of the CC. He positions it to allow visual control of aircraft in and around the LZ or DZ.

4-26. For helicopter LZs, the most desirable CC location is along the aircraft flight route, but displaced from the landing site. This helps prevent enemy EW assets from compromising the actual landing site location, even if the tactical situation dictates that the pathfinder leader remain on the site for control purposes. For an LZ with more than one landing site, or for any LZ during reduced visibility, the pathfinder leader locates the CC where it can act as a manned RP or final approach fix to provide positive navigational assistance to arriving aircraft.

4-27. The RP is an established traffic control checkpoint. It is the final navigational checkpoint for aircraft approaching the landing site or approaching air-delivery facilities in an LZ or DZ.

4-28. During the air movement phase of an air assault operation, helicopter serials also use the RP as a final coordination point for control of planned ground or aerial supporting fires in and around LZs. The air movement commander staffs the RP only when he expects tough navigational problems. He tentatively chooses its location from maps or from aerial photographic studies. He looks for an easily-identifiable point on the planned flight route to the landing site. He looks for a location that will take advantage of long-range electronic and visual navigation aids.

4-29. For single helicopter landing sites within a single LZ, the site itself offers the best location for GTA communication. Especially at night, positioning here allows the pathfinder air traffic controller to observe the final approach of helicopter formations. It helps him make sure pilots align correctly on the required landing direction. It also helps him ensure that they clear any obstacles.

4-30. The pathfinder leader organizes the control center to meet mission requirements. The control center can consist of a single pathfinder. This Soldier can operate the GTA radio for a limited period at a small site, or the control center can consist of the following staff:

LZ OR DZ COMMANDER

4-31. He supervises aircraft landings and departures, airdrops, and other pathfinder activities in the LZ or DZ. He might also serve as the GTA radio operator.

GTA RADIO OPERATOR

4-32. He operates the radio used to maintain communications with pilots. He also provides advisories for his airspace as needed.

INTERNAL NET RECORDER

4-33. Some situations require pathfinders to set up an internal net to communicate with other pathfinder elements. An internal net recorder (INR) runs this net and helps control aircraft at his HLZ. He logs details of all arrivals and departures on DA Form 7461-R, *Internal Net Record*, (Figure 4-7, page 4-12). If an aircraft fails to arrive at its destination, search and rescue medical units check the DA Forms 7461-R so they know where to focus their search. The recorder might copy the blank, reproducible form from the back of this manual onto 8½ by 11-inch paper. He might also download it from http://www.usapa.army.mil or copy it from the Army Electronic Library (AEL) CD-ROM (EM0001). Then he completes the form as follows:

PFDR Det. Write the name of the pathfinder detachment operating the landing zone.

Supported Unit. Write the name of the supported unit.

Period (DTG). Write the date and time of the mission.

Operation. Write the name of the mission.

Designation. Write the name and location of the site.

Recorder. Write your name.

No. A/C. Write the number of aircraft in the formation.

Type A/C. Write the nomenclature of each type of aircraft in the formation.

Contact Time. Write the time of the initial contact with the flight commander.

Call Sign. Write the flight commander's call sign.

Time, Arr. Write what time the aircraft or formation inserted.

Time, Dep. Write what time the aircraft or formation extracted.

Load Type, Ins. Write what type of load the aircraft inserted.

Load Type, Ext. Write what type of load the aircraft extracted.

Destination. Write the name of the aircraft's or formation's destination on leaving.

Remarks. Write anything else here that you think you need to record.

Chapter 4

LANDING SITE PARTY

4-34. The landing site party consists of a site team leader and other pathfinders and attached personnel, as required. A single pathfinder might establish and operate a small landing site for a limited time. He maintains a record of all aircraft and their respective cargos on DA Form 7461-R, *Internal Net Record*. Figure 4-7 shows an example of the completed form. A blank copy is provided in the back of this book for local reproduction on 8 1/2- by 11-inch paper. The form may also be downloaded from the Internet at Army Knowledge Online (http://www.army.mil/usapa/eforms/) or the Army Publishing Directorate Web site (http://www.apd.army.mil/USAPA_PUB_formrange_f.asp).

\multicolumn{10}{l}{**INTERNAL NET RECORD** — For use of this form see FM 3-21.38; the Proponent Agency for this form is TRADOC.}
\multicolumn{5}{l}{PFDR DET: 1-507 PFDR SECTION 2}	\multicolumn{5}{l}{OPERATION: "ROYAL COVER"}
\multicolumn{5}{l}{SUPPORTED UNIT: 1-507 PATHFINDER SCHOOL}	\multicolumn{5}{l}{DESIGNATION: LEDO LZ (YC594062)}
\multicolumn{5}{l}{PERIOD: 151430ZJUN00-161830ZJUN00}	\multicolumn{5}{l}{RECORDER: SSG ALDER}

NO. A/C	TYPE A/C	CONTACT TIME	CALL SIGN	TIME ARR	TIME DEP	LOAD TYPE INS	LOAD TYPE EXT	DESTINATION	REMARKS
5	UH-60	1120	RAVEN 22	1127	1145	PERS	-	LAWSON ARMY	1 SLINGLOAD A/C
						1.M998		AFLD	

DA FORM 7461-R, SEP 2002

Figure 4-7. Example completed DA Form 7461-R.

SITE TEAM LEADER

4-35. The site team leader reconnoiters, establishes, and operates the landing site. He supervises it and, at any time, might supervise the GTA radio operator. Some of his responsibilities include the following:

- Organizing at an objective rally point.
- Reconnoitering to determine—
    -- Long axis.
    -- Usable area.
    -- Ground slope (compute).
    -- Land heading.
    -- Best landing formation.
- Designating sling-load point(s).

- Emplacing and briefing the GTA radio operator.
- Clearing touchdown and slingload points.
- Organizing personnel and loads for air movement.
- Clearing or marking obstacles.
- Preparing for night and day missions.
- Continuing to improve the site.

EXTRA PATHFINDERS

4-36. These Soldiers operate the GTA radio and the pathfinder internal radio net (if established), position and operate navigation and assembly aids, and clear or mark obstacles. Four factors dictate the number of extra pathfinders employed:

- The size of the landing site.
- The expected density of air traffic.
- The number and type of visual and electronic aids used.
- The tactical situation.

COMMANDER

4-37. The commander can attach other Soldiers from supported units to the landing site party. The pathfinders brief and rehearse attached Soldiers. Only pathfinders reconnoiter actual landing areas, but attached personnel can—

- Reconnoiter other areas.
- Provide security.
- Help pathfinders set up and operate the landing site.
- Reconnoiter and mark assembly areas.
- Operate assembly aids.

SECTION III. LANDING SITE OPERATIONS

Before they can start using a landing site, pathfinders need only pick its location and set up communications there. They continue marking and improving the site until it can support the ground tactical plan.

COMMUNICATIONS

4-38. As soon as they arrive at the landing site, pathfinders set up communications in the GTA net. If needed, they also set up the pathfinder internal net. They monitor these radio nets continuously, unless directed otherwise, until they complete operations at the site.

4-39. Tactical situation permitting, pathfinders locate each helicopter landing site within ground communication range of the other sites and manned RPs. The range of available radios dictates whether facilities within the LZ can communicate with each other.

4-40. The commander of the landing site for utility and cargo helicopters quickly reconnoiters the area to determine the exact direction of landing. He calculates an intercept heading from the RP if necessary. He selects the location of the landing point of the lead helicopter of each flight. Then he decides if the terrain or situation dictates any change to the planned landing formation. The site commander has pathfinders or other personnel compile landing instructions for transmittal to inbound helicopters. He also has them remove or mark obstacles in or around the site.

Chapter 4

FLIGHT FORMATIONS

4-41. Ideally, all helicopters land at the same time in a planned flight formation. The landing site commander includes this information in his landing instructions to the flight leader. Pathfinders lay out the landing site in a location where helicopters will not fly directly over aircraft on the ground. The layout of the site also depends on the landing space available, the number and type of obstacles, unit SOPs, and prearranged flight formations.

LANDING ZONE AND OBSTACLE MARKINGS

4-42. For daylight operations, pathfinders use only panels or some other minimal identification means to mark LZs (Figure 4-8 through Figure 4-11, pages 4-15 through 4-18). Smoke might also be used to identify an LZ and assist the pilot in determining wind conditions. However, smoke is also easily identified by the enemy. For daylight operations, mark the number one landing point using a single VS-17 panel, with the international orange side visible. Other TDPs might be marked, as coordinated. Mar obstacles using the cerise colored side of the panel. For night operations, they use chem-lights, lanterns, field expedients, or other methods to show the direction of landing and to mark individual landing points (Figure 4-12 and Figure 4-13, pages 4-19 and 4-20). For day and night air assault operations, they mark all obstacles. (Section V provides detailed information about conducting night operations.)

4-43. At night, pathfinders can use lights of different colors (except red, which marks obstacles) to designate different helicopter sites or to separate flights within a larger formation. A lighted "T" or inverted "Y" indicates both the landing point for the lead helicopter of each flight and the direction of approach (Figure 4-14, page 4-21). Other lights mark touchdown points for the other helicopters in the flight. Each helicopter should land with its right landing gear or its right skid 5 meters left of the lights. Large cargo helicopters (CH-47) land 10 meters to the left of the lights.

4-44. For security, pathfinders and the ground unit turn off, cover, or turn all lights upside down until the last practical moment before a helicopter arrives. Then they orient the lights in the direction from which the lead helicopter is approaching, and a signalman directs its landing.

Note: Because the marking lights could be too bright for the aircrew member's NVGs, he might have to look under it to distinguish the colors. Also, aircrew members wear NVGs with filtered lenses. These filters do not allow the aircrews to see blue or green chem-lights. Colors such as yellow, orange, red, and infrared can be seen by pilots wearing ANVIS.

AIR ASSAULTS

4-45. During daylight air assault operations, pathfinders use red-colored panels or other red, easily-identifiable means to mark any hard-to-detect, impossible-to-remove obstacles such as wires, holes, stumps, and rocks. During nighttime air assault operations, pathfinders use red lights to mark any obstacles within the landing site that they cannot reduce or remove.

4-46. In most combat situations, the need for security keeps pathfinders from using red lights to mark treetops on the departure end of a landing zone. However, in training or in a rear area landing site, they do use red lights. If they cannot mark obstacles or hazards, they must fully advise aviators of existing conditions by GTA radio. In any case, the pathfinder landing site leader makes sure that pathfinders mark the most dangerous obstacles first and, if possible, that they remove them.

4-47. If required to do so by the supported unit, pathfinders can mark initial assembly points for troops, equipment, and supplies. They should choose locations that help ensure the quick, efficient assembly and clearing of the helicopter site. If the unit will use the assembly areas, the ground unit commander selects their locations. If needed, supported ground unit Soldiers go with the pathfinders to reconnoiter and mark the unit assembly areas, set up assembly aids, act as guides, and help with landing and unloading operations. Having this help ensures that the pathfinders can rapidly clear troops, supplies, and equipment from the landing points.

4-48. Pathfinders have a limited capability to secure a landing site. If they precede the initial assault elements into a landing site, Soldiers from the supported ground unit can go with them for security.

Chapter 4

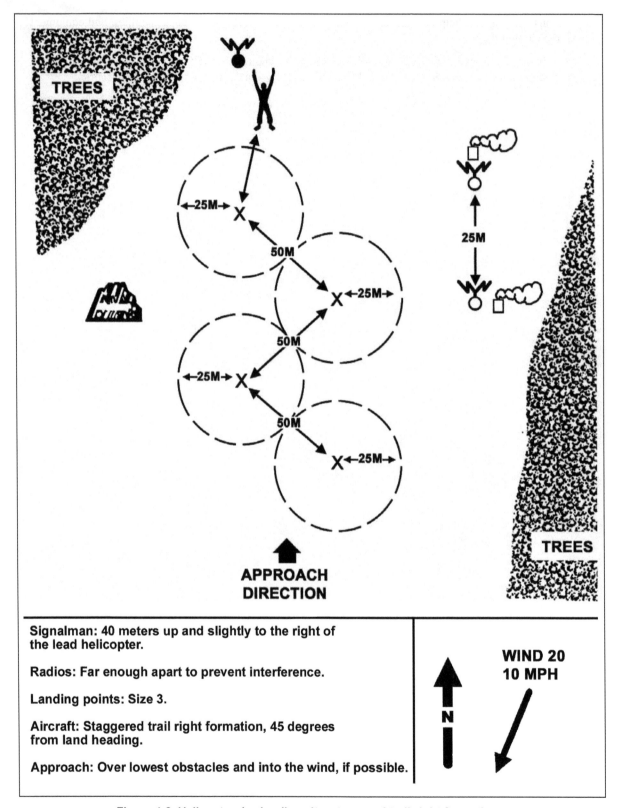

Figure 4-8. Helicopter day landing site, staggered trail-right formation.

Helicopter Landing Zones

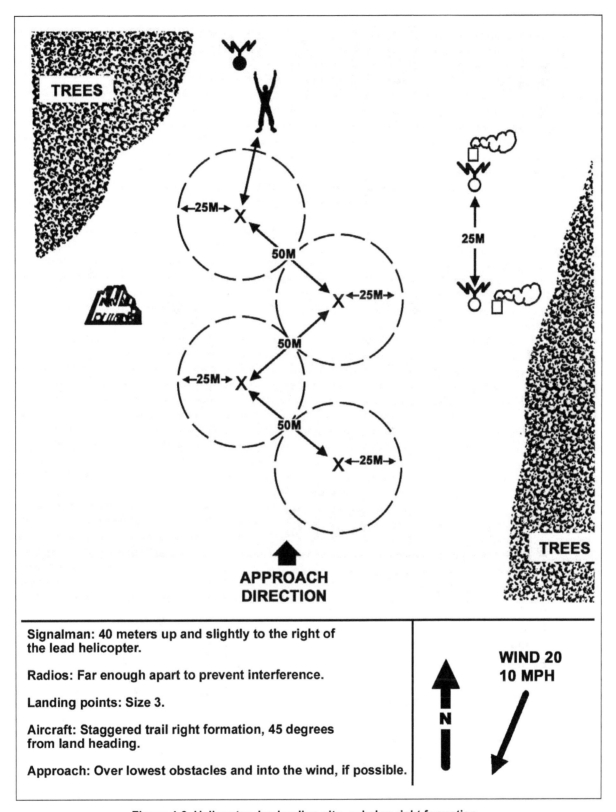

Figure 4-9. Helicopter day landing site, echelon right formation.

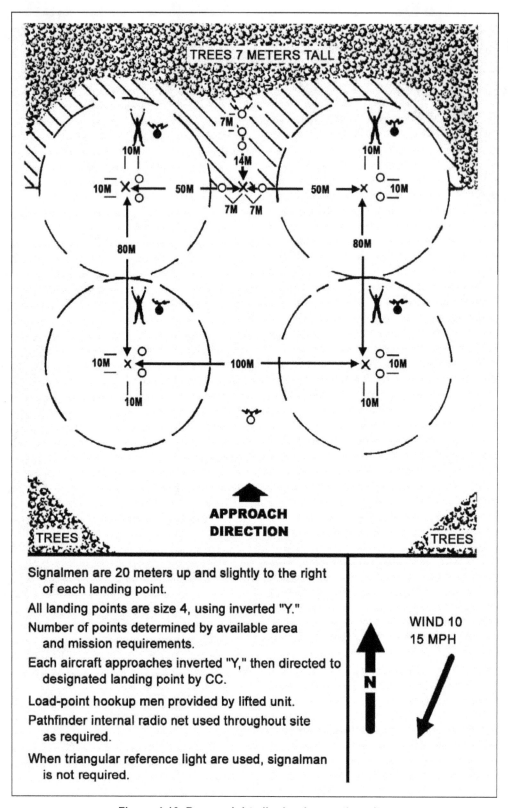

Figure 4-10. Day or night slingload operation site.

Helicopter Landing Zones

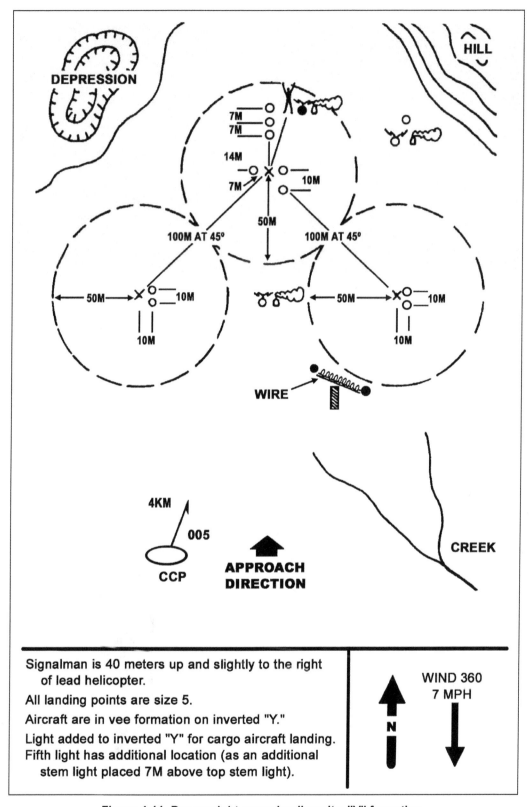

Figure 4-11. Day or night cargo landing site, "V" formation.

Chapter 4

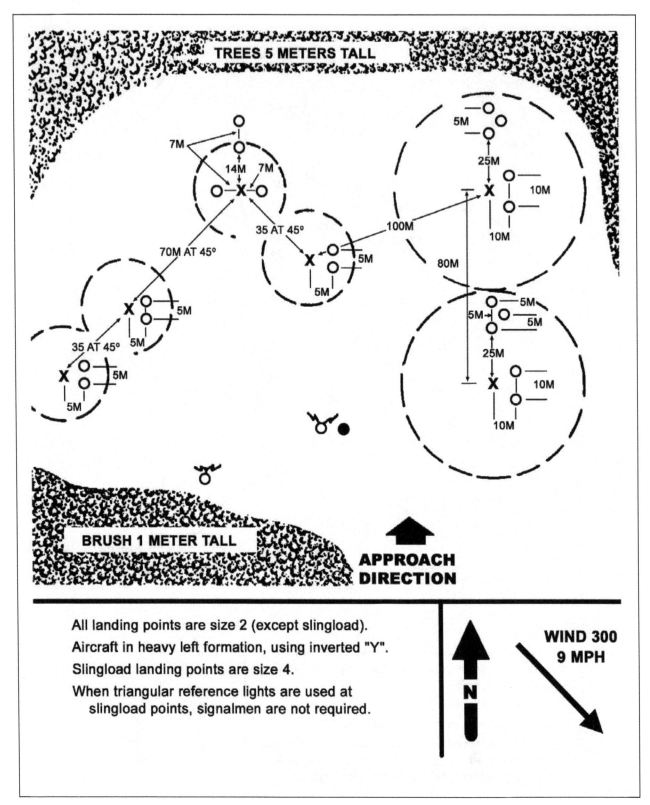

Figure 4-12. Night landing site with landing points for aircraft and slingloads.

Helicopter Landing Zones

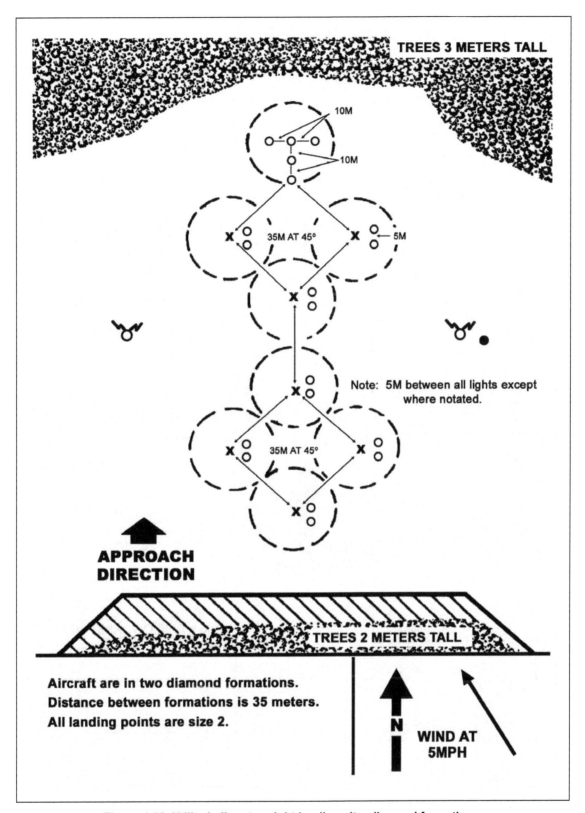

Figure 4-13. Utility helicopter night landing site, diamond formations.

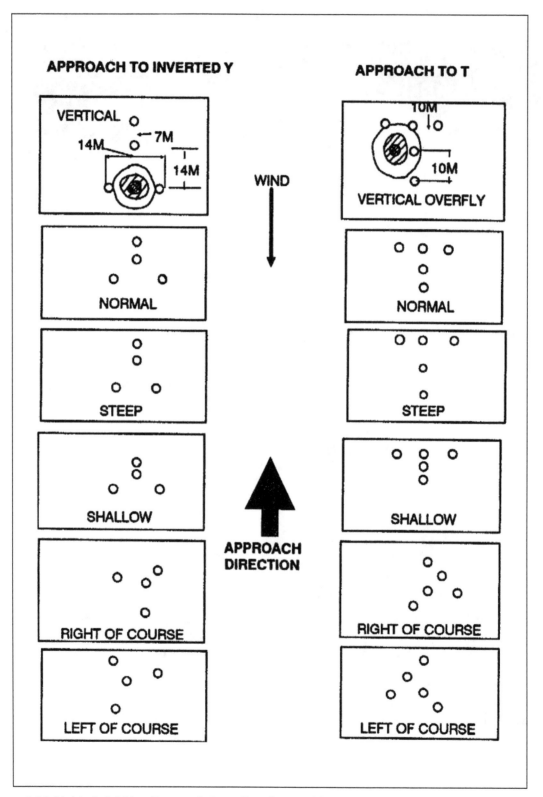

Figure 4-14. Lighted night landing symbols as the pilot would see them from different approach angles.

INTERCEPT HEADINGS

4-49. The heading from the RP (or from the CCP if the pathfinders do not use an RP) to the landing site coincides as closely as possible with the landing direction to keep the helicopter from having to turn sharply. The larger the formation, the more important this becomes. If a pilot cannot approach the landing site straight on, pathfinders will set up an intercept heading (Figure 4-15). They choose an intercept point far enough from touchdown to allow helicopters in formation a final approach of at least 1 to 2 miles. Flight leaders might need visual steering commands, time and distance information, terrain features, and electronic or visual navigation aids to help them determine the intercept point and the landing direction at the landing site.

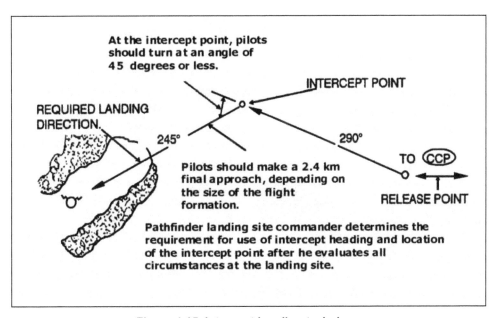

Figure 4-15. Intercept heading technique.

SECTION IV. LANDING ZONE OPERATIONS

Helicopters approach the LZ along a designated flight route. They normally travel in serials containing four or five helicopters, but they sometimes travel as platoon-sized lifts. One serial might contain a flight for each helicopter site. Flights of medium or heavy transport helicopters (CH-47) carrying artillery or other bulk cargo often arrive at LZs one or two helicopters at a time (Figure 4-16). Later flights follow at the smallest time intervals. These intervals depend on the number of helicopters in each flight, the configuration and conditions of the landing site, and the nature of the cargo to be loaded or unloaded. During planning, the aviation unit commander determines the time between successive flights. Once an operation starts, pathfinders at the site recommend any changes needed to ensure helicopter safety or expedite operations. Night operations often require more time and distance between formations.

COMMUNICATIONS CHECKPOINT

4-50. As each helicopter serial reaches the CCP on the flight route, the flight leader contacts the appropriate helicopter landing site control center.

4-51. The CC then gives the flight leader the heading from the CCP to the landing site, the landing direction, and other relevant and important information, as follows:

- Enemy situation.
- Friendly fires.

- Field elevation.
- Landing formation.
- Terrain conditions.
- Traffic situation.
- Obstacles.
- Availability of visual signals (smoke, light gun, and so forth).
- Next reporting point.

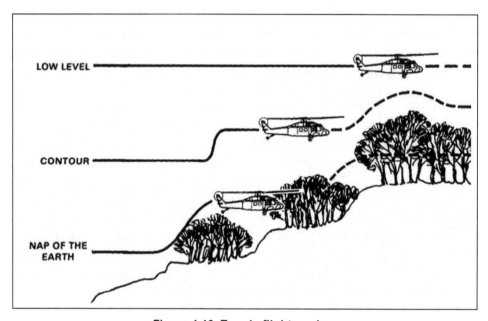

Figure 4-16. Terrain flight modes.

4-52. Before reaching the CCP, IAW instructions from the flight leader, all helicopters in a flight switch to the pathfinder control frequency.

Note: Pathfinders must stay prepared to provide ATC and navigational aid to all aircraft in and around the landing site in case those aircraft have no specified flight plan.

4-53. The helicopter formation continues along the flight route to the RP. The electronic and visual aids at the RP (if manned) help pilots navigate. As each helicopter passes over or near the RP, its flight serial leader reports this to the respective landing site CC. Then the helicopter flies directly to the assigned landing site. The CC at the individual landing site uses visual signals, steering commands, or electronic homing techniques to help any flight that cannot find its landing site.

Day Operation Signals

4-54. For daylight operations, you can use different smoke colors for each landing site. You can use the same color more than once, just spread them out. Use smoke only if you have to, because the enemy can see it, too. Try to use it only when the pilot asks for help locating his helicopter site.

Night Operation Signals

4-55. For night operations, IR strobe or other visual signals in lieu of smoke. As in daylight, red signals mean "DO NOT LAND," but you can also use them to indicate other emergency conditions. All concerned must plan and know emergency codes. Each flight lands at the assigned site according to CC messages and the visual aids displayed. You can use arm-and-hand signals to help control the landing, hovering, and parking of helicopters.

AIR CONTROL POINTS

4-56. Pathfinders might have to manage air control points (ACPs) to help aircraft en route to the LZ.

ACP PARTY RESPONSIBILITIES

4-57. The ACP party consists of two or three pathfinders, or at least one pathfinder and assistants. The party positions and operates electronic navigation aids, visual navigation aids, or both. The party also operates radios in the pathfinder internal net (if used) and the GTA net. The ACP party monitors the GTA net so they can respond at once to any pilot's request for help finding an ACP.

NAVIGATION AID ORDER

4-58. The ACP party installs navigation aids as soon as it arrives at the site or as planned. They try to set up all of the aids at the same time. However, if they cannot do this because they have too few people, or for some other reason, then they set them up in the following order:

GTA Radio

4-59. The party sets this up first. Then, if the aviation unit commander has asked them to do so, they install the electronic homing beacon. This beacon allows the party to offer long-range guidance. If they do use the beacon, the party sets it up far enough away to prevent excessive radio interference. This also helps keep the enemy from destroying the radios and the beacon at the same time.

Visual Navigation Aids

4-60. These navigation aids vary in number and type, depending on aviation unit SOPs and requirements and on the need for security. The ACP party removes any grass or brush that masks their usage of these aids, but they also plan a way to conceal the markings in case they sight enemy aircraft.

Internal Net Recorder

4-61. The pathfinder internal net recorder sets up communications with the landing zone CCs as fast as he can. He immediately reports the state of ACP readiness and any information about the local enemy situation, if any. Unless directed to operate a beacon on a definite time schedule, he constantly monitors the radio.

Security Personnel

4-62. The ACP party can include attached personnel from the supported units. These personnel provide security. They both move to their assigned locations and take up security positions, or they help set up and operate navigation aids and communications equipment.

SECTION V. NIGHT OPERATIONS

Daytime visual references (checkpoints for positive identification) are difficult to see at night. Visual aids for night navigation emit illumination. Having too few visual references can cause pilots to concentrate on a single light or group of lights in a concentrated area. This can cause visual illusions, which can then cause vertigo. To prevent this hazardous situation, pathfinders mark LZs with multiple lights and mark landing areas with two or more widely separated lights.

Chapter 4

TACTICAL LANDING LIGHTS

4-63.   The tactical landing light system provides visual cues for landing in a tactical landing site. When the aircraft approaches from terrain flight altitudes, it should use the inverted "Y" system. Aircraft normally approach a tactical landing site without the aid of the search landing light. The lighting for a tactical LZ can consist of handheld flashlights or "beanbag" lights arranged on the ground.

4-64.   Regardless of the type lighting device used, pathfinders identify the touchdown point with at least two lights. At night, they can designate different helicopter sites with lights of different colors. They might also use different colors to separate flights within a larger formation. A lighted (inverted) "Y" indicates the landing point of the lead helicopter (Figure 4-17).

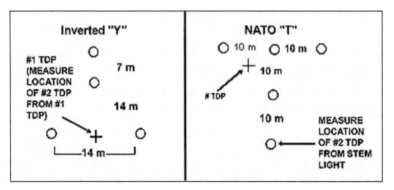

Figure 4-17. Placement of the inverted "Y" or NATO "T" at the number one touchdown point.

4-65.   At night, all landing lights should be placed in directional holes that can only be seen from the direction of approach and from above, but not from the ground. If this is not possible, the pathfinder turns his hood upside down, or keeps all lights off for security purposes until the last practical moment.

4-66.   At other touchdown points, helicopters land with the right landing gear or skid just to the left of the light (Figure 4-18). They also place a signalman at a sling-load point. Then they beam the lights in the direction from which the helicopters approach.

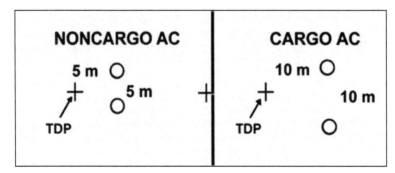

Figure 4-18. Placement of additional touchdown point markings for night use.

4-67. Pathfinders display an inverted "Y" for cargo aircraft. This marker consists of five lights. Pathfinders place the fifth light IAW prior coordination with the supporting aviation unit (Figure 4-19). The fifth light can go 7 meters from furthest stem light in the direction of landing, or 10 meters opposite the landing direction (below) the right flank light.

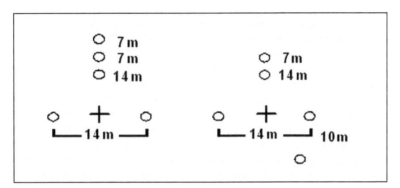

Figure 4-19. Placement of fifth light using inverted "Y," when coordinated.

4-68. Pathfinders will display a NATO landing "T" if an aircraft approaches the LZ from at least 500 above ground level (AGL), or anytime the pathfinders coordinate in advance with the supporting aviation unit.

4-69. Noncargo aircraft require a 5-meter separation between touchdown point and lights, with a 5-meter separation between lights.

4-70. Cargo aircraft require a 10-meter separation between touchdown point and lights, with a 10-meter separation between the lights.

4-71. During darkness, helicopters approach slightly steeper and slower than they would in daylight.

4-72. Vehicle headlights offer one kind of emergency night lighting. Pathfinders place two vehicles about 35 meters apart and 35 meters downwind of the landing point. They shine their headlights so that their beams intersect at the center of the landing point (Figure 4-20). The helicopter approaches into the wind, passes between the vehicles, and lands in the lighted area. This method does not work well for large helicopters.

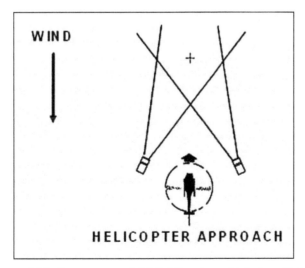

Figure 4-20. Emergency night lighting by vehicle headlights.

Chapter 4

> **CAUTION**
>
> When fully adapted to the night, the eyes grow extremely sensitive to any light. Sudden exposure to a light source causes partial to complete loss of night vision. Thus, take care to avoid exposing pilots to light sources. Also, if pilots are using NVG, avoid shining a light directly at the aircraft, or use light sources compatible with the NVG.

EXTERNAL LOADS

4-73. Employing external loads presents a challenge in the dark. Even so, the pathfinder can use one of several methods. If he lacks sufficient signalmen, he marks the load by placing three reference lights 25 meters in front of the load landing and pickup point. He spaces them in a triangle, 5 meters apart. This helps the flight crew during hookup, liftoff, and landing. On liftoff, the aircraft climbs vertically until the load clears the ground. As the helicopter begins to move forward, the pilot applies enough power to maintain a climb that allows the slingload to clear any obstacles on the liftoff path. The shorter the sling, the less altitude is required to clear obstacles.

MULTIHELICOPTER OPERATIONS

4-74. Only by using NVG can pilots fly safely in formation in a complete blackout and at terrain flight altitudes.

NIGHT VISION GOGGLES

4-75. To operate at terrain flight altitudes during low- or mid-light levels, pathfinders use night vision goggles. If the lights used in the tactical lighting and marking are too bright for night vision goggles, pathfinders must place a filter over the light cover, paint the light covers, cover them with plastic tape, or use other means to reduce the intensity of the light. The night vision goggles commonly used by aviators (AN/PVS-8) generally have a filter to prevent the cockpit instruments and lighting from blinding the aircrew. However, these filters also prevent the aircrew from observing green and blue chem-lights. These colors might be seen with the unaided eye if the aircrews adjust their goggles to look below them, but they will not be able to see the light source through the NVDs.

> **WARNING**
>
> **When your unit trains with or employs the tactical light set, wear a filter over your night vision goggles to prevent eye injury. If you do not have a filter, paint the lens cover or cover it with plastic tape to reduce light intensity.**

Helicopter Landing Zones

SECTION VI. ENVIRONMENTAL CONSIDERATIONS

The pathfinder unit can expect to support the aviation commander and ground unit commander in many climates and types of terrain. The requirements for establishing a landing site or zone are similar. For aircraft to land safely and quickly in challenging environments, pathfinders must choose and prepare LZs carefully.

PILOT INPUT

4-76. The pilot considers his experiences and his responsibilities to the crew and aircraft before determining whether a proposed landing site is safe.

4-77. Challenging climatic and terrain environments include extreme hot and cold weather and jungle, desert, and mountainous terrain. (For more detailed information on the climate, terrain, and operational aspects of these areas, see FM 90-3, FM 90-5, and FM 3-97.6.)

4-78. Each area requires the pilot to know and follow special procedures. The pathfinder who also knows these procedures can better advise and assist aviators and the supported ground unit.

COLD WEATHER

4-79. Many parts of the world experience cold weather. Extreme cold and blowing snow pose special problems in ground operations and flight. Pathfinder mission planning includes considering the problems presented by ice, snow, or rain. The pathfinder's knowledge of flight procedures helps him advise the pilot about the existing surface conditions.

COMMUNICATIONS

4-80. Most locations allow generally-good radio communications. However, atmospheric electricity, such as the aurora borealis, can disrupt them. These events could disturb or block some frequencies. Mountainous terrain also restricts communications. Pathfinders might need to set up relay stations. "Radio skipping" happens often in cold weather areas. Radio operators often hear long-distance radio traffic on tactical FM networks.

NAVIGATION

4-81. In snow-covered areas with flat terrain, pilots might need marked and manned RPs. When aircraft fly over loose snow, the air movement lifts the snow and circulates it into a snow cloud. This often produces a zero-visibility condition known as "whiteout," through which the pilot must take off or land blind (Figure 4-21). Whiteout conditions place extra demands on the landing site party.

SURFACE CONDITIONS

4-82. The pathfinder evaluates the surface of the ground to see whether aircraft can land without sinking too deep into the snow. He can use a tactical vehicle to test the hardness of the surface. The landing site party might also try to determine the degree of ground slope, and whether obstacles lie under the cover of snow at each landing point.

Distance Between Aircraft

4-83. Pathfinders might need to increase the distance between aircraft to 100 meters and the size of the landing point to 100 meters in diameter.

Landing Point Markings

4-84. Marking the landing points presents other problems. A pilot's depth perception is impaired in snow-covered areas. A signalman on the ground provides a useful reference for estimating height. In daytime, pathfinders mark touchdown points so the pilot can find a clear and safe landing area.

Chapter 4

Whiteouts

4-85. If the tactical situation permits, the GTA radio operator advises the pilot of the surface conditions so the pilot can plan how to approach. Using the echelon left or right landing formation reduces the effect of snow clouds (also called "whiteouts") on subsequent landings. The pathfinder plans to stagger aircraft arrivals to let the snow clouds settle.

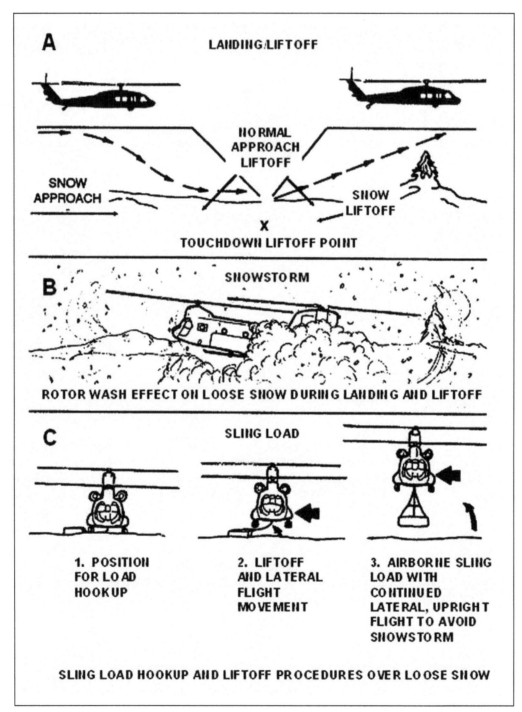

Figure 4-21. Lessening the effects of loose snow on the ground.

Multiple Landing Sites

4-86. Depending on the mission requirements, climatic conditions, and the expected times of the landings, the pathfinder leader might decide to use multiple landing sites.

Night Approaches

4-87. Aircraft making night approaches to snow sites need a visual reference point on the ground such as runway or tactical landing lights. These lights help the pilot judge the angle of descent and rate of closure. He plans the approach to land short of the touchdown point. This ensures that he does not overshoot the point and have to decelerate rapidly in the snow cloud produced by his own aircraft. Approaching short allows the pilot to maintain airspeed after leveling off, and to keep the aircraft in front of the snow cloud until touchdown.

Adjustment of Inverted "Y"

4-88. If he coordinates with the flight commander before the landing, the pathfinder can adjust his inverted "Y" forward 10 meters in front of his designated Number 1 touchdown point. This way, the landing site party takes advantage of all usable areas on the site.

SIGNALMAN

4-89. The pathfinder leader positions any extra personnel to act as signalmen for aircraft approaching other touchdown points. While aircraft approach and land, he makes sure that signalmen remain in safe areas. Other signalmen should also control the loading of personnel on the aircraft, as instructed by the crew chief or the crew. The technique for landing on snow with a slingload resembles other types of approach, but the pilot hovers at a higher altitude because of the load (A, Figure 4-21). He has a hard time judging the height of the slingload (the height above the ground) as it nears the snow surface. He relies on a signalman to keep him informed. To avoid building up a snow cloud, the pilot puts the load on the ground as fast as he can (B, Figure 4-21).

SLINGLOAD OPERATIONS

4-90. The CH-47 requires a sling length of at least 50 feet. Other aircraft allow a shorter sling. Normally an aircraft hovers during hookup and liftoff with a slingload. Doing this above snow produces a snow cloud (B, Figure 4-21). The pilot must expect this and plan for it. In fact, when operating over snow-covered terrain, the pilot can use the most common technique—hovering the helicopter over the load while the ground crew attaches the sling to the hook—or not.

4-91. The pilot can land to the left of the load, but close enough for hookup personnel to attach the sling to it.

4-92. When ready for liftoff, the pilot starts a slow, vertical ascent, with enough lateral movement to position the aircraft over the load (C, Figure 4-21). He keeps ascending until the load clears the ground, and then he checks hover power, starts accelerating, and continues to climb.

WARNING

Rotor wash increases the risk of frostbite. Make sure you and anyone else on the ground dresses for the conditions and keeps or uses a face mask and goggles.

Chapter 4

STATIC ELECTRICITY

4-93. During cold weather, static electricity creates serious problems. Moving an aircraft through the air, brushing snow and ice from an aircraft, or dragging steel cables over the snow can generate static electricity. During external load operations, aviators key the FM radio just before load pickup. This discharges the aircraft's static electrical charge. Because the charge rapidly builds up again, hookup personnel use a grounding device to avoid electrical shock (Chapter 5 says more about static discharge wands).

SAFETY

4-94. Accumulated ice on aircraft structural and moving parts presents a danger to nearby ground personnel. The aircraft can accumulate ice up to three-quarters of an inch thick during flight in temperatures and altitudes where icing conditions exist. During flight at less extreme temperatures, this ice begins to loosen and fall off. Ice might shed while the helicopter loses altitude during the landing approach and during touchdown, and pieces of ice shed by the main rotor can fly outward as much as 300 feet. Ground personnel should stay a safe distance away from helicopters during landing and shutdown (after flight in icing conditions), and passengers should not exit until the rotor blades have stopped.

JUNGLE

4-95. Jungle areas impede military operations. Jungle areas promise heat, humidity, rainy seasons, and other weather conditions that reduce aircraft performance.

COMMUNICATIONS

4-96. Jungle tends to obstruct military lines of communication. Thick vegetation, irregular terrain, and adverse atmospheric conditions screen radio transmissions. The ground or supported might have to use radio relays. They might also have to staff and mark the CCP. If communications are limited in range, pathfinders might also have to provide GTA communications to advise and direct the pilot to the landing site.

LANDING SITES

4-97. Jungle conditions mean small landing sites that can handle only a few aircraft at a time. Small landing sites also mean a reduced allowable cargo load (ACL). Pathfinders evaluate surface conditions at the landing site to make sure the aircraft will not sink or bog down in the soil. Then they survey the site for vines, trees, and other obstructions in the approach path and near the touchdown point.

NAVIGATION

4-98. On an approach to a jungle landing site, the pilot avoids using a high rate of descent. He uses a steep enough angle of descent to just clear any obstacles. He normally uses a ten-to-one obstacle ratio, but for a jungle operation, he should reduce this ratio to no less than five to one. Due to density altitude problems in tropical areas, the aircraft might not be able to develop enough lift to clear tall obstacles. So, the pathfinder leader considers obstacle height on the approach and departure ends. When site size and terrain conditions permit, the pilot might run the liftoffs and landings. However, the small size of a jungle site, soft terrain, or obstacles can keep him from doing so.

LIGHTS

4-99. The tactical situation might restrict the use of lights in nighttime jungle LZ operations.

SECURITY

4-100. Success of the ground unit commander's mission relies on site security. Because jungle terrain provides cover and concealment, landing site security presents a constant challenge. The pathfinder team leader coordinates with the flight commander to set a specific time to light the site.

LIFTOFFS AND LANDINGS

4-101. The pathfinder orients the site to the direction of the wind. He keeps departure obstacle ratios low due to climatic conditions, jungle vegetation, and helicopter's reduced lift capability. Because ground effects reduce the aircraft's lift efficiency, the pilot hovers as low as possible and lingers no longer than necessary.

DESERT

4-102. The typical desert is a dry, barren region, generally treeless and sandy. It has environmental extremes, with violent and unpredictable weather changes. Its terrain conforms to no particular model. Frequent clear days offer unequaled visibility and flight conditions, but a sudden sandstorm immediately halts all operations. Successful desert operations require special training, acclimatization, and great self-discipline.

COMMUNICATIONS

4-103. In desert operations, the radio offers the best way to communicate. The low, rolling terrain allows good radio range. Due to the increased distances involved in military desert operations, FM radio communications might prove inadequate, especially in the higher FM frequencies. Pathfinders, aircraft, and ground crew must all have high-frequency radio equipment. Sand or dust in equipment or a poor electrical ground cause most communication problems. Due to the increased distances between land force units engaged in desert operations, helicopters might provide air or ground relay or help deploy ground radio rebroadcast facilities.

NAVIGATION

4-104. Many of the conditions experienced in cold weather operations resemble those in desert operations. Pathfinders and pilots find distances and altitudes hard to judge in the desert. The lack of definable terrain features makes navigation difficult, especially at night and over long distances. Also, the sameness of the terrain can influence a pilot to pay less attention to his surroundings. Pathfinders might have to mark and man release points.

LANDING SITES

4-105. The climatic conditions in the desert profoundly affect the setup and operation of landing sites. Most importantly, the pathfinder must consider density altitude, wind, and sand (dust). Sand on a landing site can produce brownout conditions similar to those in snowy areas, so the same precautions apply. This makes a rocky area a better landing site than a sandy hollow, depression, or valley.

WIND

4-106. Desert winds generally calm down for an hour or two around sundown. Another calm occurs before sunrise. Other than those times, desert winds can drive dense clouds of dust and sand with hurricane force. Strong winds naturally raise dense clouds of dust and sand, and rapid temperature changes often follow strong winds. The pathfinder leader must consider what times of day the wind will allow him to operate the landing site.

4-107. The extreme heat often experienced in the desert also affects the aircraft's ACL. When supporting a ground unit, the pathfinder leader coordinates with the aviation element to determine the ACL for each type of aircraft. Both the minimum distance between aircraft and the size of the landing point might increase in desert operations: 100 meters between aircraft, 100-meter-diameter landing points. In daylight hours, ground-crew members mark the touchdown points. They paint sandbags a bright color or mark them using some other quick method. Ideally, they use signalmen.

4-108. When establishing a landing site, the pathfinder leader considers taxi procedures. When an aircraft must taxi, the pilot moves it into a vertical position as quickly as possible to reduce the amount of sand (dust) the engine sucks in as well as to avoid a brownout. Pilots should avoid taxiing over the same area repeatedly.

LIFTOFFS

4-109. Pilots will not try a normal liftoff in a sandstorm. Helicopters with wheels and airplanes should make a running-type takeoff. Helicopters with skids should make a maximum performance liftoff.

LANDINGS

4-110. When they can, pilots should use a running-type landing to reduce sand intake. If a pilot can make a running landing, he keeps the touchdown roll to a minimum to keep from overloading the landing gear. If the terrain does not permit a running landing, the pilot lands at a greater-than-normal angle. He should never land from a hover.

SAFETY

4-111. Ground crew personnel should wear clothing that will protect them against the sand blown around by the rotor wash. Each person on the ground should take special care to keep the sand out of his eyes, ears, nose, and mouth. Goggles, earplugs, and cloth masks provide adequate protection for facial areas. Other ground crew procedures resemble those for cold weather operations.

MOUNTAINS

4-112. Mountains have rugged, divided terrain with steep slopes and few natural or man-made lines of communication. Weather fluctuates seasonally from extreme cold, with ice and snow, to extreme heat. Also, it can switch between the two extremes very quickly. This unpredictability greatly affects operations.

COMMUNICATIONS

4-113. Mountainous terrain often limits or restricts communications. To maintain communications within the AO, aircraft might have to limit operations to the vicinity of the unit. Other aircraft can serve as radio relay stations. Pathfinder units might also have to set up radio relays at the RP, CCP, or both.

4-114. Mountain conditions challenge aviators in pathfinder operations more than any other conditions. For precise flying in mountainous areas, pilots need large-scale terrain maps.

4-115. Since intervening terrain degrades GTA communications, providing navigational aid and control over extended ranges might prove difficult.

WIND

4-116. The main weather hazard in the mountains is wind. Even moderate winds (11 to 20 knots) can produce significant turbulence over mountain ridges. Predicting wind conditions is difficult. The windward side of a mountain maintains a steady direction of airflow, though the strength of the wind might vary. The leeward side has turbulent winds with strong vertical currents. This turbulence might prevent assault landings and require pilots to fly at higher altitudes. This naturally increases the risk of detection and destruction.

DENSITY ALTITUDE

4-117. In the mountains, density altitude can vary a lot between PZs and LZs. It can also vary greatly from one time of day to another. It normally peaks in the late afternoon, and drops to its lowest point at dawn.

NAVIGATION

4-118. In the mountains, the helicopter offers the best way to rapidly move forces. In the offense, air assault operations can insert forces into the enemy's rear area and bypass or envelop his defenses. In the defense, helicopters can move reinforcements and reserves rapidly.

LANDING SITES

4-119. Mountainous regions offer few, if any, airfields for fixed-wing aircraft, and few LZs suitable for multiple helicopters.

4-120. If the enemy situation allows, pathfinders set up LZs on the windward side of the mountain because that side offers more stable winds.

4-121. When they can only find LZs designed for single aircraft, planners increase in-flight spacing. This places an extra load on each crew. When conducting multiship operations into a small LZ, the pathfinder controller should allow sufficient time between liftoff and landing for the turbulent air generated during the departure of the previous helicopter to stabilize. Otherwise, the pilot of the incoming craft will experience that turbulence and lose lift.

4-122. A pilot must touch down very carefully on the typical small, rough, sloped mountain LZ. Depending on the angle of the slope and on the aircraft's available torque, the pilot might be able to make a normal slope landing. Pilots of larger craft, such as cargo helicopters, might have trouble positioning the entire fuselage in the available area. Once the cockpit extends over the landing area, the pilot cannot see the ground. He must rely on the crew chief and signalman to direct him.

4-123. During a mountain approach to an LZ surrounded by uneven terrain, the pilot has a hard time determining the actual aircraft altitude and rate of closure. Where the terrain slopes up to the LZ, a visual illusion occurs. The pilot might think he is flying too high and closing too slowly. If the terrain slopes down to the LZ, he might feel he is flying too low and closing too fast. Employing a signalman on the ground gives the pilot a visual reference to adjust his controls. He might need more than one signalman.

SITE ASSESSMENT

4-124. Pathfinders should determine the following information while reconnoitering and selecting a mountain site:

- The size, slope, amount of surface debris, and the area covered by shadows and obstacles in and around the site.
- The approximate direction, speed, and characteristics of the wind.
- The inbound route, if necessary. When the pilot cannot land due to a steep slope, the aircraft might terminate at a hover to off-load troops and supplies.
- The departure route. Departure routes should orient into the wind and over the lowest obstacles.

SECTION VII. APPROACH PATH CONSIDERATIONS

Pilots should try to land their aircraft into the wind; however, the terrain and its effect on the wind might require a crosswind landing. If so, the pilot for single-rotor helicopters should plan the approach so that the wind blows from the left side of the aircraft. This helps the pilot overcome the effects of torque, reduces power requirements, and helps him control the heading. Other considerations include vertical air currents, escape routes, terrain contour and obstacles, and the position of the sun.

VERTICAL AIR CURRENTS

4-125. Updrafts on the approach path make landing easier. However, severe vertical air currents (updrafts or downdrafts) might require the pilot to approach downwind.

ESCAPE ROUTES

4-126. The pathfinders and pilots should plan one or more escape routes along the approach path for the pilot to use if he must go around and try the approach again.

TERRAIN CONTOUR AND OBSTACLES

4-127. The height of terrain and obstacles along the approach path should permit the pilot to conduct a shallow approach angle into the landing site. When possible, the pathfinders select a landing point on or near the highest terrain feature.

POSITION OF THE SUN

4-128. Though the pilot first considers wind direction and nature of the terrain when choosing the approach path, he must also consider the relative location of the sun and shade. To keep the pilot from having to adjust from one light condition to another, the pathfinder makes sure that if the landing point falls in a shaded spot, the whole approach path does as well. When the sun rises or falls to just above the horizon, avoid using an approach path that faces directly into it.

Chapter 5
External Loads

Carrying cargo and equipment outside the helicopter eliminates many of the problems that other modes of transportation have. Helicopters move cargo by external slingload when—

- The cargo compartment cannot hold the load.
- The load exceeds the helicopter's internal load limitation.
- The ground crew must load or unload the cargo at once.
- Landing zone conditions prevent the aircraft from touching down.

Pathfinder-qualified Soldiers prepare to organize and control external load pickup or drop-off sites as an integral part of LZ operations. The supported unit provides a detailed load plan, to include rough weights and sequences of load movement. This ensures the correct and rapid movement and placement of cargo.

LANDING POINTS

5-1. Conditions such as a dusty surfaces, darkness, or obstacles often require pathfinders to increase the minimum spacing between loads and landing points. This reduces the number of helicopters that can safely operate at the site at the same time, the size of the mission that can be supported, and the overall speed of the operation.

TYPES OF LOADS

5-2. All external loads fall under one of three types: high density, low density, or aerodynamic. Each exhibits unique characteristics in flight. Pathfinders determine the type, size, and weight of the load during the planning phase of the operation.

HIGH DENSITY

5-3. The high-density load offers the best stability.

LOW DENSITY

5-4. The low-density load offers the least stability.

AERODYNAMIC

5-5. The aerodynamic load lacks stability until the airstream stabilizes the load. The ACL depends on the type of aircraft, the age of the airframe, the altitude above sea level, the temperature, the humidity, and the aviation unit's SOP.

Chapter 5

UNIT RESPONSIBILITIES

5-6. Most slingload operations involve four units. Each has pathfinders who perform specific functions.

SUPPORTED UNIT

5-7. The supported unit moves equipment and rigs the loads. Pathfinders in the supported unit check the weight, rigging, and positioning of all external loads to ensure helicopter safety. Ideally, the supported unit provides hookup personnel for individual loads. In the supported unit, pathfinders assist in—

- Selecting, preparing, and controlling the PZ.
- Coordinating in advance with the supporting unit.
- Rigging the loads.
- Furnishing slings, straps, clevises, and any other slingload equipment required for the move.
- Checking for improper rigging and weight in excess of the aircraft's ACL.

AVIATION UNIT

5-8. This is the aviation unit that will fly the loads. They—

- Provide advice and technical help to the supported unit, as required.
- Ensure that the loads fall within the transporting aircraft's ACL.
- Provide assistance in the recovery and return of slingload equipment.
- Advise the supported unit on load limitations.
- Advise the supported and receiving units on the suitability of selected LZs and PZs.
- Establish coordination with the supported and receiving units.

RECEIVING UNIT

5-9. The receiving unit—

- Selects, prepares, and controls the LZ.
- Provides trained ground crews to guide the aircraft and de-rig the loads.
- Coordinates with the supporting unit for the control and return of the slingload equipment.
- Inspects the rigging of back loads.

PATHFINDER UNIT

5-10. In the pathfinder unit, pathfinders—

- Provide advice and aid to the supported, aviation, and receiving units.
- Provide expertise in the planning and execution of both PZ and HLZ operations.
- Supervise the rigging and inspection of all the loads.
- Provide ground guidance and air traffic control during the slingload.
- Ensure that the loads fall under the transporting aircraft's ACL.

EQUIPMENT

5-11. Cargo nets and slings make up an essential part of the external load operation. During an inspection, they require the same level of attention that the cargo receives. Any evidence of frayed or cut webbing justifies replacement of the affected component. When they assemble slings, pathfinders should avoid sewing up torn slings or substituting nonstandard parts in the field. Slings must meet the critical

External Loads

strength requirements specified in FM 10-450-3. The Army's inventory includes a variety of equipment adapted or designated for use in slingload operations.

AERIAL-DELIVERY SLINGS

5-12. Aerial-delivery slings (ADSs) were originally designed to deliver heavy loads by air (Table 5-1). They have been adapted for use in air assault operations. ADSs come in a variety of sizes and strengths, as shown in FM 10-450-3.

Usage	Loop Slings	Vertical Pendant Pounds	Thicknesses	Available Lengths (In Feet)	
Pendant	2-Loop [1,2]	8,900	4	3 feet	16 feet
				9 feet	20 feet
				11 feet	120 feet
				12 feet	
	3-Loop	13,500	6	60 feet	140 feet
	4-Loop	17,800	8	3 feet	16 feet
				9 feet	20 feet
				11 feet	28 feet
				12 feet	
	6-Loop	27,000	12	60 feet	120 feet
	9-Loop	42,000			
Part of sling set	2-Loop [1,2]	5,600	4	3 feet	16 feet
				9 feet	20 feet
				11 feet	120 feet
	3-Loop	8,500	6	60 feet	140 feet
	4-Loop	11,200	8	3 feet	16 feet
				9 feet	20 feet
				11 feet	28 feet
				12 feet	
	6-Loop	17,000	12	60 feet	120 feet
[1] Identified by colored thread stitched lengthwise down the middle of the strap.					
[2] Three-foot donut ring tensile strength for this sling equals 10,000 pounds. Using dual rings increases tensile strength to 17,500 pounds.					

Table 5-1. Aerial delivery specifications for the Type XXVI sling.

Chapter 5

HITCHES

5-13. When connecting ADSs to metal air items or directly to the load, loaders use one of the following hitches (Figure 5-1).

Choker

5-14. Pull the free-running end of the sling around the point of attachment. Draw it between the loops of the sling's standing end. After making sure that the cotton buffer is in its proper place, "milk" down the keeper on the standing end to secure the sling.

Basket

5-15. Separate the loops of the sling at one end. Place the sling over the suspension point. Ensure that the cotton buffer is in its proper place. To secure the sling, "milk" down the keeper towards the suspension point.

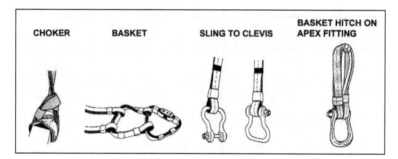

Figure 5-1. Hitches.

NETS AND CONTAINERS

5-16. The Army has many types of cargo containers. However, the 5,000- and 10,000-pound cargo nets and the A-22 cargo bag are the ones most often used to transport cargo externally. FM 10-450-3 describes how to inspect both the large cargo net and the A-22 cargo bag (Figure 5-2). It also provides rigging instructions. Avoid overloading the nets; use them with loads that fall within the aviation unit's prescribed limits. Pick up the nets rather than drag them across the ground, because dragging them can cause them to snag on something and damage the net or the thing it snags. Use a canvas insert when carrying items small enough to slip through the netting.

Small (5,000-Pound Capacity) Cargo Net

5-17. This olive drab net can carry up to 5,000 pounds or 125 cubic feet of cargo (NSN 1670-01-058-3811, line item number [LIN] 2776).

Large (10,000-Pound Capacity) Cargo Net

5-18. This larger net can carry up to 10,000 pounds or 380 cubic feet of cargo (NSN 1670-01-058-3810, LIN NO 2708). It is 18 feet wide and can transport boxed or bulky loads (Figure 5-2).

External Loads

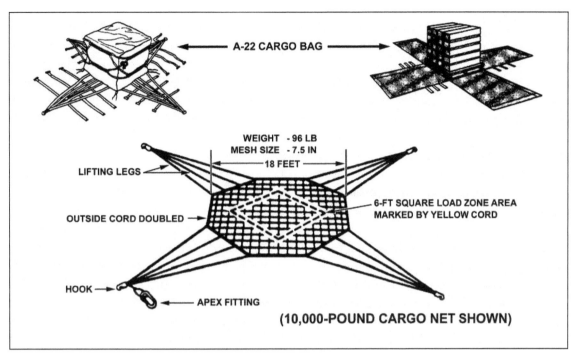

Figure 5-2. Cargo nets and bag.

A-22 Cargo Bag

5-19.   The A-22 cargo bag, with or without its canvas cover, can externally transport standard palletized loads, loose cargo, ammunition, oil drums, and other general items whose total weight falls under 2,200 pounds (Figure 5-3).

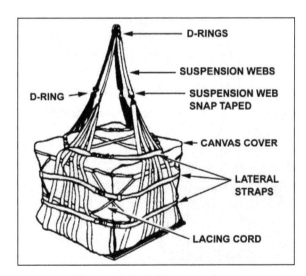

Figure 5-3. A-22 cargo bag.

Chapter 5

Suspension Clevises

5-20. Clevises come in three sizes.

Large

5-21. This clevis (NSN 4030-00-090-5354) has a rated capacity of 12,500 pounds (pendant) with a 7,875-pound sling-to-lifting provision point of attachment. Adding more large clevises as attaching points increases rated capacity as follows:

- Two large clevises increase rated capacity to 15,750 pounds.
- Three large clevises increase rated capacity to 23,625 pounds.
- Four large clevises increase rated capacity to 31,500 pounds.

Medium

5-22. This clevis (NSN 1670 4030-00-678-8562, Figure 5-4) has a rated capacity of 6,250 pounds (pendant) with a 3,750-pound sling-to-lifting provision. Adding more medium clevises as attaching points increases rated capacity as follows:

- Two medium clevises increase rated capacity to 7,500 pounds.
- Three medium clevises increase rated capacity to 11,250 pounds.
- Four medium clevises increase rated capacity to 15,000 pounds.

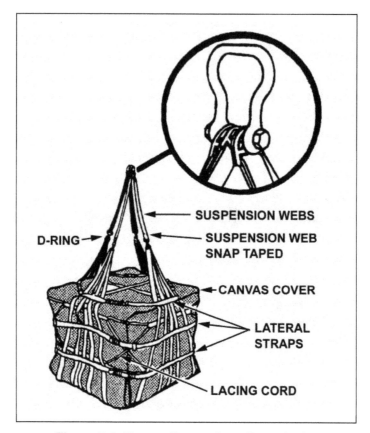

Figure 5-4. Upper sling and medium clevis.

Small

5-23. This clevis (NSN 1670 4030-00-360-0304) has a rated capacity of 6,250 pounds (pendant) with a 3,750-pound sling-to-lifting provision. Adding more small clevises as attaching points increases rated capacity as follows:

- Two small clevises increase rated capacity to 7,500 pounds.
- Three small clevises increase rated capacity to 11,250 pounds.
- Four small clevises increase rated capacity to 15,000 pounds.

REACH PENDANTS

5-24. A reach pendant is a synthetic rope assembly with an attached, stiffened reach tube and a loop on each end. The built-in reach tube enables the hookup man to place the pendant's top eye on the helicopter cargo hook while the helicopter hovers at a higher distance over the load (Figure 5-5). Two reach pendants are authorized for use with slingloads. To use either pendant with a sling set, remove the sling set apex fitting pin; place the pendant's lower eye in the apex fitting; and reinstall the apex fitting pin.

11,000-Pound Capacity

5-25. The 11K, NSN 4020-01-365-3115, part number DSG-5-11K, measures about 5 feet long and has an 11,000-pound safe working load capacity. The top eye is black with a small diameter loop, while the bottom eye is green with a larger diameter loop. The safe working load capacity is stamped on the reach tube.

25,000-Pound Capacity

5-26. The 25K, NSN 4020-01-337-3185, part number BOS-14-K7, measures about 5 feet long and has a 25,000-pound safe working load capacity. The top eye is black with a small diameter loop, while the bottom eye is also black, but has a larger diameter loop. The safe working load capacity is stamped on the reach tube.

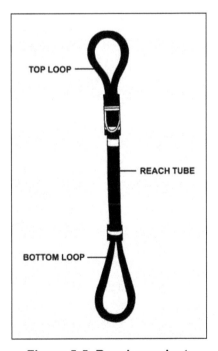

Figure 5-5. Reach pendant.

Chapter 5

Inspection

5-27. Inspect the reach pendants *before and after* use. Check for cuts and tears in the nylon-urethane plastic sheath on each loop. If the white strength member (third layer) shows, remove the pendant from service.

Cleaning

5-28. Clean the reach pendant with a mixture of warm water and mild dish or laundry detergent. You can use mineral spirits to remove oil and grease. You can treat the top and bottom eyes with silicone spray. However, do not use silicone spray on the reach tube.

Storage

5-29. Store the reach pendants in a clean, dry area out of direct sunlight. Prolonged exposure to sunlight will deteriorate the strength of reach pendants.

> **CAUTION**
> Avoid getting silicone spray on the reach tube. Avoid using chemical cleaners on reach pendants. Chemicals may weaken the strength members of the pendant. If a pendant becomes contaminated with chemicals, remove it from service.

POLYESTER ROUNDSLINGS

5-30. Use polyester roundslings as the primary vertical pendant (Figure 5-6). You can use one of three hitches to attach roundslings to the load. The lifting capacity of polyester roundslings varies with the size of the sling and the type of hitch used to attach the load. Each sling has two identification tags permanently sewn to the eye and eye sleeve. These identify the size and capacity of the roundsling as well as other information needed for its safe use. Roundslings are also color-coded by size. Table 5-2 lists roundsling lengths and lift capacities.

Storage

5-31. Store roundslings in a clean, dry, cool area out of direct sunlight. Prolonged exposure to sunlight will deteriorate the strength of roundslings.

Inspection

5-32. Inspect each polyester roundsling before and after every use. Remove it from service if you find any of the following:

- Missing or unreadable identification tags.
- Acid or alkali burns.
- Melted, charred, or weld-splattered portions.
- Any holes, tears, cuts, snags, embedded particles, broken or worn stitching, or abrasive wear that exposes the core fibers.
- Knots in any part of the roundsling.
- Distortion, excessive pitting, corrosion, or broken fitting(s).
- Any other condition that causes doubt as to the strength of the roundsling.

External Loads

> **CAUTION**
> Avoid dragging roundslings on the floor or over rough surfaces. Never twist them or join them together with knots.

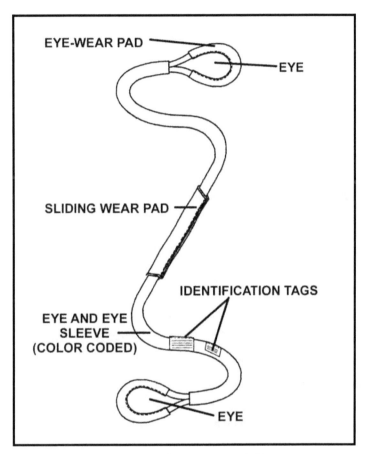

Figure 5-6. Polyester roundslings.

Part No.	Length (In Feet)	Color	Lift Capacity			Weight (In Pounds)
			Choke	Vertical	Basket	
PRS2E008	8	GREEN	4,200	5,300	10,600	4
PRS2E017	17	GREEN	4,200	5,300	10,600	10
PRS3E008	8	YELLOW	6,700	8,400	16,800	5
PRS3E017	17	YELLOW	6,700	8,400	16,800	11
PRS5E030	30	RED	10,600	13,200	26,400	26
PRS7E065	65	BLUE	17,000	21,200	42,400	75
PRS7E070	70	BLUE	17,000	21,200	42,400	81

Table 5-2. Safe working loads (lift capacities) of polyester roundslings.

Chapter 5

SERVICE LIFE OF AERIAL-DELIVERY SLINGS

5-33. The first person to use a sling must date-stamp it with the calendar or Julian date in 1-inch letters. He can use orange-yellow parachute-marking ink, strata blue parachute-marking ink, or an orange-yellow tube-type marker. He marks near the first keeper at both ends of the sling. This date determines the date of the next inspection. Every six months, the current user reinspects the sling; strikes through the last date in the same color it was written in; and in either of the other two colors, marks the date he reinspected the sling. *Every single user* inspects *every single sling* before and after *every single use*. If the condition of the sling seems questionable, he removes the sling from service (Figure 5-7).

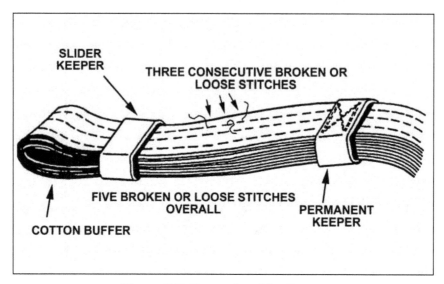

Figure 5-7. Unserviceable slings.

GENERAL INSPECTION

5-34. When inspecting nylon air items, note that if you find more than three consecutive broken or loose stitches, or five or more broken or loose stitches overall in the sewn portion, the item is unserviceable. After rigging the load with any nylon air item, put cotton buffers in place to prevent any nylon-to-nylon or nylon-to-metal contact. Look for the following:

- Inspection date that has already passed (an inspection is overdue).
- Foreign matter or chemicals such as mildew, paint, or grease.
- Cuts.
- Frays.
- Burns.
- Broken stitches.
- Missing cotton buffers, sliding keepers, or permanent keepers.
- Rust.

CARGO STRAP

5-35. The A7A cotton or nylon cargo strap measures 188 inches long and has a rated capacity of 500 pounds. A friction adapter located on one end of the strap has a thick-lipped metal floating bar. Supply issues this strap with one metal D-ring. Inspect this piece of equipment for cuts or frays.

External Loads

CARGO TIE-DOWN EQUIPMENT

5-36. Check the tie-downs for serviceability.

CGU-1B Tie-Down Strap

5-37. The CGU-1B cargo tie-down device has a rated capacity of 5,000 pounds. You can adjust the length of this device.

15-Foot Tie-Down Strap

5-38. The 15-foot cargo tie-down strap, issued with a quick-fit strap fastener, has a rated capacity of 5,000 pounds.

Load Binders

5-39. The two load binder types are rated for 10,000 pounds and 5,000 pounds. The 10,000-pound capacity load binder has its rating stamped on the side.

METAL AIR ITEMS

5-40. Thoroughly inspect metal air items for rust, stripped threads on the nuts or bolts, burrs, cracks, bent or twisted metal, or oil. When using any clevis assembly, tighten the nut hand-tight only.

Inspection

5-41. Use the Type IV link assembly (NSN 1670-00-783-5988) to build a 3-foot donut or to connect one ADS to another (Figure 5-8). This link assembly has a rated capacity of 12,500 pounds. When inspecting the Type IV link assembly, look for the following deficiencies:

- Hard to rotate or irregularly rotating aluminum buffers.
- Bent or cracked posts.
- Bent slide connectors.
- The absence of a metallic "click" when it locks.

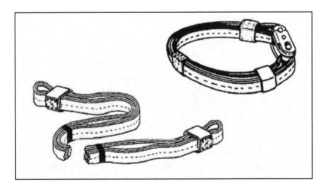

Figure 5-8. Three-foot apex (donut) ring.

25 April 2006   FM 3-21.38   5-11

Chapter 5

Points of Attachment

5-42. In slingload operations, the clevis assemblies serve as points of attachment from the aircraft to the load.

Tightening

5-43. When using any clevis assembly, tighten the nut by hand only. Tape both ends of the nut and bolt to prevent slippage during use. Choose only case-hardened nuts and bolts. Never mix items. The bolt heads have case-hardened marks such as ticks, numbers, letters, or a combination of all three.

LARGE-CAPACITY SLING SETS

5-44. The new 10,000-pound and 25,000-pound capacity sling sets are similar, except for a few minor differences. All components have identifying marks. You may only exchange apex fittings between sets. Take care not to mix up the other components. Table 5-3 compares these two large-capacity sling sets, and Figure 5-9 shows one.

Type Sling		*10,000-Pound Sling*	*25,000-Pound Sling*
Capacity:		10,000 pounds	25,000 pounds
Apex fitting	Color:	Brushed aluminum	Gold steel
	Pin diameter:	1 1/8-inch diameter	1 1/2-inch diameter
	Weight:	4 1/2 pounds	10 pounds
Sling rope	Color:	Olive drab	Black
	Length:	12 feet	12 feet
	Diameter:	7/8 inch	1 1/4 inch
Chain links-quantity:		110 to 115 links	86 to 88 links
NSN:		1670-01-027-2902	1670-01-027-2900
Total weight:		52 pounds	114 pounds

Table 5-3. Large-capacity sling sets.

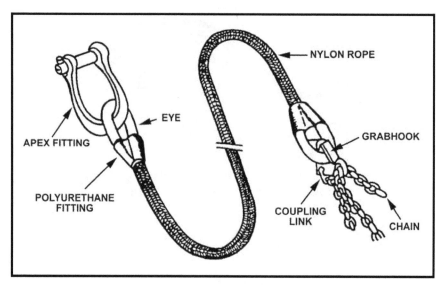

Figure 5-9. 25,000-pound capacity sling set.

External Loads

> **CAUTION**
>
> Each sling set has four legs. Each leg has a rated capacity of one-quarter of the total capacity of the set. On some loads, you will use up to six legs. However, remember that adding two legs does not increase the rated capacity of the entire set.

5-45. The nylon rope assembly for each set has an interwoven eye located at each end. A polyurethane fitting covers the eye to protect the leg from abrasion and ultraviolet radiation (Figure 5-9). Each double-braided rope connects to a grabhook assembly. Figure 5-10, Figure 5-11, and Figure 5-12 show a coupling link, sling leg-numbering sequence, and a grabhook, respectively. Though the grabhooks for the two sets look alike, you cannot interchange them because they have different ratings.

5-46. FM 10-450-3 and TM 10-1670-295-23&P discuss how to inspect the rope sling sets. FM 10-450-3 also provides sling-conversion tables.

5-47. Secure the cross pin on each apex fitting with a 3/8-inch bolt, a castellated nut, and a cotter pin.

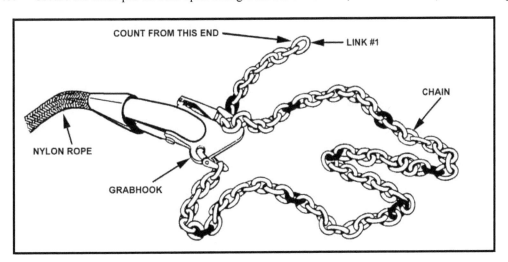

Figure 5-10. Coupling link.

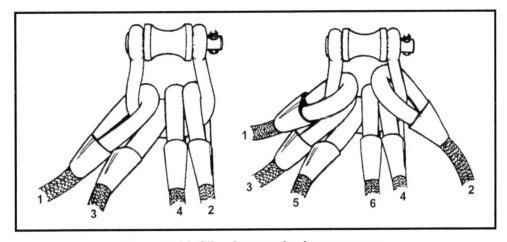

Figure 5-11. Sling leg-numbering sequence.

Chapter 5

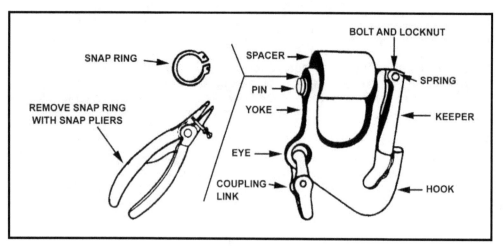

Figure 5-12. Grabhook.

AIRCRAFT LOAD LIMITATIONS

5-48. The structural strength of the cargo hook assembly determines the maximum weight that any aircraft can carry with an external slingload. In most cases, the tensile strength of the hook does not limit the weight that an aircraft can lift; the allowable cargo load does. In fact, the capacity of the cargo hook assembly usually exceeds the ACL.

TENSILE STRENGTH

5-49. Cargo hook tensile strengths for US Army aircraft show—

- UH-1H/UH-1N Iroquois – 4,000 or 5,000 pounds (Figure 5-13).
- UH-60A/60L Blackhawks – 8,000 or 9,000 pounds (Figure 5-14).
- CH-47D Chinook – 26,000 pounds (Figure 5-15, page 5-18).

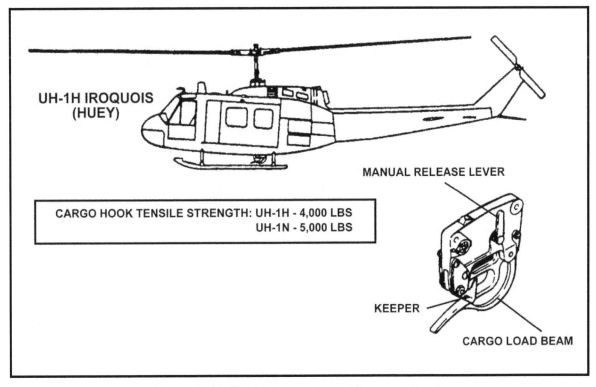

Figure 5-13. UH-1H Iroquois and its cargo hook.

Chapter 5

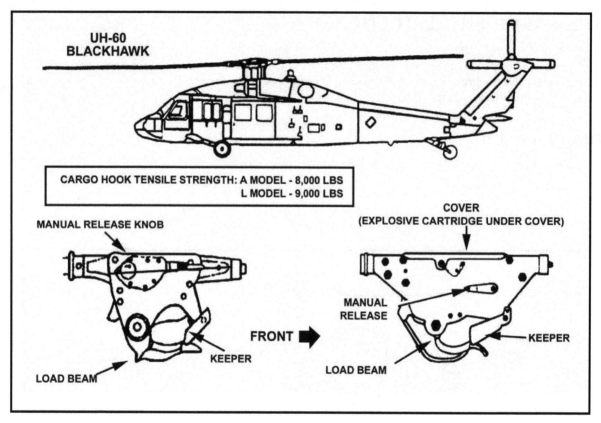

Figure 5-14. UH-60 Blackhawk and its cargo hooks.

External Loads

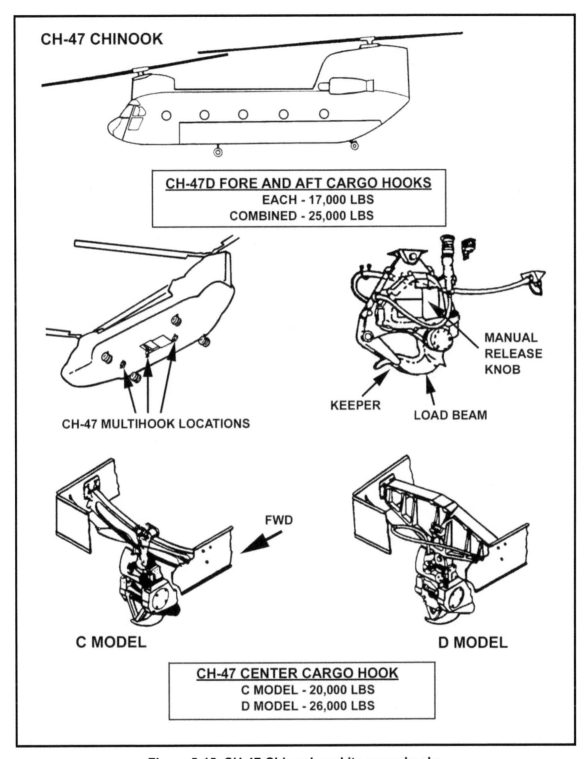

Figure 5-15. CH-47 Chinook and its cargo hooks.

UH-1H

5-50. When transporting external loads with a UH-1H, use a nylon donut or web ring to attach the load to the aircraft. The cargo hook on the UH-1H is stationary; using an apex with a heavy load would bind the hook and shear it off. The cargo hook tensile strengths for the UH-1H is 4,000 pounds; for the UH-1N, it is 5,000 pounds.

UH-60 BLACKHAWK

5-51. When using the 10,000-pound apex to secure an external load to the UH-60, you must also use the aluminum spacer. The spacer is not required, or recommended, when using a 25,000-pound apex. However, if you use the 25,000-pound apex with spacer, the cargo hook must be manually operated by an aircraft crewmember or a member of the hook-up team. *Never* use a donut or web ring on a UH-60. The web ring will bind on the hook and prevent the crew from releasing the load in an emergency. The tensile strength of the UH-60 cargo hook system is, for the UH-60A, 8,000 pounds and for the UH-60L, 9,000 pounds.

STANDARD WEIGHTS

5-52. When using a UH-60 Blackhawk for airlift, coordinate closely with the aviation unit for the ACL. For the standard weights of petroleum, oils, and lubricants (POL), for external loads only, see Table 5-4. Standard vehicle and artillery weights follow in Table 5-5 and Table 5-6.

Fuel	*55-Gallon Drum*	*500-Gallon Blivet*
Motor gasoline (MOGAS)	404 pounds	3,400 pounds
Gasoline (JP4/JP8)	410 pounds	3,500 pounds
Diesel fuel	457 pounds	3,800 pounds
Lube oil (30 weight)	479 pounds	4,000 pounds

Table 5-4. POL for external loads only.

Vehicle	Weight
M998/M1038 Truck, Cargo, 1 1/4-ton (HMMWV)	5,200 pounds (empty) 7,700 pounds (loaded)
M966 TOW Missile Carrier (HMMWV)	6,050 pounds (empty) 8,200 pounds (loaded)
M416 1/4-Ton Trailer	580 pounds
M101A2 3/4-Ton Trailer	1,350 pounds
M105A2 1 1/2-Ton Trailer	2,750 pounds
M35A2 2 1/2-Ton Truck	12,000 pounds (add 500 pounds if equipped with a winch)
M149 1 1/4-Ton Water Trailer	2,540 pounds (empty) 6,060 pounds (full)
M149A1 1 1/4-Ton Water Trailer	2,540 pounds (empty) 6,060 pounds (full)
M149A2 1 1/4-Ton Water Trailer	2,800 pounds (empty) 6,320 pounds (full)

Table 5-5. Standard vehicle weights.

Artillery	Weight
M101 105-mm howitzer	4,600 pounds (add 300 pounds if equipped with shields)
M102 105-mm howitzer	3,160 pounds (add 170 pounds for section equipment)
105-mm ammunition	60 pounds (each box)
105-mm ammunition	47 pounds (each carton)

Table 5-6. Standard artillery weights.

AIR ITEMS REQUIRED FOR COMMON STANDARD LOADS

5-53. Pathfinders require several types of expendable rigging supplies to complete the rigging of the loads discussed in this paragraph. These supplies include 1/4-inch cotton webbing (80-pound test), 3/8-inch diameter rope (3,180-pound test), 7/16-inch diameter nylon rope (4,500-pound test), type III nylon cord (550-pound test), pressure-sensitive tape, cellulose wadding or paperboard energy-dissipating material, and canvas or felt padding. Pathfinders should obtain sufficient supplies of these items before rigging the loads. To rig loads with ADSs and with more than one suspension point, twist an ADS once for each 3 feet of sling length. This reduces vibration in the sling during flight. The nylon and chain multileg sling sets and the 10,000- and 25,000-pound capacity sling sets do not require the twists. FM 10-450-3 discusses preparation and rigging for the following loads in detail.

Chapter 5

CARGO NET

5-54. A 5,000-pound-capacity (15 feet square) or 10,000-pound-capacity (18 feet square) nylon cargo net requires one A7A cargo strap or length of rope. With this the pathfinder can secure the net together on top of the load to prevent smaller items from falling out of the net.

PERFORATED STEEL PLANKING

5-55. Perforated steel planking (PSP) requires—

- Two 16-foot, two or three-loop ADSs.
- One 3-foot ADS with one type IV link assembly (for donut).

FUEL DRUMS

5-56. One or two rubber or fabric fuel drums (blivets), each of which contains 500 gallons of fuel and a 10,000-pound-capacity sling set.

CONCERTINA WIRE

5-57. The items required to move this load depend on the amount of concertina wire in the load.

CARGO BAG

5-58. The A-22 cargo bag has a maximum capacity of 2,200 pounds.

SLINGLOAD THEORY

5-59. The behavior of an external load in flight can greatly affect the performance of the aircraft carrying it. High drag coefficients reduce airspeed. This means that the task takes longer or does not get finished if the allotted time for the task expires. Therefore, whoever prepares the load must try to reduce the drag of the load on the aircraft. A high drag coefficient can also endanger the aircraft and crew. Because of this, the pilot must "punch" if he thinks that continuing to fly the load could endanger his crew or aircraft. To stabilize a load, the loaders should consider the following:

ADDITION OF WEIGHT TO THE LOAD

5-60. The heavier a load, the less air pressure will disturb it. Thus, carrying heavier loads assures greater stability. However, make sure the load does not exceed the rated capacity of the equipment or the ACL of the aircraft.

STREAMLINING OF THE LOAD

5-61. Long, symmetrical loads fly crosswise to the direction of flight. This causes a lot of drag on the aircraft. Loads tend to stabilize if the center of gravity (CG) is located in the first one-third of the load. Either adjust the load or, if needed, add weight to move the CG toward one end or the other. The heavier end of the load will "seek" the direction of flight and the load will stabilize. The lighter tail end of the load will act just like the fins on a dart.

AIRSPEED OF THE AIRCRAFT

5-62. The least desirable method is to have the aircraft fly slow to try to keep the load from destabilizing. This burns extra fuel and takes more time to do less work. Prepare the loads so that the aircraft can fly safely at speeds of 60 knots or more.

External Loads

SLING LENGTH

5-63. Lengthening the slings that attach the load to the aircraft reduces the load's stability in flight. The shorter, the better, as long as the sling measures at least 6 feet long. Also, the more vertical the attached sling, the less stress on those that are more horizontal. Figure 5-16, page 5-22, shows how sling angle affects load stress.

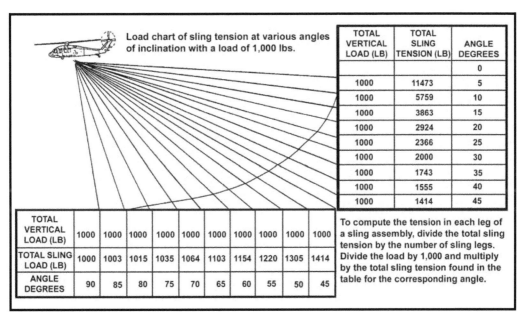

Figure 5-16. Load chart of sling tension at various angles of inclination with a load of 1,000 pounds.

EFFECT OF VERTICAL SLING

5-64. A vertical sling carrying 3,000 pounds has 3,000 pounds of stress on it. That means the stress equals the weight of the load.

EFFECT OF 45-DEGREE SLING

5-65. A 45-degree sling carrying 3,000 pounds has 4,242 pounds of stress on it. That means the stress equals nearly one-and-a-half times the weight of the load.

EFFECT OF 5-DEGREE SLING

5-66. A 5-degree (almost horizontal) sling carrying 3,000 pounds has 34,419 pounds of stress on it. That means the stress equals more than ten times the weight of the load.

HOOKUP AND RELEASE PROCEDURES

5-67. Hooking up a load requires a team effort. The signalman must position the aircraft over the load. He does this so the slingload team can discharge the static electricity and attach the load to the aircraft as quickly and safely as possible. Most of the time, the air crew releases the load. This seldom requires any ground crew except the signalman.

GROUND CREW PROTECTIVE MEASURES AND EQUIPMENT

5-68.   Working around hovering helicopters exposes ground crews to a variety of dangers. Leaders must do everything they can to ensure the safety of the ground crews. The crews themselves should use the following safety equipment (Figure 5-17).

Helmet

5-69.   This protects the wearer from head injuries caused by flying debris. It also protects him if his head were to get caught between the aircraft and the load, for example. Wearers must keep helmets securely fastened.

External Loads

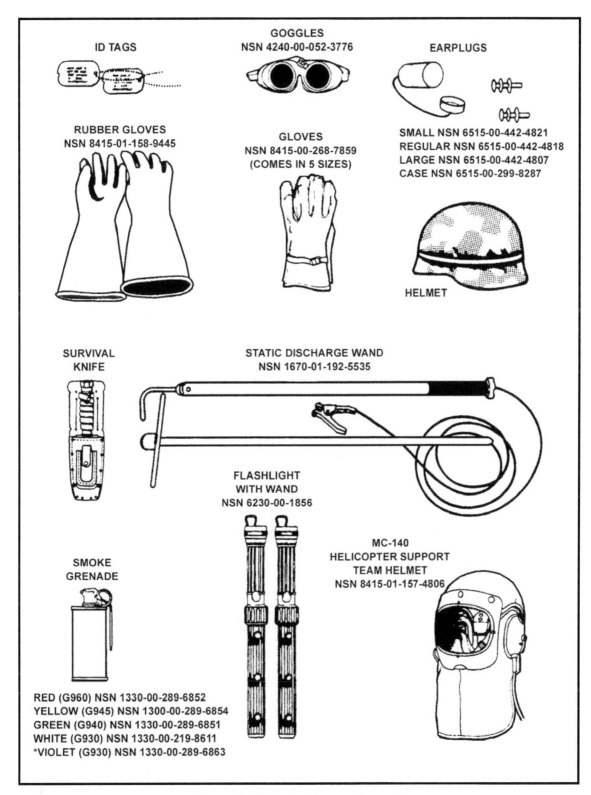

Figure 5-17. Protective equipment.

Protective Mask or Dust Goggles with Respirator

5-70. In high dust or debris environments, each crewmember wears a mask or goggles. This protects the crewmembers' faces, eyes, and respiratory systems from the airborne particles stirred up by the rotor wash. The mask protects better than the goggles but can cause problems with depth perception (important for signalmen).

Earplugs or Suitable Substitute

5-71. These protect against the excessive noise associated with hovering aircraft. They also prevent debris from entering the ear canal.

Hand Protection

5-72. Marine Corps and Navy personnel must wear gloves designed to protect electrical workers against burns due to static discharges. Everyone else (US Army, USAF, and USCG) should wear leather gloves to help protect the hands and fingers. Whoever must use the static wand to discharge static electricity should wear gloves designed for adequate protection from static discharge burns.

- Inspect shockproof gloves before and after each operation. Check for excessive wear, fraying, holes, and tears. Do not use a torn glove. Even a small hole leaves a person unprotected from static electric shock.
- Check each glove for holes by filling it with water and squeezing it while holding the open end closed. Or, blow air into it like a balloon and submerge it in water. Any holes will cause air bubbles.

Static Discharge Wand

5-73. The static discharge wand protects the hookup man from electrical shock by grounding the cargo hook. In flight, the helicopter stores static electricity. This electrical charge increases with the weight of the helicopter, with low humidity, and with the amount of debris blown around by the rotor system (dust, sand, or snow). Thunderstorms can cause huge discharges of static electricity. When the helicopter lands and touches the ground, this charge grounds. However, while the helicopter remains airborne, such as when it hovers to make a slingload drop, the charge stays in the aircraft. As soon as the ground-crew member connects the apex fitting to the cargo hook, he becomes a path for an electrical charge to follow into the ground. This charge can cause severe electrical burn or injury.

- To avoid the possibility of a static electric shock, ground the cargo hook (connect the helicopter to the ground) using grounding stakes and static discharge wands. (The stakes and wands may be field-expedient or manufactured.) Because these wands connect the helicopter to the ground, the electric charge dissipates. This protects the hookup man from receiving a shock when he connects the apex fitting to the cargo hook.
- Inspect the static discharge wand to make sure it is in serviceable condition. Drive the grounding stake opposite the ground crew's exit direction. This keeps them from tripping on the cable as they leave.
- Drive the stake into the ground until it seats firmly—at least 6 to 8 inches in firm ground and 24 inches in sandy or loose soil. Drive the stake in at a 45-degree angle away from the side of the load, in case someone falls on it. Connect the cable clamp to the vertical shaft of the stake.
- When operating on concrete or asphalt surfaces, position the loads as close to the edge of the surface as you can. This allows you to drive the grounding stake into the ground.
- Do not hold the static discharge wand within 14 to 16 inches of the metal hook end—a strong static charge can jump as far as 12 inches. During the hookup operation, the static discharge wand must stay in contact with the cargo hook. If contact fails, all ground-crew members must pull back from the hook until someone can reestablish contact between the wand and the aircraft's cargo hook.

Other Equipment

5-74.   Use smoke grenades to mark the location of the landing site or to indicate wind direction. Use flashlights with wands to give arm-and-hand signals at night.

SAFETY

5-75.   In addition to using the proper equipment, Soldiers must also follow these other safety measures:

- Wear long-sleeved shirts with the sleeves rolled down and fastened. Button your shirt collar. Tuck shirttails or jacket bottoms into your trousers.
- Police the operational area thoroughly before conducting slingload operations. This cuts down on the amount of debris thrown about by rotor wash.

5-76.   Stay alert during hookup and release operations; sound judgment and common sense hold the keys to success. Stay ready to get clear of the load. Soldiers have been crushed between the aircraft and loads. Some have had loads dragged over them; others took an unwanted ride when they somehow entangled themselves with the load. Whenever you have to make the hookup, take special care. Slings under tension can easily crush an arm or leg against the load. Some of the particular hazards associated with loads include—

Cargo Extensions or Projections

5-77.   Gun tubes, landing gear, missile launchers, bridge planks, and so forth can interfere with or injure you by striking or tripping you. Stand clear of such projections or position yourself so you can clear the load at once.

Sharp Projections, Hooks, Handles, Racks

5-78.   If possible, avoid these. Examples include protruding handles or levers such as tarpaulin tie-down hooks, door handles, spare-tire racks, and similar projections. Sharp edges can cause serious injury. You can quickly get hooked to the load if your clothing or equipment catches on something. Keep alert and ready to move out of danger immediately.

Top-Heavy or Narrow-Based Loads

5-79.   Treat with caution any top-heavy or narrow-based loads that the rotor wash could blow over. If possible, lay this kind of load on its side before starting the hookup. If you cannot do this, position the crew on the side or end of the load that is least likely to tip. Again, stay ready to move away from the danger quickly.

High Loads

5-80.   High loads can seriously injure you if you climb up on them to hook them up. Rotor wash can sweep you off, or you might have to jump to avoid a dangerous situation. Pay attention to where you stand. Try to stand on a lower projection or step rather than on top of the load. This way, if the aircraft makes contact with the load, it does not catch you in between. Also, try to work from a crouched position or from your hands and knees. Keep solid footholds and handholds, and stay ready to move quickly out of the way if you need to. If possible, back a vehicle up to the load and use it as a working platform. (Move it out of the way before the aircraft starts to lift the load.)

GROUND CREW EMERGENCY CONDUCT

5-81.   When an aircraft hovering over a slingload suffers an emergency severe enough for the pilot to have to set the aircraft down, he will do so. This can happen all at once such as in a controlled crash. For

Chapter 5

this reason, whenever an aircraft seems to be having trouble, all members of the ground crew should clear the slingload point by moving to a location coordinated with the aviation unit. Once they have moved far enough away, they should each take a prone position or seek cover until the aircraft lands. Two responsibilities require special note:

Signalman

5-82. Face the aircraft; move to a safe spot.

Hookup Men

5-83. Try to work along the same side of the load as your assembly area, or as coordinated. This way, you do not have to climb over or go around the load to seek safety. You can instead move directly off and away from the load. If the load is a heavy piece of equipment, you might want to keep the load between you and the aircraft while you are moving. This offers you some protection if the aircraft were to crash.

GROUND CREW DUTIES

5-84. Normally, the ground crew consists of one signalman and two hookup men, with one hookup man acting as static wand man.

Signalman

5-85. Duties of the signalman include the following.

Before the Aircraft Arrive(s)

5-86. Direct the positioning of the load. Supervise the inspection of the load for proper routing of the slings and proper preparation. Ensure that the load is ready to fly.

As the Helicopter(s) Approaches

5-87. Station yourself 20 meters in front of the load where you can best maintain eye contact with the crew. Give the arm-and-hand signal of "assume guidance." As the helicopter nears the load, use arm-and-hand signals to position the cargo hook directly over the load, close enough that the hookup men can place the apex fitting onto the cargo hook. During this time, position yourself so the pilot can see your signals easily. Because the pilot of an Army aircraft sits on the right side of the aircraft, you will usually stand just to the right of the aircraft. If the terrain forces you to stand somewhere else, make sure the pilot can see you at all times.

During the Hookup Process

5-88. Watch the cargo hook and apex fitting. After hookup, the pilot hovers the aircraft until the hookup men clear away from the load. When they have moved clear, you will signal the aircraft upward slowly, so the sling legs gradually take up the load. You must do this to make sure the sling legs clear the load. If the sling legs foul, motion the pilot downward, and then instruct him to cut away the load. If you did a good job of hooking up the load, and if the load suspends properly below the aircraft, then give the aircraft the signal to depart. Then move quickly aside to clear the helicopter's path.

External Loads

> **DANGER**
>
> AT NO TIME WILL THE SIGNALMAN OR ANY OTHER MEMBER OF THE SLINGLOAD TEAM ALLOW A SUSPENDED LOAD TO PASS OVER HIS HEAD.

Hookup Men

5-89. Duties of the hookup men include the following:

- One of you handles the static discharge wand and the cargo hook. The other controls the apex fitting of the slingload. Together, you must complete the hookup fast to reduce helicopter hover time and to reduce your exposure time under the helicopter.
- Position yourselves by the load so that, while the helicopter hovers over the load, you can quickly complete the hookup (Figure 5-18). You must also make sure the signalman can continually observe the operation.
- When the helicopter moves into the correct position for hookup, whichever one of you is the static wand man must ground the aircraft. Touch the static wand to the cargo hook (Figure 5-19, page 5-28) and keep it there to maintain a continuous ground.

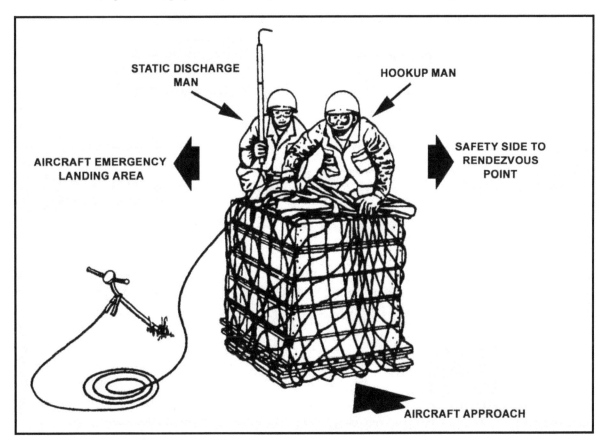

Figure 5-18. Position of hookup team.

Chapter 5

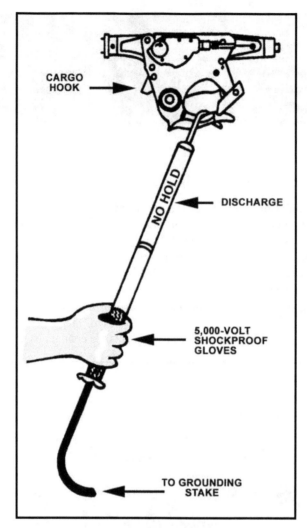

Figure 5-19. Grounding technique.

- Once the static wand man grounds the aircraft, the other hookup man places the apex fitting onto the cargo hook, then checks to make sure that the hook is properly closed (and locked, if required).
- After you properly hook up the load to the aircraft, both of you must move quickly aside to the location coordinated with the aviation unit. If the signalman learns that any of the legs have fouled, he notifies the pilot at once. Also, you will have to rehook the load.

RELEASE PROCEDURES

5-90. For this mission, leaders refer to the hookup men as the "cargo release team." As the helicopter approaches the site, the pilot takes instructions from the signalman, who guides the aircraft into position for cargo release. The cargo release team stands by, unless it must release the load manually. The signalman directs the aircraft to set the load on the ground. He gives the release signal. At this time, the apex fitting should fall free of the cargo hook. If it does not, the signalman has the aircraft hover, then he directs the cargo-release team to move under the helicopter and manually release the load from the hook. The load clears the hook. After the release, everyone moves out from under the aircraft. The signalman directs the aircraft to depart and quickly moves out of its path. If the pilot cannot activate the cargo hook from within the helicopter, and if cargo release personnel open it, then ground-crew members must use the following emergency cargo release procedures:

External Loads

- If a donut ring or basket hitch is used, try to disassemble the apex/donut. Pass the pin/ADS through the hook.
- If the cargo hook is attached to a clevis or apex fitting, unscrew the nut on the clevis or fitting and remove the pin.
- If necessary, derig the load so the aircraft can set down.

HOOKUP PROCEDURES DURING WHITEOUTS OR BROWNOUTS

5-91. The hazards of these conditions (snow or dust) prevent the use of a signalman or a hovering hookup.

- Rig the load with a 20-foot or a 40-foot extension (as required) using 20-foot ADS with two or three loops and the appropriate number of type IV link assemblies. Place an apex fitting at the end of the extension.
- Lay the extension to the left of the load. The aircraft approaches normally, then taxis to the location of the apex fitting and stops. Once the aircraft lands, the hookup person moves to the aircraft and attaches the apex fitting to the cargo hook. The aircraft suspends the load and departs as directed by the GTA.
- When attaching the extension to skid-equipped helicopters, such as the UH-1H, take care that the sling goes forward of but not through the skid. Then attach it to the cargo hook.

WARNING

Before the operation begins, coordinate the ground crew's evacuation route to a rendezvous point. Proper coordination with the liaison officer or helicopter crew prevents confusion. Helicopter emergency procedures depend on terrain, wind direction, and pilot choice. Good coordination also prevents the helicopter and ground crews from moving in the same direction.

SLINGLOAD INSPECTION RECORD

5-92. To improve slingload safety, the Department of the Army implemented inspection procedures for all Army equipment moved by the slingload method of air delivery. These procedures went into effect 1 October 1997. All Army loads require inspection by a qualified inspector before the arrival of the supporting aircraft. The inspector completes the Slingload Inspection Record. (Figure 5-20, page 5-30, shows an example completed DA Form 7382-R, *Sling Load Inspection Record*.) This form is used to inspect all loads, to include nonstandard, or unique, loads. The commander with high risk approval authority (usually the first colonel in the chain of command) is the approval authority for a nonstandard load, and will be annotated in the remarks block of the DA Form 7382-R.

INSPECTOR QUALIFICATIONS

5-93. Inspectors must hold the grade of E-4 or more. They must also either be a pathfinder, a slingload inspector course graduate, or air assault- qualified.

Chapter 5

DISTRIBUTION OF THE SLINGLOAD INSPECTION RECORD

5-94. Reproduce the slingload inspection record onto 8 1/2 by 11-inch paper, get it through official distribution channels, or download it from the AEL. Complete the inspection record in triplicate. Copies of the completed form are distributed as follows:

- Give a copy to the supporting aviation unit.
- Securely tape or tie a copy to the load.
- Give a copy to the supported unit.

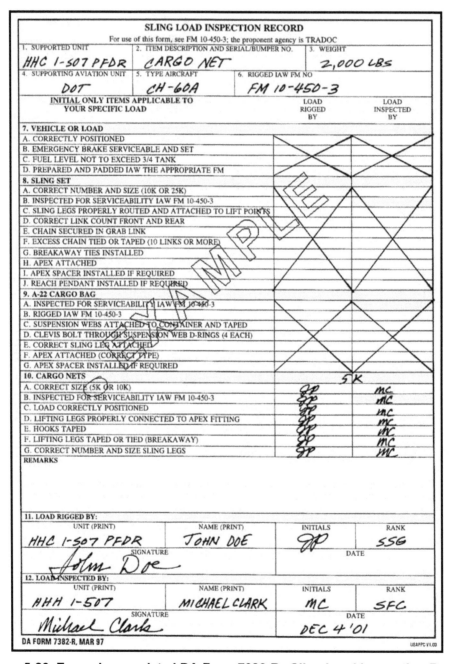

Figure 5-20. Example completed DA Form 7382-R, *Sling Load Inspection Record*.

THIS CHAPTER IMPLEMENTS STANAG 3570.

Chapter 6
Drop Zones

The ground unit commander designates the drop zone, usually with the drop zone support team leader's (DZSTL's) technical help. The drop zone is where drop aircraft deliver personnel and equipment by parachute or free drop. The commander selects a DZ location that best supports the tactical plan. In the case of tactical training, the commander checks the USAF assault zone availability report (AZAR) to see if an approved DZ already exists within the tactical area. If the AZAR does not include a DZ in that area, the commander must assess the tactical situation before choosing a DZ location.

SECTION I. SELECTION FACTORS

The commander uses the drop zone selection factors discussed in this section to analyze the suitability of a drop zone.

AIRDROP AIRSPEEDS

6-1. The speed of the aircraft (airspeed) determines how long the aircraft will remain over the drop zone. Table 6-1 shows airspeeds for rotary-wing aircraft in knots indicated airspeed (KIAS). Table 6-2, page 6-2, shows the same thing, but for fixed-wing aircraft, by aircraft type and load.

Type of Aircraft	Airspeeds
UH-1 Huey	50 to 70 knots (optimum 70 knots)
UH-60 Blackhawk	65 to 75 knots (optimum 70 knots)
CH-46 (USMC)	80 to 90 knots
MH-53 (USAF)	80 to 110 knots (optimum 90 knots)
CV-22 Osprey (USAF)	80 to 110 knots (optimum 90 knots)
CH-47	80 to 110 knots (optimum 90 knots)
CH-46/53 (USMC)	80 to 110 knots (optimum 90 knots)
CH-54 Skycrane	65 to 75 knots (optimum 70 knots)
CH/HH3 (USAF)	70 to 90 knots
MC-130 Combat Talon I and II	70 to 90 knots
C-130/141/17/5	130 to 135 knots (personnel/door bundles)
C-7A Caribou	90 to 120 knots
C-27A (Aeritalia G-222)	125 knots
C-46 Commando/C-47 Sky Train	104 to 125 knots
DC-3 (Contract Aircraft)	104 to 125 knots
CASA-212	90 to 110 knots

Table 6-1. Airspeeds for rotary-wing aircraft.

Chapter 6

Type of Load	Airspeeds		
	C-130	C-141 or C-5	C-17
Personnel Static Line	130	130 to 135 (130 is ideal)	130 to 135 (130 is ideal)
Personnel HALO and HAHO	110 to 150	130 to 180	138 to 145
Container delivery system combination and Equipment	130 to 140 (See note)	150	140 to 150
Heavy equipment	140	150	150
Free fall (free drop)	140	150	140 to 150
High velocity CDS	130 to 140 (See note)	150	140 to 150
Wedge	130 to 140 (See note)	150	140 to 150
Ahkio sled	130 to 140 (See note)	150	140 to 150
Combat rubber raiding craft (CRRC)	130 to 140 (See note)	150	140 to 150
Door bundle	130	130 to 135 (130 is ideal)	130 to 135 (130 is ideal)
Simulated airborne training bundle (SATB) (does not apply to C-17)	Use same load as for actual drop	Use same load as for actual drop	Not applicable
High Speed, Low-Level, Aerial Delivery System (HSLLADS)	En route airspeed		
Note: Use this type of load when gross weight exceeds 120,000 pounds. For combination drops, use the higher airspeed KIAS. (A combination drop exists when the same or different type aircraft drop different types of loads in the same pass over the DZ.)			

Table 6-2. Airspeeds for fixed-wing aircraft.

DROP ALTITUDE

6-2. The DZSTL measures drop altitude in feet AGL (Table 6-3) from the highest point on the DZ (the highest field elevation) to the aircraft. In combat (wartime) operations, airborne and airlift commanders jointly determine drop altitudes. Table 6-4 shows drop altitudes, by load and aircraft type, in feet AGL.

A	Distance from highest field elevation in DZ to desired altitude of aircraft, in feet.	800	Feet AGL
B	Highest field elevation in feet above sea level, rounded up to next 50 (for example, round 505 up to 550).	+ 550	Feet field elevation
C	Drop altitude in feet indicated.	1,350	Feet indicated

Table 6-3. Example calculation of drop altitude in feet indicated.

Drop Zones

6-3.   Table 6-4 shows airdrop altitudes for different types of training missions. (For more information on drop altitudes, see AFI 11-231 and AFI 11-410.)

6-4.   The aircraft altimeter displays altitude in feet indicated (feet above sea level), not in AGL (feet above the highest point on the ground). Thus, the pilot might request the drop altitude in "feet indicated." You can calculate this simply by following this example:

- Obtain the drop altitude, that is, the distance in feet from the highest point on the drop zone (field elevation) to the desired altitude of the aircraft. In this example, drop altitude equals 800 feet (A, Table 6-3).
- Obtain the highest field elevation in feet above sea level. Round this number up to the nearest multiple of 50 (round 537 up to 550, for example) (B, Table 6-3). For purposes of obtaining the drop altitude in feet indicated, use this number for field elevation.
- Sum the two numbers you obtained to yield drop altitude in feet indicated (C, Table 6-3).

Type of Load	Time of Day (Light Conditions)	Rotary Wing Aerial Delivery Altitudes
Personnel	Day or Night (includes limited visibility)	1,500 Feet AGL
Bundles	Day	300 Feet AGL
	Night (includes limited visibility)	500 Feet AGL
Note: If the rotary wing aircraft is flying 90 KIAS or faster, then it can drop personnel as low as 1,250 feet AGL.		

Type of Load	Fixed Wing Aerial Delivery Altitudes
Planning	1,000 feet AGL
Combat operations (war)	Determined jointly by airborne and airlift commanders
Tactical training	800 feet AGL
Basic airborne training	1,250 feet AGL
HALO (minimum opening)	2,500 feet AGL
Simulated airborne training bundle-personnel (SATB-P)	500 feet AGL
Tactical training bundle (TTB)	Use drop altitude of simulated load

Table 6-4. Airdrop altitudes for rotary- and fixed-wing aircraft.

TYPE OF LOAD

6-5.   The type of load is considered when estimating the drop zone time requirement, or how many bundles or personnel can be exited in a single pass over the drop zone. This is a consideration as a commander may request a DZ capable of exiting a certain amount of jumpers in a single pass, or may need to know how many jumpers can exit over a preselected DZ. For personnel, allow one second for each jumper after the first. For example, ten jumpers minus the first jumper equals nine jumpers. Multiply nine times one second. Allow nine seconds for all ten jumpers to get out the door. For equipment, allow three seconds for each door bundle after the first. For example, five bundles minus the first bundle equals four bundles. Multiply four times three seconds each. Allow twelve seconds to get the equipment out the door. There is no set time to wait between exiting bundles and personnel. However, the jumpmaster team must ensure all bundles have exited the aircraft, and that no unsafe conditions exist, before they start exiting personnel IAW Chapter 10 of FM 3-21.220. Bundles and personnel must never exit at the same time.

Chapter 6

> **DANGER**
> Never allow personnel and bundles to exit the aircraft at the same time.

6-6. For container deliver system (CDS) and heavy equipment, the time requirement is already factored into the minimum computed air release point (CARP) DZ sizes found in AFI 13-217.

METHODS OF DELIVERY

6-7. The type of airdrop determines method of delivery. The three methods are low-velocity, high-velocity, and free-drop trips. The method then normally determines the location of the control center. Table 6-5 shows the minimum airdrop altitudes, by aircraft, load, and parachute type.

USAF Fixed-Wing Aircraft: Door Bundles		
Type of Parachute	Altitude for C-5, C-17, and C-141	Altitude for C-130
G-14	300 feet AGL	300 feet AGL
T-10 cargo	300 feet AGL	400 feet AGL
C-5, C-17, C-141: Container Delivery System		
Type of Parachute	Number Parachutes or Containers	Airdrop Altitude
Planning drop altitude	NA	600 feet AGL
G-12D	Single canopy 1 to 6 containers	475 feet AGL
	7 or more containers	575 feet AGL
	2 or 3 parachutes	525 feet AGL
G-12E	Single canopy 1 to 40 containers (130 KIAS)	425 feet AGL
	Single canopy 1 to 40 containers (140 to 150 KIAS)	375 feet AGL
	2 or 3 parachutes	550 feet AGL
G-14	1 or 2 containers	300 feet AGL
	3 containers	400 feet AGL
12- to 22-foot high-velocity ring-slot parachute	NA	100 feet plus vertical distance for the load being drop
26-foot high-velocity ring-slot parachute	NA	100 feet plus vertical distance for the load being drop
SATB-C	NA	See parachute type being simulated

Table 6-5. Minimum aerial delivery altitudes.

Drop Zones

C-130: Container Delivery System		
Type of Parachute	Number Parachutes or Containers	Airdrop Altitude
Planning drop altitude	Single canopy 1 to 6 containers	600 feet AGL
G-12D/E	7 or more containers	400 feet AGL
G-12D	2 or more parachutes	600 feet AGL
	2 or more parachutes	600 feet AGL
G-12E	2 or more parachutes	550 feet AGL
CRRC (G-12D/E)	NA	600 (boat only) otherwise use personnel drop
G-14	1 or 2 containers	400 feet AGL
	3 containers	500 feet AGL
12- to 22-foot high-velocity ring-slot parachute	NA	100 feet plus vertical distance for the load being drop
26-foot high-velocity ring-slot parachute	NA	100 feet plus vertical distance for the load being drop
SATB-C	NA	See parachute type being simulated

C-5, C-17, C-141, C-130: Heavy-Drop Equipment			
Type of Parachute	Cluster Size (Number of Canopies or Bundles)	Altitude for C-5, C-17, and C-141	Altitude for C-130
Planning drop altitude	NA	1,100 feet AGL	1,100 feet AGL
G-12D	NA	650 feet AGL	2 to 3 parachutes 650 feet AGL
G-12E	NA	550 feet AGL	2 to 3 parachutes 550 feet AGL
G-11A	1	900 feet AGL	900 feet AGL
	2 to 7	1,100 feet AGL	1,100 feet AGL
	8	1,300 feet AGL	1,300 feet AGL
G-11B	1	700 feet AGL	700 feet AGL
	2 to 4	750 feet AGL	750 feet AGL
	5 to 7	1,100 feet AGL	
	8	1,300 feet AGL	
G-11C/X	1 to 2	975 feet AGL	1,050 feet AGL
	3 to 4	1,025 feet AGL	1,100 feet AGL
	5	1,075 feet AGL	1,150 feet AGL
	6 to 7	1,125 feet AGL	1,200 feet AGL
	8	1,225 feet AGL	1,300 feet AGL
SATB-H	NA	See parachute type being simulated	See parachute type being simulated

NOTES:
1. Combination drops use the highest airdrop altitude. A combination drop exists when either of the following occurs:
   * When *different* aircraft drop different types of loads in same pass over DZ.
   * When different type loads exit *same* aircraft in same pass over DZ.
2. Minimum airdrop altitude for heavy equipment using the 5,000-pound parachute release is 1,000 feet AGL or by parachute type, whichever is higher.

Table 6-5. Minimum aerial delivery altitudes (continued).

LOW-VELOCITY AIRDROP

6-8. Low-velocity airdrops are used for sensitive equipment and personnel. The parachute slows the rate of the descent to prevent damage to equipment or injury to personnel.

HIGH-VELOCITY AIRDROP

6-9. High-velocity airdrops are used to deliver certain supply items. The load must be rigged in an airdrop container with an energy dissipater attached to its underside and a ring-slot parachute attached to the top. The chute stabilizes the load and reduces the rate of fall, ensuring an acceptable landing shock.

FREE DROP

6-10. Free drops are used for nonsensitive items only. This type of load has no parachute to stabilize or slow its rate of descent. Loads may require special packaging to prevent damage from impact.

ADDED RISK

6-11. When determining the suitability of the DZ and considering the method of delivery around populated or built-up areas or airfields, the pathfinder also considers the added risk of injury to personnel or damage to buildings when using high-velocity or free-drop methods.

OBSTACLES

6-12. To ensure a safe airdrop, and to ensure Soldiers can recover and employ airdropped personnel and equipment, the ground unit commander should assess the risks of obstacles on the DZ and adjacent areas.

OBSTACLES TO PERSONNEL

6-13. This includes anything, natural or manmade, that could harm a parachutist or prevent mission accomplishment.

OBSTACLES TO EQUIPMENT

6-14. This includes anything, natural or manmade, that could damage or hinder the recovery of equipment.

Trees

6-15. Trees 35 feet (which is the distance from the top of a personnel parachute to the harness) or higher that would impede recovery of personnel or equipment present an obstacle.

Water

6-16. Water at least 4 feet deep and 40 feet wide, and within 1,000 meters of any edge of the surveyed DZ is an obstacle.

Power Lines

6-17. Power lines carrying 50 or more volts can kill a jumper.

Drop Zones

> **DANGER**
>
> Set up the DZ away from power lines. A 50-volt shock can kill a jumper. Even if it does not, it could cause him to fall, and that could kill him.

6-18. Try to site the DZ at least 1,000 meters from a power line. If you cannot, and a power line is located within 1,000 meters of any boundary of the DZ, then you must coordinate with the local power company to shut off the power to that line NLT 15 minutes prior to TOT. If this is not possible, then the flying mission commander, aircrew, and jumpmaster must assess the risk. They should consider at least the following:

- Type of jump.
- Jumpers' experience.
- Aircrew's experience.
- Ceiling.
- Surface and altitude wind limits required to approve, suspend, or cancel.

6-19. To further minimize risks, they should consider how they might alter the mission profile to raise or lower drop altitudes, change the DZ run-in or escape headings, or remove inexperienced jumpers from the stick. Also, if they can, they should clearly mark power lines with lights, smoke, or VS-17 panels.

> **DANGER**
>
> Set up the DZ away from power lines. A 50-volt shock can kill a jumper. Even if it does not, it could cause him to fall, and that could kill him too.
>
> Also, never try to climb power line poles to position or affix markings to the poles or the lines themselves.

6-20. Figure 6-1 shows an example safety zone for when power lines fall within 1,000 meters of the drop zone.

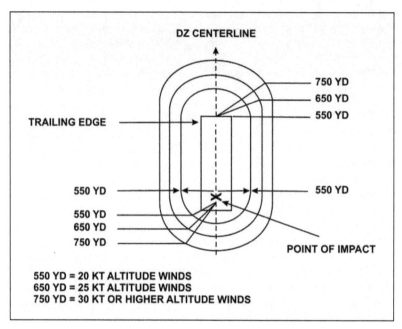

Figure 6-1. Recommended safety zones for high-tension lines.

Other Obstacles

6-21. This includes anything else, such as barbed wire fences, swamps, rocks, ditches, steep inclines, or gullies, that could injure parachutists, damage or prevent the recovery of equipment, or interfere with the mission.

ACCESS

6-22. Ground unit commanders should avoid any DZ that has a major obstacle between it and the objective area. Ground unit commanders should also make sure the area has adequate routes to conduct troop movement and to recover equipment.

SIZE

6-23. Ground unit commanders must use the following minimum peacetime drop zone sizes for fixed wing aircraft, unless a waiver is issued. During wartime and contingency operations, the commander at the appropriate level may waive the DZ size. AFI 13-217 provides information about waivers.

COMPUTED AIR RELEASE POINT

6-24. The USAF prescribes the sizes of computed air release point DZs during peacetime drop operations.

Heavy Equipment

6-25. The minimum CARP DZ size (Table 6-6, top section) measures at least 600 yards (549 meters) wide by 1,000 yards (915 meters) long for one platform. Add 28 meters (30 yards) to the length and width for each 100 feet above 1,100 feet.

Personnel

6-26. Table 6-6, bottom section, shows the CARP DZ size for personnel. The CARP DZ size for one jumper is at least 549 meters (600 yards) by 549 meters (600 yards). For each additional jumper, add 64 meters (75 yards) to the length of the DZ.

Heavy Equipment			
Altitude (Agl In Feet)	Width	Drop Zone Length	
		One Platform	Additional Platforms
To 1,100	600 Yards	1,000 Yards	Add 400 yards (C-130) or 500 yards (C-17 or C-5) to trailing edge for each additional platform.
Above 1,100	Add 30 yards to DZ width and length for each 100 feet above 1,000 feet (Add 15 yards to each side of the DZ).		
Personnel			
Altitude (Agliin Feet)	Width	Drop Zone Length	
		One Platform	Additional Platforms
To 1,000	600 Yards	600 Yards	Add 75 yards to trailing edge for each additional parachutist. When using CAPES, add 100 yards each instead.
Above 1,000	Add 30 yards to DZ width and length for each 100 feet above 1,000 feet (Add 15 yards to each side of the DZ).		

NOTES:
1. For day visual formations, increase width by 100 yards (50 yards each side). For SKE formation, increase width by 400 yards (200 yards each side). Official sunset to sunrise, increase width by 100 yards for single ship visual drops (50 yards each side) or 200 yards for visual formations (100 yards each side).
2. Official sunset to sunrise, increase length by 100 yards for visual drops (50 yards each end).
3. For personnel formations, minimum DZ basic width using center PIs is 1,240 yards for 2-ship elements and 1,800 yards for 3-ship elements. When using offset PIs, minimum basic width is 1,100 yds for 2-ship elements and 1,300 yds for 3-ship elements.

Table 6-6. Size criteria for tactical airlift drop zones, personnel, and heavy equipment.

Container Delivery System

6-27. Table 6-7 shows the CARP DZ sizes for the container delivery system.

Altitude (AGL in Feet)	Width	Number of Containers		Length
		Single	**Double**	
CDS (C-130)				
To 600 feet AGL	400 yards	1 2 3 4 5 to 8	1 to 2 3 to 4 5 to 6 7 to 8 9 or more	400 yards 450 yards 500 yards 550 yards 700 yards
Above 600 feet	Add 40 yards to DZ width and length for each 100 feet above 600 feet (Add 20 yards to each side of the DZ).			
CDS (C-17)				
To 600 feet AGL	450 yards	1 2 3 4 to 8 9 to 14 15 to 20	1 to 2 3 to 4 5 to 6 7 to 16 17 to 28 29 to 40	590 yards 615 yards 665 yards 765 yards 915 yards 1,065 yards
Above 600 feet	Add 40 yards to DZ width and length for each 100 feet above 600 feet. Add 20 yards to each side of the DZ.			

High Velocity (HV) CDS (Using 12-, 22-, or 26-Foot, Ring-Slot Parachutes)

Altitude (AGL in Feet)	Width	Length
Less than or equal to 3,000 feet AGL	580 yards or 530 meters	660 yards or 604 meters Add 50 yards or 46 meters to the trailing edge for each additional row of containers
More than 3,000 feet AGL	Add 25 yards or 23 meters to each side and 100 yards or 91 meters to each end for every 1,000 foot increase in drop altitude.	

High Altitude Airdrop Resupply System (HAARS) CDS

Altitude (AGL in Feet)	Width	Number of Containers	Length
Less than or equal to 3,000 feet AGL	500 yards or 457 meters	1 to 8 containers	1,200 yards or 1,098 meters
		9 or more containers	1,900 yards or 1,739 meters
More than 3,000 feet AGL	Add 25 yards or 23 meters to each side and 50 yards or 46 meters to each end for every 1,000 foot increase in drop altitude.		

High Speed Low Level Aerial Delivery System (HSLLADS)

Altitude (AGL in Feet)	Width	Length
NA	300 yards or 274 meters	600 yards or 549 meters

Table 6-7. Size criteria for tactical airlift drop zones, Container Delivery System.

Drop Zones

Additional Size Requirements

6-28. For each additional platform on a C-130, add 366 meters (400 yards) to the length of the DZ. For each additional platform on a C-17, C-5, or C-141, add 458 meters (500 yards). For multiple aircraft not flying in trail formation, add 100 yards to the width of all CARP DZs. From official sunset to sunrise, add 100 yards to the length and width of all CARP DZs. For SKE formations, increase the width by 400 yards. For SKE formation, you need not add the 100 yards when the aircraft are not flying in trail.

6-29. For C-17s flying in personnel formations, the minimum width for a basic DZ, using center PIs, is 1,240 yards for two ship elements, or 1,800 yards for three ship elements. When using offset PIs, the minimum width is 1,100 yards for two ship elements, and 1,300 yards for three.

Note: Multiply yards by 0.9144 to convert them to meters; divide meters by the same number to convert them to yards.

Army VIRS and GMRS Drop Zones

6-30. For the verbally initiated release system (VIRS) and for the ground-marked release system (GMRS), allow a minimum size of 300 yards by 300 yards (275 meters by 275 meters). To determine the required size of Army VIRS DZs, use the D=RT formula (Figure 6-2). For personnel jumps, allow a 100-meter buffer zone at the leading and trail edges of the DZ. If local regulations permit, the local commander can waive these buffer zones.

D = RT

Determine additional size requirements.

D = Length of DZ in meters.

R = Aircraft's rate of speed in meters per second (MPS). To convert knots to meters per second—
- Multiply the number of knots by 0.51.
- Do not round this number up or down.

T = Time required to exit each load:
- Parachutists (personnel) require 1 second each, after the first, which is free. The formula for computing the total seconds required to drop personnel is (N - 1) x 1, with N equal to the total number of personnel. Thus, ten personnel require—

  (10 – 1) X 1 = 9 X 1 = 9 seconds

- Door bundles require 3 seconds each, after the first bundle. The formula for computing the total seconds required to drop bundles is (N – 1) x 3, with N equal to the total number of bundles. Thus, three bundles require—

  (3 – 1) X 3 = 2 X 3 = 6 seconds

EXAMPLE PROBLEM

What is the minimum GMRS DZ length needed for a C-130 to drop ten parachutists?

D = Length of DZ in meters (unknown).

R = 66.30 meters per second (130 x 0.51).

T = 9 seconds (1 second per parachutist, not counting the first).

SOLUTION

D = R x T

D = 66.3 MPS X 9 seconds = 596.7 meters
(Round up to nearest whole number, which is 597.)

D = 597 meters of usable DZ required.
For personnel drop zones, add a 200-meter buffer—100 meters on the leading edge and 100 meters on the trailing edge—to total 797 meters for the drop zone. (The commander can waive this requirement.)

Figure 6-2. Example application of D=RT formula.

Drop Zones

PARACHUTISTS OR BUNDLES

6-31. To calculate the maximum number of either parachutists or bundles that a GMRS or VIRS DZ of given length can accept in one pass, use the T=D/R formula (Figure 6-3). You must know the type of aircraft and drop speed, and type of exit. The T=D/R formula may also be used to calculate the same information for a CARP DZ. In this case, measurement is from the PI to the trail edge of the DZ, minus the buffer zone (personnel only). Minimum length for CARP DZ is 3 seconds. In all cases, once the PI is established, the DZ time must be recalculated from the PI to trail edge, minus the required buffer.

T = D / R

Calculate number of parachutists or bundles that a GMRS DZ of given length can accept in one pass.

- **T =** Amount of time in seconds that the aircraft will be over the DZ.
- **D =** Distance of DZ in meters (length).
- **R =** Rate of aircraft's speed expressed in meters per second. To convert knots to meters per second, multiply the knots by .51. Round this number up to the nearest whole number.

EXAMPLE PROBLEM

How many parachutists from a C-130 can a 750-meter-long GMRS drop zone accept on each pass?

- **T =** The number of parachutists that can drop on a 750-meter long GMRS DZ.
- **D =** 550 meters (750-meter drop zone less 100-meter buffer at each end).
- **R =** 130 x 0.51 = 66.3 rounded up to 67.

SOLUTION

- **T** = D/R
- **D/R** = (550/67) = 8.2
- **T =** = 8 seconds (always round down).
- **DZ** Can accept nine parachutists per pass: eight parachutists, at one each second, plus one free.

Figure 6-3. Example application of T=D/R formula.

LOAD DRIFT UNDER PARACHUTE

6-32. To calculate the amount of drift experienced by a load under a parachute, use the D=KAV formula (Figure 6-4). Always round up to the next whole number.

D=KAV

Calculate drift

- **D =** The amount of drift in meters.
- **K =** Load drift constants:
  - Personnel .... 3.0 meters
  - Bundle .... 1.5 meters
  - Equipment .... 1.5 meters
  - Container delivery system (CDS) .... 1.5 meters
  - Tactical training bundle .... 2.4 meters
- **A =** Express drop altitude in hundreds of feet: For 800 feet, say "8;" for 850, say "8.5."
- **V =** Velocity of the wind (Use either surface wind speed or MEW).

EXAMPLE PROBLEM

For a drop altitude of 800 feet and a wind speed of 11 knots, calculate a jumper's drift:

- **K =** Load drift constant for jumper (personnel) = 3 meters.
- **A =** Drop altitude = 800 feet, so in this example, A = 800/100 = 8.
- **V =** Wind speed = 11 knots.

SOLUTION

- **D =** K x A x V
- **D =** 3 x 8 x 11
- **D =** 264, in the example conditions, a jumper drifts 264 meters.

Figure 6-4. Example application of D=KAV formula.

WIND

6-33. Measuring wind on the drop zone entails measuring both surface wind and mean effective wind. Use an authorized wind-measuring device to measure surface (ground) wind speed, especially for personnel and heavy equipment operations.

6-34. Mean effective wind (MEW) refers to the average wind from ground level to drop altitude. Measure the magnetic azimuth to the balloon and note the reciprocal heading. This gives you the MEW direction to report. Use the pilot balloon (PIBAL) to measure MEW. PIBAL circumferences include—

- 10 grams for day—57 inches.
- 30 grams for day—75 inches.
- 10 grams for night—74 inches.
- 30 grams for night—94 inches.

6-35. At night, attach a small, liquid-activated light or 6-inch chem-light to the balloon to aid in observation. Table 6-8A (this page) and 6-8B (page 6-16) show the PIBAL charts for the 10- and 30-gram helium balloons, respectively.

10-GRAM HELIUM BALLOON

Inflate balloon to 57-inch circumference for day and 74-inch circumference for night.

ELEVATION ANGLE	\	DROP ALTITUDE IN FEET											ASCENSION TABLE	
		500	750	1000	1250	1500	1750	2000	2500	3000	3500	4000	4500	TIME	ALT (FT)
	70	02	02	01	01	01	01	01	01	01	01	01	01		
	60	03	02	02	02	02	02	02	02	02	02	02	02		
	55	03	03	03	03	03	03	03	03	03	03	03	03		
	50	04	04	03	03	03	03	03	03	03	03	03	03	0:10	80
	45	05	04	04	04	04	04	04	04	04	04	04	04	0:20	170
	40	06	05	05	05	05	05	05	04	04	04	04	04	0:30	250
	35	07	06	06	06	06	05	05	05	05	05	05	05	0:40	330
	30	08	07	07	07	07	07	07	07	06	06	06	06	0:50	400
	25	10	09	09	09	08	08	08	08	08	08	08	08	1:02	500
	24	11	10	09	09	09	09	08	08	08	08	08	08	1:10	540
	23	11	10	10	09	09	09	09	08	08	08	08	08	1:20	610
	22	12	11	10	10	10	10	09	09	09	09	09	09	1:30	670
	21	12	11	11	10	10	10	10	10	10	10	10	10	1:43	750
	20	13	12	11	11	11	11	11	10	10	10	10	10	1:50	790
	19	14	13	12	12	11	11	11	11	11	11	11	11	2:25	1000
	18	15	13	13	12	12	12	12	12	11	11	11	11	2:44	1100
	17	16	14	13	13	13	13	12	12	12	12	12	12	3:05	1250
	16	17	15	14	14	14	13	13	13	13	13	13	13	3:49	1500
	15	18	16	15	15	14	14	14	14	14	14	14	14	4:30	1750
	14	19	17	16	16	16	15	15	15	15	15	15	15	5:11	2000
	13	21	19	18	17	17	17	17	15	15	15	15	15	6:34	2500
	12	22	20	19	19	18	18	18	18	17	17	17	17	7:58	3000
	11	24	22	21	21	20	20	20	19	19	19	19	19	9:22	3500
	10	27	25	23	23	22	22	22	21	21	21	21	21	10:44	4000
	09	30	27	26	26	25	24	24	24	23	23	23	23	12:08	4500

Table 6-8A. Conversion chart for 10-gram helium (pilot) balloons.

30-GRAM HELIUM BALLOON

Inflate balloon to 75-inch circumference for day and 94-inch circumference for night.

ELEVATION ANGLE	DROP ALTITUDE IN FEET												ASCENSION TABLE	
	500	750	1000	1250	1500	1750	2000	2500	3000	3500	4000	4500	TIME	ALT (FT)
80	01	01	01	01	01	01	01	01	01	01	01	01		
70	03	03	03	02	02	02	02	02	02	02	02	02		
60	04	04	04	04	04	04	04	04	04	04	04	04		
55	05	05	05	05	05	05	05	05	05	04	04	04	0:10	120
50	06	06	06	06	06	06	06	06	05	05	05	05	0:20	240
45	07	07	07	07	07	07	07	07	07	06	06	06	0:30	360
40	09	08	08	08	08	08	08	08	08	08	08	08	0:42	500
35	10	10	10	10	10	10	10	09	09	09	09	09	0:50	600
30	12	12	12	12	12	12	12	11	11	11	11	11	1:02	750
25	15	15	15	15	15	15	14	14	14	14	14	14	1:10	830
24	16	16	15	15	15	15	14	14	14	14	14	14	1:17	1000
23	17	17	16	16	16	16	15	15	15	15	15	15	1:48	1250
22	18	18	17	17	17	17	17	16	16	16	16	16	2:10	1500
21	19	19	18	18	18	18	17	17	17	17	17	17	2:34	1750
20	20	20	19	19	19	19	18	18	18	18	18	17	2:56	2000
19	21	20	20	20	20	20	19	19	19	19	19	18	3:43	2500
18	22	22	21	21	21	21	21	20	20	20	20	20	4:31	3000
17	23	23	23	22	22	22	22	22	21	21	21	21	5:21	3500
16	25	25	24	24	24	24	23	23	23	23	22	22	6:09	4000
15	27	27	26	26	25	25	25	25	24	24	24	24	7:00	4500
14	29	29	28	27	27	27	27	27	26	26	26	25		
13	31	30	30	30	30	29	29	29	28	28	28	27		

Table 6-8B. Conversion chart for 30-gram helium (pilot) balloons.

FORWARD THROW

6-36. This refers to the effect of inertia on a falling object. An object that leaves an aircraft moves at the same speed as the aircraft. The parachutist (or bundle) continues to move in the direction of flight until the dynamics of gravity and the parachute take effect. The forward throw distance is the distance along the aircraft flight path traveled by a parachutist or cargo container after exiting the aircraft, until the parachute fully opens and the load is descending vertically. Forward throw distance for rotary-wing and STOL aircraft equals half the aircraft speed (KIAS), expressed in meters. Table 6-9 shows the forward throw distance from a fixed-wing aircraft.

Load	Forward Throw Distances for Fixed-Wing Aircraft		
	C-5	C-130	C-17
Personnel or Door Bundle	229 meters (250 yd)	229 meters (250 yd)	229 meters (250 yd)
Heavy Equipment	668 meters (730 yd)	458 meters (500 yd)	640 meters (700 yd)
CDS	N/A	503 meters (550 yd)	663 meters (725 yd)
TTB	N/A	147 meters (160 yd)	147 meters (160 yd)
NOTE: To convert yards to meters, multiply yards by 0.9144. To convert meters to yards, divide meters by 0.9144.			

Table 6-9. Forward throw distances for fixed-wing aircraft.

Chapter 6

APPROACH AND DEPARTURE ROUTES

6-37. Ground unit commanders must choose adequate routes for the aircraft to and from the DZs. They consider—
- Enemy situation and location.
- Obstacles to the aircraft such as television towers or high-tension lines.
- Terrain higher than the drop zone.
- Adjacent air operations and flight routes.
- No-fly areas.

SECTION II. DROP ZONE SUPPORT TEAM

The drop zone support team plans, establishes, and operates day and night drop zones for personnel and resupply missions flown by fixed-wing and rotary-wing aircraft. The DZST is responsible for accomplishing the mission on the DZ. In operations without the USAF special tactics team, the DZST will shoulder the overall responsibility for the conduct of operations on the DZ. The DZST represents both the airborne and airlift commanders. The DZST leader assumes all the responsibilities normally associated with the USAF STT and the DZSO.

ORGANIZATION

6-38. The DZST must have at least two members. It might need more, depending on the complexity of the mission. However, additional team members do not need to be DZSTL qualified. The senior member of the DZST functions as the team leader. He must hold the rank of NCO (sergeant or above in the US Army, E-4 or above in the USAF or USMC), an officer, or the civilian equivalent. He must have completed the appropriate initial training as a DZST member and must satisfy current parent service requirements. To conduct personnel and heavy equipment drops, he must also hold current jumpmaster qualification.

MISSIONS

6-39. Primary missions of the DZST include wartime CDS drops to battalion or smaller units. They also make peacetime, visual, and meteorological condition drops, with one to three aircraft, for personnel, CDS, and heavy equipment. Secondary missions include wartime drops of brigade-sized or larger units, peacetime drops of C-130, Adverse Weather Aerial Delivery System (AWADS) involving one to three aircraft, or visual meteorological conditions (VMC) drops of four or more aircraft.

NOTE: Any authorized personnel, other than qualified combat controllers, who perform DZSTL duties, are restricted to formation airdrops of four or less aircraft. The only exception is on a military range with active range control.

EQUIPMENT FAMILIARIZATION

6-40. The DZST leader must know how to use equipment to set up, mark, and operate the drop zone. Depending on the mission, this equipment includes--

ANEMOMETER

6-41. An anemometer is an instrument used to measure wind velocity. There are currently three types of anemometers approved for use in support of airborne operations: AN/PMQ-3A, DIC and DIC-3, and turbometer. The AN/ML433A/PM and meters that use floating balls or devices in a tube (sensor-based devices) are *not* authorized for use during personnel or cargo airdrop operations. Other anemometers not

Drop Zones

tested and recommended for use should be employed only after a command-initiated risk assessment is completed. Regardless of the method or device used to measure the wind on the DZ, the airborne commander must ensure winds fall within the limitations for the type of drop being conducted.

Messages

6-42. The following USAIS messages authorize several commercially available anemometers for use in drop zone operations:

- DTG 101000Z Mar 94, Subject: Use of Anemometers During Airdrop Operations.
- DTG 212000Z Oct 94, Subject: Use of TurboMeters During Static Line Airdrop Operations (personnel drops).

AN/PMQ-3A

6-43. This is a handheld or tripod-mounted omnidirectional anemometer (NSN: 6660-00-515-4339). It is capable of providing wind speed and direction. Because of its size, cost, and weight (10 pounds with all components), it is not ideal for light Infantry units in operational environments. With the trigger pressed down, the correctly oriented anemometer gives wind direction in degrees. It can read the wind from 0 to 15 knots on the low scale, and from 0 to 60 knots on the high scale. The anemometer requires recalibration every six months.

DIC and DIC-3

6-44. One piece, handheld, compact, lightweight, factory-calibrated devices, these commercially purchased anemometers are approved for use during airborne operations. The DIC and DIC-3 use folding cups to catch the wind and electronically display wind speed, but not direction. During use, it is critical that the cups are fully extended to ensure an accurate reading. The device is omnidirectional and does not need to be oriented with wind direction to provide accurate readings. Post manufacture calibration methods are not available. The DIC and DIC-3 can depict wind data in knots, miles per hour, kilometers per hour, or meters per second. The additional features of the DIC-3 are the ability to display peak wind velocity over a given period, and average wind speed over two time periods. Because the DIC and DIC-3 cannot be calibrated, they must be checked before use by—

- Ensuring fresh batteries are installed.
- Turning on the anemometer in a no-wind condition, such as in a building or enclosed vehicle. If any reading other than zero is displayed, the device is unserviceable and must be turned in for disposal or returned to the manufacturer.
- Conducting a three-anemometer check by comparing the wind reading on three anemometers at the same time under identical conditions. Discard the anemometer that reads differently then the other two. This is most accurate if all anemometers are of the same type.

TurboMeter

6-45. This anemometer is stocked under NSN 1670-00-T33-9004. It can also be commercially purchased. It is a small, lightweight, electronic wind speed indicator. It does not display direction, but when turned into the wind, it depicts wind data in knots, miles per hour, meters per second, and feet per second. For the most accurate results, the TurboMeter must be oriented within 20 degrees of the wind direction, with the wind entering the rear of the meter. Because the TurboMeter cannot be calibrated, conduct the same preoperation and three-anemometer check as when using the DIC/DIC-3 anemometer.

VS-17 Marker Panel, Aerial

6-46. The two-sided VS-17 marker panel (NSN 8345-00-174-6865) measures 2 feet wide by 6 feet long. One side is international orange. The other side of the panel is cerise (red). Six tie-down points permit attachment to stakes. The short ends in the stowage pocket have three snap fasteners. When folded, the panel's olive drab green should show. Pathfinders should display the panel side whose color contrasts best against the surrounding area.

Light, Marker, Ground Obstruction

6-47. One BA-200 battery powers this "beanbag light" (NSN: 6230-00-115-9996). Interchangeable, colored plastic domes offer different colors of light. These markers work well in light holes or on the surface. The ground crew secures the markers with tent pegs or by filling the bottom with sand or rocks.

Drop Zones

RAISED-ANGLE MARKER

6-48. This locally constructed raised-angle marker (RAM) marks the PI on CARP DZs. It consists of five VS-17 panels. Most rigger units have the ability to construct a RAM (Figure 6-5).

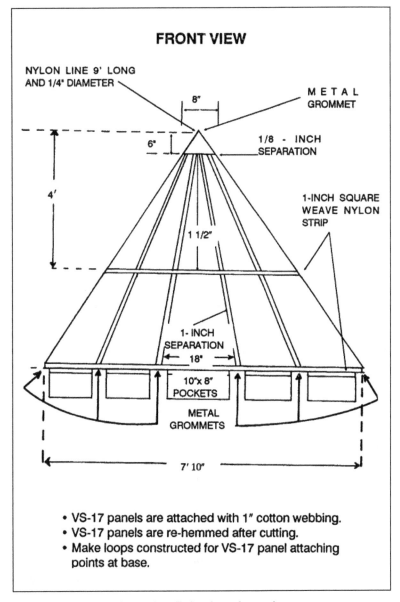

Figure 6-5. Raised-angle marker.

WHELEN LIGHT

6-49. This light attaches to the top of one of two types of batteries originally used with the AN/PRC-77. To place the light into operation, the user seats it on top of the battery. Different colored domes offer different colors of light. The unit buys this light locally. The batteries are as follows:

- Dry battery BA-4386/U.
- Lithium battery BA-5598/U.

M-2 Light Baton

6-50. Two BA-30s power this flashlight (NSN: 6230-00-926-4331). Different lenses (stored in the base compartment) change the color of the light. This light works best in a light hole or on top of the ground attached to a tent peg.

Aerial Marker, Distress

6-51. This omnidirectional flashing (strobe) light (NSN 6230-00-67-5209) has a very long range. An optional directional cover snaps on top for tactical operations. Other snap-on caps change color and function. The black cap, for example, makes the strobe light invisible except to devices that can "see" infrared.

Mirror, Emergency Signaling, Type II

6-52. Pathfinders can use the signal mirror (NSN 6350-00-105-1252) to signal aircraft by reflected sunlight. The back of the mirror has a set of instructions for proper use and aiming. The signal mirror works even on hazy days. It works in all directions—not just when the user faces the sun—and the intended viewer can see it from as far away as the horizon.

Pilot Balloon

6-53. Pathfinders use the 10- or 30-gram rubber balloon to measure the mean effective wind. They fill the balloon with helium until the balloon inflates to the specified circumference. National stock numbers for PIBALs follow:

- NSN 6660-00-663-7933, balloon, meteorological, 10-gram.
- NSN 6660-00-663-8159, balloon, meteorological, 30-gram.

Lighting Unit

6-54. This light (NSN 6660-00-839-4927) attaches to the PIBAL for night operations. Overinflating the PIBAL compensates for the weight of the light so it can ascend at the same rate as it would without the light. Water or any other fluid will activate the PIBAL's wet-cell battery. Below 50 degrees Fahrenheit, warm water activates the light faster. A 6-inch chem-light may be used as a lighting unit in place of the wet-cell battery.

Drift Scale

6-55. This slide-type scale uses a 90-degree angle to measure the ascent of the PIBAL. Pathfinders use the drift scale to compute the mean effective wind. The local Training Support Center produces the drift scale. Pathfinders can also use the pocket transit (small enough to carry in a pocket), theodolite (NSN 6675-00-861-7939) with built-in clinometer (NSN 6675-00-641-5735), or the separate clinometer (NSN 6675-01-313-9730).

AN/PRC-119A (SINCGARS) Radio

6-56. This man-portable radio (NSN 5820-01-267-9482) allows FM radio contact with aircraft. It also permits navigational aid (NAVAID) for aircraft with FM-homing capabilities. Without power-increasing accessories, it transmits between 4 and 16 kilometers.

AN/PRC-113 (HAVE QUICK) RADIO

6-57. This man-portable UHF/VHF AM radio (NSN 5820-01-136-1519) has a quick, jam-resistant, ECCM transceiver. Pathfinders use it for short ranges—5 to 16 miles—for tactical, ground-to-ground, or ground-to-air communication.

AN/PRC-117F (ALSO KNOWN AS RT-1796) RADIO

6-58. This man-portable radio can transmit and receive in the 30 to 512 MHz frequency range. Thus, it can be used for FM, AM, and SATCOM communications. With this one radio system, a Ranger radio operator can communicate with any other radio system used in Ranger operations. The 117F operates in three distinct frequency ranges.

- VHF low band – 30 MHz to 89.99999 MHz.
- VHF high band – 90 MHZ to 224.99999 MHz.
- UHF band – 225MHz to 512MHz.
- 110 programmable radio nets.

6-59. The 117F outputs 20 watts of power in the 90 mHz to 400 mHz range and 10 watts in the upper and lower frequency ranges. The 117F is menu driven. It uses Vinson, ANDVT, Fascinator, and KG-84 embedded encryption. It operates on 26 volts of DC power (VDC), and requires two BA-5590 nonrechargeable batteries. It has one H-250 handset, a VHF blade antenna with a flexible adapter base, a VHF/UHF flex antenna, a KDU remote-control cable, a wide battery box, and the AN/PRC-117F transceiver. It uses the AV-2040 satellite antenna used for SATCOM communications. With batteries installed, the 117F weighs 15.9 lbs.

ASIP RADIO

6-60. The ASIP is an FM, VHF, low-radio system with built-in communications security (COMSEC) and a built-in test (BIT). Its frequency range is 30,000 to 87,975 MHz. It can be used man-packed or vehicle-mounted. To power up in manpack configuration requires 13.5 VDC, which is provided by a single BA5590 battery. In vehicular mode, it operates on 27.5 VDC, which it draws the vehicle's battery. Four power settings include LOW (200 to 400 meters), MEDIUM (440 meters to 5 kilometers), HI (5 to 10 kilometers), and PA (10 to 40 kilometers). The latter setting (PA) is only used when the ASIP is vehicle-mounted. It sends data at the rates of 600, 1,200, 2,400, 4,800, or 16,000 bits per second.

Chapter 6

COORDINATION

6-61. The drop zone coordination checklist provides the DZST leader with a tool for coordinating before the mission without having to communicate with the aircraft (Figure 6-6).

---

1. Confirm the following:
   - Mission.
   - Drop zone location.
   - Drop zone name.
   - Number of bundles and parachutists.
   - Joint air attack team (JAAT) sequence number.
   - Time on target.
   - Weather decision time.

2. Verify the current DZ survey (AF Form 3823).

3. Verify the following information:
   - Type of drop (HE, CDS, or personnel).
   - Type and number of aircraft.
   - Time between flights and passes.
   - Number of racetracks.
   - Drop speed and heading.
   - Drop altitude: AGL IND.
   - Type of parachute.
   - Ground quick disconnects.

4. Confirm the following DZ information:
   - Type of markings (GMRS, CARP, VIRS).
   - Code letter.
   - Timing points.
   - Primary drop signal.
   - Alternate drop signal.
   - Primary no-drop signal.
   - Alternate no-drop signal.
   - Mission cancellation signal.
   - Obstacle markings.

5. Coordinate DZ support capabilities:
   - Communications available.
   - Frequencies and call signs.
   - Acquisition aids available.
   - NAVAIDs.
   - MEW equipment.

6. Coordinate airspace.

7. Confirm aircraft (mission) commander's name, unit, and telephone number.

8. Enter DZST leader's name, rank, unit, and telephone number.

9. Follow DZ reporting procedures for scoring, incidents, and accidents.

Figure 6-6. Drop zone coordination checklist.

SUPPORT REQUIREMENTS

6-62. The DZSTL ensure that support requirements for the drop zone control group are coordinated and in place no later than one hour before TOT. The two support groups are a complete support group and a partial support group. If the drop zone is 2,100 meters or longer or 20 seconds or more in exit time, or if more than one aircraft is executing the mission, then a complete control group must be used. If none of these situations exist, then a partial control group may be used.

CONTROL GROUPS

6-63. Control groups consists of--

- An assistant DZSTL who is DZSTL qualified (complete control group) or not (partial control group).
- One (partial control group) or two (complete control group) front-line-ambulance (FLA) qualified medical personnel for personnel drops and heavy equipment. These personnel are not needed for CDS drops, depending on local rules and regulations.
- One (partial control group) or two (complete control group) wind-measuring devices. One is located at the control center with the DZSTL. In complete control groups, the second is located with the assistant DZSTL at the highest location on the drop zone.
- Malfunction officer with camera, who must be a qualified and current rigger IAW AR 59-4.
- Parachute recovery detail with recovery kit.
- Vehicles with drivers.
- Road guards.
- Military Police, if required to control traffic or provide crowd control.
- Boat detail for PE drops only.

Rescue Boat

6-64. A boat detail is required for personnel drops if a water obstacle is within 1,000 meters of any edge of the drop zone, at least 40 feet wide at the widest point, and at least 4 feet deep at its deepest point. If the water is at least 4 feet deep, but less than 40 feet wide, a boat detail is not required. However, jumpers must still use approved life preservers. The DZSTL may declare any body of water an obstacle based on jumper safety.

6-65. Units may supplement the requirements in this paragraph. When assessing DZ risk for a training parachute jump, the commander should consider the distance from the water obstacle to the DZ and the depth and width of the water obstacle.

6-66. The following factors may also enter into risk assessment of a water obstacle: the bottom, the current, the water temperature, the number of obstacles, the equipment available to reduce the risk, jumper experience, available or artificial light, and the importance of the DZ to mission success.

Personnel

6-67. The OIC, NCOIC, and boat operators must all be qualified and licensed to operate the boats and the issued boat motors. Each boat needs one primary and one assistant operator and two recovery personnel, ideally one of whom is lifeguard qualified and combat lifesaver certified. Everybody in the boat should be a strong swimmer.

6-68. The DZSTL must--

- Determine if a follow-on assessment of the DZ has been conducted to confirm the current status.
- Ensure the OIC or NCOIC is fully briefed on the plan. Ensure all boat detail personnel have been trained and have all necessary equipment available to conduct the mission.
- Read all applicable regulations, FMs, and SOPs. Ensure copies are available throughout the mission.

6-69. The Jumpmaster must--

- Ensure that, if approved life preservers are used, they have been inspected within the last 180 days and are serviceable.
- Ensure that all jumpers have received training on life preserver wear, fit, and use (to include manual inflation).
- Ensure all personnel have received prejump training within the 24 hours before drop time, with special emphasis on unintentional water landings.

Time Requirements

6-70. The OIC or NCOIC ensures that at least two boats must be in place one hour before TOT. At least 10 minutes before TOT, both boats must be in the water with their engines running. Otherwise, a no-drop situation exists.

Communications

6-71. Two-way communications with the DZSTL must be established at least an hour before TOT, and maintained throughout the jump operation.

Drop Zones

Coverage

6-72. To ensure that the entire obstacle is accessible to the boat detail, each water obstacle might require a different type of coverage.

Equipment

6-73. Each recovery boat team needs the following equipment:

- A rubber boat (RB-10) or solid-bodied boat of comparable size, with operable outboard motor.
- Enough fuel and oil to complete the mission.
- Life vest or other floatation device for each boat detail member, and as many extras as they can carry for jumpers who might not already be wearing a B5 or B7 flotation device (water wings).
- One life ring with attached rope.
- One FM and one handheld radio, each with spare battery.
- One each shepherd's crook and grappling hook.
- One long backboard for CPR.
- One aid bag with resuscitation equipment.
- One 120-foot long rope and four sling ropes with end-of-line bowlines and snap links.
- Four paddles.

6-74. For night operations, add the following:

- Two operational night vision devices with two sets of batteries.
- One spot light.

Note: Jumpers wearing B5s or B7s need no life jackets.

BASIC EQUIPMENT LIST

6-75. The DZSTL should maintain an inventory of the following basic equipment to support the mission:

- VS-17 panels.
- Smoke grenades or flares.
- White lights such as an M-2 light baton.
- Air traffic control light (B-2).
- Signal mirror.
- Strobe light.
- Binoculars.
- Anemometer required for personnel and heavy equipment drops, recommended for measuring the wind before all types of drop.
- Compass.
- PIBAL kit with helium.
- Night vision goggles, for night drops.
- Other equipment as needed, based on premission coordination or unit SOP.

DUTIES OF THE LEADER

6-76. The DZST leader establishes and operates the DZ. He selects the locations of the control center, PI, and release point. He bears the ultimate responsibility for accomplishing the mission. Specifically, the leader—

- Makes sure the DZ reaches full operational status one hour before drop time.
- Conducts premission coordination.
- Opens the DZ through range control. After the mission, accounts for all personnel, air items, and equipment, then closes the DZ.
- At least one hour before the drop, reconnoiters the DZ on the ground or from the air for obstacles or safety hazards.
- Establishes communication with departure airfield control officer not later than (NLT) one hour before drop time.
- Controls all ground and air MEDEVACs.
- Submits postmission reports to the appropriate agencies.
- Operates all visual acquisition aids.
- Ensures no-drop signals are relayed to the drop aircraft.
- Ensures all DZ markings display correctly.
- Establishes a ten-minute window. Ensures pathfinders continuously monitor surface winds, starting NLT twelve minutes before time on target (TOT). This includes the ten-minute window plus two extra minutes to relay a no-drop signal, if needed. For example, if TOT is 0700 hours, then the ten-minute window (plus two minutes) begins at 0648 hours. If at any time during the ten-minute window the winds exceed allowable limits, the DZST leader relays a no-drop to the aircraft. Once he calls a no-drop, he establishes a new ten-minute window (without an extra two minutes). For example, if the winds pick up at 0655 hours, the leader calls a no-drop. The new ten-minute window counts from the time of the no-drop and extends to the new TOT ten minutes after that, at 0705 hours.
- Takes surface wind readings from the control center location and from the highest point of elevation on the DZ when the DZ is 2,100 meters in length or longer, when exit time is 20 seconds or more, or for a multiple aircraft operation.
- Calls a no-drop when surface winds exceed the limits shown in Table 6-10.

Type Of Load	Surface Wind (In Knots)

Personnel
    Land
    Water
	
	13
	17

HALO or HAHO
    Land
    Water
	
	18
	20

Equipment without ground disconnects	13
Equipment with ground disconnects	17
CDS using G-12 parachutes	13
CDS or door bundles using G-13 or G-14 parachutes	20
USAF tactical training bundles and simulated airborne training bundles	25
High-velocity CDS at HAARS	No Restrictions
Free drop	No Restrictions
For USAF personnel and additional equipment, see *AFI 13-217*.	

Table 6-10. Surface wind limits for airdrops.

Drop Zones

CONTROL CENTER

6-77. The DZST leader controls and observes the airborne operation from the control center. Pathfinders also take wind readings here. The DZST leader should position all radios, signaling devices, and appropriate forms at the control center. The type of mission determines the location of the control center.

PERSONNEL DROPS

6-78. Locate the control center at the PI.

CDS DROPS

6-79. Locate the control center 200 yards to the 6 o'clock of the PI.

OTHER DROPS

6-80. For free drops, heavy equipment, high velocity CDS, HAARS, and AWADS (ceiling less than 600 feet), locate the control center off the DZ where you can see both the approaching aircraft and the PI. For example, the wood line might obstruct the leading edge. If so, it would not make a good control center location for these types of drops.

ALL GMRS AND VIRS DZS

6-81. Locate the control center at the RP.

SIGNALS

6-82. When voice control does not work, the ground support team uses visual signals to the aircraft. Two of the most important visual signals are no-drop and mission cancellation.

6-83. To communicate a no-drop situation to the aircraft, scramble the shape designator and remove the markings or any other previously coordinated DZ signal.

6-84. The drop aircraft pilot should continue to fly racetracks if coordinated until you give the signal indicating clear to drop. You can signal no-drop when—

- Winds exceed the maximum limitations for that type of drop.
- You see vehicles moving on the DZ.
- Rotary wing aircraft fly in close proximity to the DZ.
- You see anything else unsafe on the DZ.

6-85. Decide in mission coordination how many no-drop passes the pilot must fly before the mission is automatically cancelled and the pilot can begin his return to base.

6-86. Cover signals for clear-to-drop also. You may decide to indicate clearance to drop by emplacing DZ markings. You can also use this means if you have no smoke. If you plan to use smoke, decide what each color of smoke will mean, but avoid using red to mean clear-to-drop.

6-87. At night, your clear-to-drop signals could include any means coordinated in advance such as shade-designator illumination, a flashing white light, a green light, and so on.

6-88. Multiple signals are best. For example, FM and smoke for clear-to-drop, or scrambled code letter and FM for no-drop (Figure 6-7).

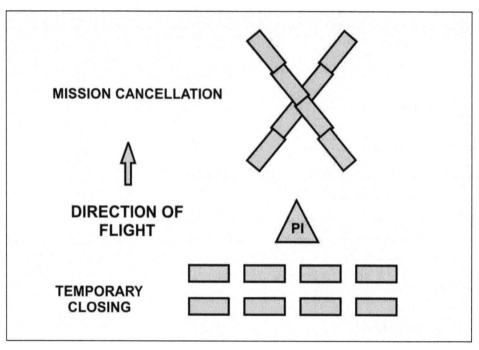

Figure 6-7. Drop zone cancellation and closing markers.

DETERMINATION OF RELEASE POINT LOCATION

6-89. To determine a release point on a GMRS drop zone, Air Force fixed wing VIRS drop zone, or Army rotary wing VIRS drop zone, complete the following steps (Figure 6-8):

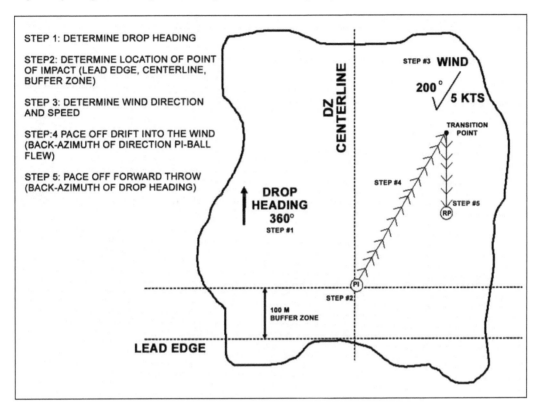

Figure 6-8. Release point location.

STEP 1--DETERMINE DROP HEADING

6-90. If the drop zone was surveyed and an AF IMT 3823, *Drop Zone Survey*, was published for the drop zone, then the DZSTL uses the magnetic course indicated. The drop zone might have been surveyed as a circular DZ, or a tactical assessment might have been done on it. It might be established as an ARMY VIRS. In the latter case, the DZSTL determines the drop heading based on the long axis, wind direction, and obstacles on the approach and departure ends of the DZ.

STEP 2--DETERMINE POINT OF IMPACT

6-91. The PI for personnel is the centerline of the drop zone 100 meters from the leading edge. The PI for bundles is the centerline of the DZ, but *on* the leading edge. These points may be adjusted forward, left or right. For CDS and heavy equipment, the DZSTL uses the surveyed PI locations shown on the AF IMT 3823. If a tactical assessment was done in lieu of an AF IMT 3823, he uses the standard PI locations for CDS and heavy equipment from the CARP dummy tree.

STEP 3--DETERMINE WIND DIRECTION AND SPEED

6-92. The DZSTL uses the PIBAL to determine the MEW. If he has no PIBAL, then he must use the surface wind direction and speed. Once he determines the wind direction and speed, he calculates a D = K x A x V formula for drift in meters.

Chapter 6

STEP 4--PACE OFF THE DRIFT IN METERS INTO THE WIND

6-93. This should be the reciprocal heading of the PIBAL direction. If a PIBAL was not used, then a field-expedient means of determining wind direction may be used. If the direction and distance of the drift are paced into the wood line, the PI is adjusted as necessary, but only forward, left, or right.

Example: 90 knots drop speed = 45 meters forward throw.

GROUND-MARKED RELEASE SYSTEM

6-94. The GMRS offers the DZSTL a way to identify the release point to the drop aircraft without using a radio. The pilot uses the ground markings to adjust his flight path 100 meters to the right of the corner panel or light, and parallel to the approach-corner panel or light axis. (This discussion uses the words "panel" and "light" interchangeably.)

PATTERNS

6-95. Use VS-17 panels to mark the DZ with an inverted "L," "H," or "T" pattern. The selected pattern must be coordinated far in advance.

Inverted "L

6-96. The inverted "L" has four panels:

- The approach panel.
- The corner panel.
- The alignment panel.
- The flanker panel.

"H" and "T"

6-97. Align these other panels with and orient them on the corner panel. Due to side-angle-vision limitations in the C-5, use the seven-panel "H" and six-panel "T" patterns.

VS-17 PANELS

6-98. Figure 6-9 shows panel emplacement for "H" and "T" patterns (add an inverted "L" figure). Distances and azimuths are measured from the upper right corner of each panel to the upper right corner of the next, and from center mass of the selected RP. During daylight airdrops, the marker panels should be raised at a 45-degree angle from the ground toward the aircraft approach path to increase the aircrew and jumpmaster's ability to see them.

Drop Zones

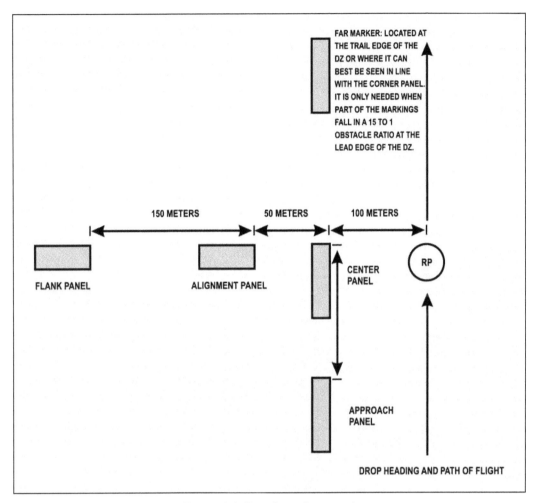

Figure 6-9. Panel emplacement.

Chapter 6

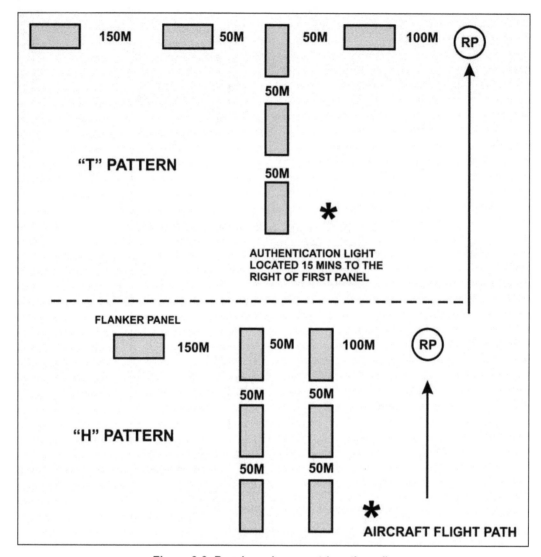

Figure 6-9. Panel emplacement (continued).

Corner Panel

6-99.   Set up the corner panel 100 meters to the left of the RP (90 degrees from drop heading). Orient the long axis of the panel so it is parallel with drop heading.

Alignment Panel

6-100.   From the corner panel, move 50 meters in the same direction as above and emplace the alignment panel. Orient the long axis of the panel so it is perpendicular (90 degrees) from drop heading.

Approach Panel

6-101.   Place the approach panel 50 meters in front of the corner panel, on a back azimuth (opposite) from the drop heading. Orient the long axis of the panel so it is parallel with drop heading.

Flanker Panel

6-102. Place the flanker panel 150 meters to the left of the alignment panel, as seen from the drop heading. Orient the long axis of the panel so it is perpendicular (90 degrees) from drop heading, and parallel to the alignment panel.

LIGHTS

6-103. At night, replace panels with lights (use one light for each panel). Do not use chem-lights for DZ markings. For operations requiring security, night DZ markings should be visible only from the direction of the aircraft's approach. If flashlights are used, they should be equipped with simple hoods or shields and aimed toward the approaching aircraft. Omnidirectional lights, fires, or improvised flares may be screened on three sides or placed in pits with the sides sloping toward the direction of approach. Use directional lights for the approach, corner, alignment, and flanker. If necessary, you can use the directional light holes for the far code letter and line up the base light with the corner light. Figure 6-10, page 6-36, provides construction requirements for Army code letters. Mark the release point with some type of identifiable light source to distinguish it from all other DZ markings.

Chapter 6

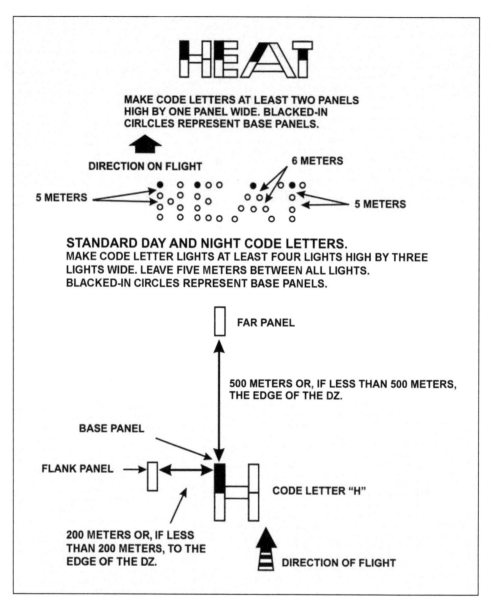

Figure 6-10. Horizontal clearance and marker construction.

Marking Considerations

6-104. Place the markings where obstacles will not mask the pilot's line of sight. The DZ markings must be clearly visible to the aircrew on approach as early as possible. If conditions preclude placing the markings at the computed point, the DZSTL may have to adjust the location of the intended PI, ensuring the new PI location complies with the requirements for the type of airdrop. Advise both the aircrew and user of the change in PI location. As a guide, use a mask clearance ratio of 1 to 15 units of horizontal clearance. For example, suppose you must position a DZ marker near a terrain mask, such as the edge of a forest on the DZ approach. The trees measure 10 meters (33 feet) high. The markings would require 150 meters (492 feet) of horizontal clearance from the trees (Figure 6-11).

Drop Zones

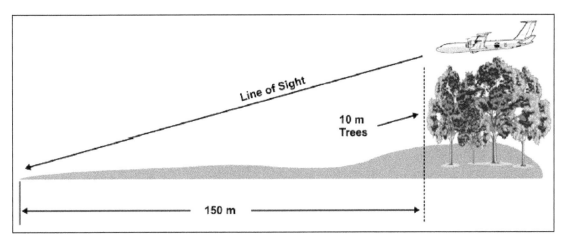

Figure 6-11. The 15-to-1 mask clearance ratio.

6-105. If any of the GMRS markings fall within a 15-to-1 mask clearance ratio on the approach end of the drop zone, and it is not feasible to adjust the selected PI, you can place an Army code letter (H, E, A, T) or a far (marker) panel on the trailing edge of the DZ. However, before doing so, you must coordinate this during either the DZST or aircrew mission briefing. Using a code letter will distinguish this DZ from other DZs in the area. The code letter is located at the end of the DZ or where the pilot can see it best, and aligned with the corner and approach panel, parallel to drop heading.

6-106. During daylight airdrops, the marker panels should be slanted at a 45-degree angle from the surface toward the aircraft approach path to increase the aircrew and jumpmaster's ability to see them. If security permits, smoke (other than red) may be displayed at the release point or corner marker to assist in DZ acquisition.

ARMY VERBALLY INITIATED RELEASE SYSTEM

6-107. The Army VIRS method establishes the release point on the DZ through radio communications. If tactically feasible, a code letter can mark the RP. However, the aircraft initiates the drop on verbal command from the ground.

6-108. Emplace a standard Army code letter with VS-17 panels (for daytime operations) at the release point. Position the base panel of this code letter exactly on the RP. Use code letter H, E, A, or T. Make the letter at least two panels high by one panel wide (Figure 6-12, page 6-38).

Chapter 6

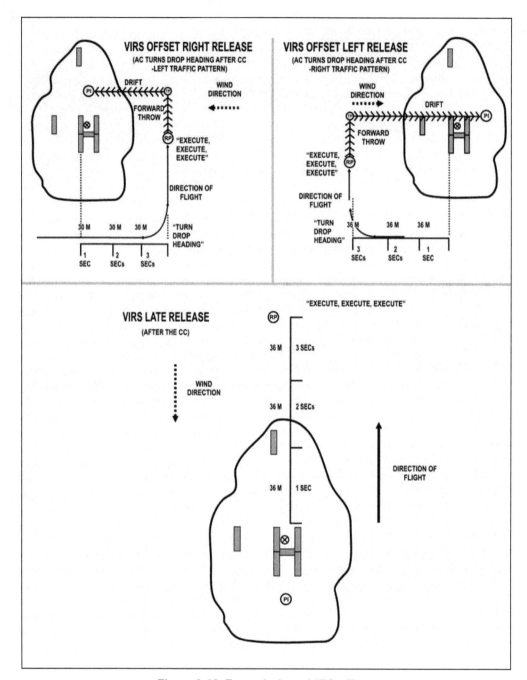

Figure 6-12. Example Army VIRS offset.

6-109. Emplace a flank panel to the left of a code letter at a distance of 200 meters or on the edge of the DZ, whichever is closer. Emplace a far panel 500 meters from the code letter along the drop heading or at the end of the DZ, whichever is closer. Position each panel with its long axis parallel to the drop heading and raised 45 degrees back toward the code letter. The DZSTL and radio operator position themselves at the release point.

Drop Zones

6-110. At night, replace the panels with lights. Make the code letter at least four lights high by three lights wide, with 5 meters between each light. To limit ground observation, you may place the code letter, flank, and far light in holes as follows:

- Place the code letter and far light in directional holes.
- Place the flank light in a bidirectional hole (toward RP and direction of aircraft approach).
- If the RP falls off the DZ, hide the markings, or if the DZSTL cannot see the aircraft, he can change the parachute drop to a jumpmaster-directed release operation using the wind streamer vector count (Figure 6-13).

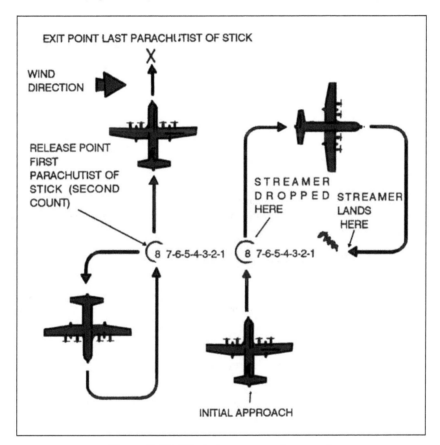

Figure 6-13. Wind streamer vector count.

- If the RP falls off the DZ and the DZSTL cannot, due to the tactical situation, position himself at the RP, then he can conduct an offset release (late, left, or right). To do this, he determines how many seconds the aircraft must fly past him before initiating the release. He gives the aircraft steering corrections to fly over the RP, just as in a standard VIRS. However, when the aircraft has flown a set distance past the control center, the Pathfinder commands the pilot to "turn drop heading" or "execute." In Figure 6-14, the drop speed is 70 KIAS. The RP falls about 80 meters off the DZ, and the old and new control centers are 118 meters apart. Multiplying 70 KIAS by .51 equals 36 meters per second of flight. The 3 second offset places the RP about 118 meters from the control center or code letter. The DZSTL, code letter, and control center are positioned on the DZ at a distance from the RP that is rounded off to the nearest second.

Note: These same procedures may be used when the tactical situation prevents the pathfinder from positioning himself on the release point, but he must remain in a concealed location and call the VIRS drop offset from his position.

AIR FORCE VERBALLY INITIATED RELEASE SYSTEM

6-111. When using USAF VIRS, the DZST leader verbally guides the pilot over the RP to align the aircraft for the drop. Figure 6-14 shows an example USAF VIRS transmission.

INITIAL RADIO COMMUNICATION

AIRCRAFT: T2S26, THIS IS HERC 30, OVER.
DZST: HERC 30, THIS IS T2S26, AUTHENTICATE DELTA FOXTROT, OVER.
AIRCRAFT: T2S26, THIS IS HERC 30, GOLF, OVER.
DZST: HERC 30, T2S26--NOT IN SIGHT. CONTINUE, OVER.

ONCE THE AIRCRAFT IS ABOUT ONE MINUTE OUT

DZST: HERC 30, THIS IS T2S26, HAVE YOU IN SIGHT, TURN LEFT.
DZST: (ELIMINATE CALL SIGNS) TURN LEFT. . . STOP TURN.
DZST: ON COURSE, STAND BY. (5 SECONDS FROM DROP).
DZST: EXECUTE, EXECUTE, EXECUTE, T2S26 OUT.

Figure 6-14. Example USAF VIRS transmission.

6-112. The leader uses this method when the tactical situation prevents use of regular markings or when aircraft pilots could not see regular markings from the air.

6-113. He establishes the VIRS DZ just as he would establish a GMRS or rotary-wing VIRS release point. (Figure 6-8, page 6-30, shows how to determine the location of the release point.) Unlike those release points, however, the USAF VIRS DZ RP requires no markings.

6-114. The leader sets up communications with the drop aircraft and at least two FM, VHF, and UHF radios on the DZ.

6-115. He transmits concise instructions to the aircraft. To align the aircraft on the desired inbound heading, he gives left and right turns. When the aircraft lines up on course, the pathfinder signals STOP TURN. About five seconds before the release, or at some other moment (as briefed), he signals STANDBY.

6-116. When the aircraft reaches the predetermined release point, the pathfinder leader gives an EXECUTE three times.

6-117. When transmitting the MEW to the aircraft, he makes sure to identify it as such. He states the altitude used to obtain it. He also provides pertinent details about any erratic winds or wind shears reported by other aircraft.

AIR FORCE COMPUTED AIR RELEASE POINT

6-118. The DZST leader and DZ party mark the point of impact on a surveyed DZ. The aircraft navigator computes the release point from the air.

COORDINATION

6-119. Coordinate authentication markings with the aircrew.

CODE LETTER ELEVATION

6-120. Never elevate the panels in the code letter.

Drop Zones

PERSONNEL BUFFER ZONE

6-121. There is a minimum buffer of 300 yards on the lead, left, and right sides of the DZ, and minimum buffer of 200 yards on the trail edge of the DZ.

MARKERS

6-122. Markers differ for day and night.

Day Operations

6-123. For day operations (Figure 6-15), pathfinders mark the point of impact with a RAM (Figure 6-5, page 6-20) and an Air Force code letter (optional), which could be a "J," "C," "A," "R," or "S" (Figure 6-16). This applies to rectangular drop zones. They use "H" or "O" for circular drop zones. Each letter must measure at least 35-feet square, and requires at least nine panels flat on the ground.

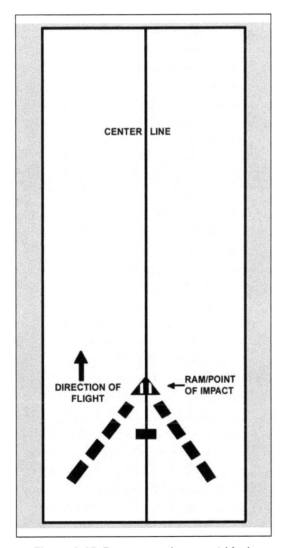

Figure 6-15. Drop zone placement (day).

Figure 6-16. Code letters.

Night Operations

6-124. For night operations (Figure 6-17), mark the point of impact with—

- A code letter (made of at least nine lights) placed at the point of impact.
- One flanker light placed 250 meters to the left and right of the point of impact. If terrain restricts the light placement to less than 250 meters, the aircrew will be briefed.
- A trailing edge amber light placed 1,000 meters, centerline, from the shape designator at the PI or at the trailing edge of the surveyed DZ, whichever is closer to the PI (optional). Usually, an amber rotating beacon is used.

Drop Zones

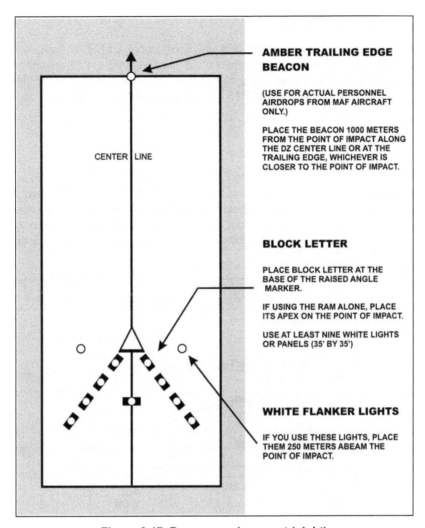

Figure 6-17. Drop zone placement (night).

AUTHENTICATION

6-125. Authentication varies for day and night operations.

Day Operations

6-126. During day operations, the DZSTL may authenticate or identify different sites by specifying drop times, drop headings, or alternating panel colors, or whatever he coordinates.

Night Operations

6-127. During night operations, the DZSTL may authenticate or identify different sites by replacing one light in the code letter with any color light except white.

OTHER FORMS OF CARP ZONES

6-128. Some other forms of CARP drop zones are random approach, area, and cicular drop zones. The GUC may also choose to place the point of impact randomly to better serve the mission.

Chapter 6

RANDOM APPROACH DROP ZONE

6-129. A random approach DZ is a variation of a previously surveyed DZ. It must be big enough for multiple run-in headings. Any axis of approach may be used as long as the resulting DZ meets the minimum criteria for the load or personnel being airdropped, and as long as it is within the boundaries of the original, surveyed DZ. In all cases, the DZSTL performs a safety-of-flight review before using a random approach DZ.

AREA DROP ZONE

6-130. An area DZ (Figure 6-18) has a start point (A), an endpoint (B), and a prearranged flight path (line-of-flight) over a series of acceptable drop sites between A and B. The distance between A and B is no more than 15 nautical miles. Changes in ground elevation within one-half NM of centerline should be no more than 300 feet. The reception committee can receive the drop anywhere between A and B within one-half NM of centerline. Once the pilot identifies and locates the prebriefed signal or electronic NAVAID, he can make the drop.

Note: Area DZs only apply to C-17 operations when crews are SOLL II qualified.

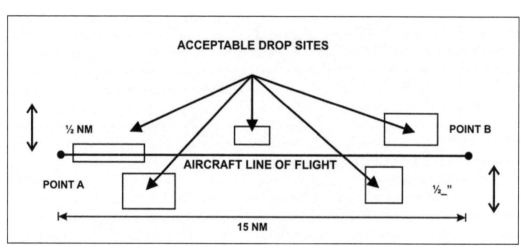

Figure 6-18. Area drop zone.

CIRCULAR DROP ZONE

6-131. The size of the DZ is governed by mission requirements and usable terrain. The PI of a circular DZ is normally at the DZ center to allow for multiple run-in headings. For specific missions, the PI location may be adjusted to allow for dropping loads such as sequential heavy equipment (HE) loads or mass container delivery system (CDS) loads on circular DZs. However, this limits the run-in heading to only one direction. In all cases, the minimum DZ dimensions for the type and number of loads being dropped must fit within the surveyed circular DZ. The DSZTL computes the circular drop zone as shown in Figure 6-19 to determine whether the minimum DZ fits into the surveyed circular DZ. When the PI has been relocated, he should use Option 2. The DZSTL calculates and records the size of the circular DZ using Option 1 on the DZ survey form. This prevents confusion and reduces the risk of off-DZ drops if the circle center point is used as the PI.

Drop Zones

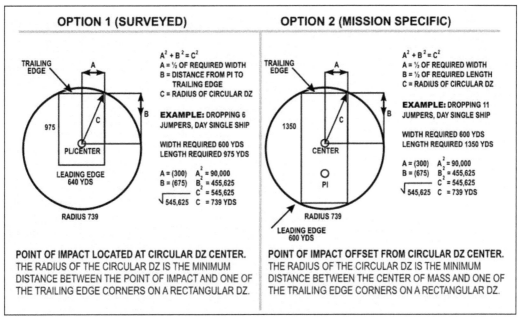

Figure 6-19. Computation of circular drop zone.

RANDOM POINTS OF IMPACT

6-132. When mission requirements dictate, the DZSTL may use the RPI placement option. He has two options:

Option 1

6-133. The mission commander notifies the DZSTL at least 24 hours in advance that RPI placement will be used. When the DZ is established, the DZSTL randomly selects a point on the DZ and establishes that point as the PI for the airdrop. The DZSTL ensures that the DZ meets the minimum size requirements for the type of load and that the entire DZ falls within the surveyed boundaries.

Option 2

6-134. The mission commander or supported force commander may request the DZ established with the PI at a specific point on the DZ. Requests should be made at least 24 hours in advance. The requestor ensures that the DZ meets minimum size criteria for the type of load, and that the entire DZ falls within the surveyed boundaries.

MULTIPLE POINTS OF IMPACT

6-135. An MPI airdrop is authorized if everyone involved has been properly briefed. An MPI airdrop is the calculated dispersal, both laterally and longitudinally, of airdropped loads to predetermined locations on a DZ. The DZ must meet the minimum size requirements for each PI, and the DZSTL must provide the precise location of each PI to the aircrews. Offset PIs are surveyed PIs 250 yards left and right of the surveyed PI. The DZ width must be increased to meet the distance criteria from the DZ edge to the PI. This manner of placement reduces the effects of wake turbulence across the DZ.

> *Note:* Personnel airdrops from C-17s in formation may require offset (laterally displaced) points of impact.

ASSAULT ZONE AVAILABILITY REPORT

6-136. The Zone Availability Report (ZAR) is a consolidated list of DZs and LZs maintained by HQ AMC for use by DoD aircraft. The direction and guidance for DZ and LZ operations is AFI 13-217. The ZAR currently contains both CONUS and OCONUS surveys forwarded by the owning command. Overseas zones are not controlled by AMC, but will be included, as they are also forwarded by the owning commands.

6-137. To request survey of a new or existing zone, the commander contacts 720th STG/DOO, Hurlburt Field FL (DSN 579-6055). He should send new or updated DZ surveys to his nearest wing/group tactics office for a safety of flight review. He forwards completed DZ, LZ, and HLZ surveys to HQ AMC/DOKT for inclusion in the ZAR.

6-138. To obtain a completed survey, he can use the fax-on demand system at Scott AFB, IL (DSN 576-2899), (Com (618) 256-2899). The Internet site available for military (.mil) users is located at https://amc.scott.af.mil/do/dok/zar.htm.

Purpose	Address	Phone	Internet
To request a survey of a new or existing zone	720th STG/DOO, Hurlburt Field FL	DSN 579-6055	NA
To submit or obtain a completed survey	HQ AMC/DOKT, 402 Scott Drive, Unit 3A1, Scott AFB, IL 62225-5302	DSN 576-2899 COM 618 256-2899	https://amc.scott.af.mil/do/dok/zar.htm (.mil users only)

AF IMT 3823, DROP ZONE SURVEY

6-139. A drop zone survey is required for airborne operations. The two types of surveys are tactical and existing surveyed drop zones. Completing a DZ survey requires a physical inspection of the DZ and documentation of findings on AF IMT 3823. The using unit may complete the survey. The using unit is the one whose equipment or personnel is being airdropped. For exercises and joint training operations, users complete the survey and ensure the DZ meets the criteria for operational and safety standards. The user physically inspects the DZ before use to identify and evaluate potential hazards to the airdropped personnel or equipment, to man-made or natural structures, and to ground personnel. The DZST is qualified to survey the DZ and complete the AF IMT 3823. After completing all blocks that apply, the DZST sends the survey to the nearest active duty tactics office for review by the appropriate radio operator. The radio operator then forwards the survey to HQ, AMC TACC/DOOXY, who determines the proper approval authority and obtains the approval. After approval, the TACC/DOOXY enters the survey into the BBS, where it is then available for use. These procedures are used to approve surveys for all AMC, ACC, and AMC/ACC gained aircraft.

SAFETY-OF-FLIGHT REVIEW

6-140. The nearest group tactics office completes a safety-of-flight review on all DZ surveys. This review ensures that an aircraft can safely enter and leave the DZ. The review includes an in-depth chart study of the terrain features along the route of flight from the IP to about 4 nautical miles past the DZ trailing edge. For a complete list of regional group/wing tactics offices see https://amc.scott.af.mil/do/dok/zar.htm.

Drop Zones

TACTICAL ASSESSMENT

6-141. During exercises and contingencies, when time or situation prevent the completion of a full DZ survey, such as to support highly mobile ground forces, the using unit must at least complete a tactical DZ survey.

6-142. Though using the AF IMT 3823 (discussed later in this chapter) is preferred, it is not required for a tactical survey. Requests and surveys may be sent electronically. As much information as practical should be obtained and forwarded for review. The unit sends requests for a final review of the tactical survey to the designated exercise or contingency airlift, or to the senior representative of the special operations airlift component.

6-143. When using a tactical DZ (Table 6-11), the airlift unit assumes responsibility for aircraft safety of flight; the receiving unit assumes responsibility for injury to personnel or damage to equipment or air items. The DZ size is determined by the mode of delivery, load dispersal, and discussion with the receiving unit about air item recoverability and load survivability.

Type Drop	*Aircraft*	*Day or Night*	*Point of Impact* *
CDS	C-130	Day	At least 200 yards/183 meters
		Night	At least 250 yards/229 meters
	C-17	Day	At least 225 yards/206 meters
		Night	At least 275 yards/251 meters
Personnel	All USAF fixed-wing aircraft	Day	At least 300 yards/274 meters
		Night	At least 350 yards/320 meters
Heavy Equipment		Day	At least 500 yards/457 meters
		Night	At least 550 yards/503 meters
* Point of impact shown in distance from the leading edge of the drop zone and centerline.			

Table 6-11. Favorable conditions for airdrops on tactically assessed DZs.

INSTRUCTIONS FOR COMPLETION

6-144. This paragraph explains how to complete AF IMT 3823, *Drop Zone Survey*, shown completed in Figures 6-20A and 6-20B (pages 6-51 and 6-52). All blocks must be completed. The completer should write "NA" in blocks that do not apply. When performing a safety-of-flight review on a foreign DZ, the completer should enter as much information as possible on AF IMT 3823. At a minimum, he must provide information for blocks 4D, 6A, 6B, 7, 9A-F, and 9H. He should attach a copy of the foreign DZ to the safety-of-flight review.

Block 1A

6-145. Enter DZ name.

Block 1B

6-146. If the survey will be sent to HQ AMC/DOTK for inclusion in the ZAR database, then enter only "NA." If the survey is for local use, then the group tactics office should complete this block.

Block 2A

6-147. Enter the country where the DZ is located.

Block 2B

6-148. Enter the state, province, or territory.

Block 3

6-149. Enter map series, sheet number, edition, and date of map used.

Blocks 4A1 through 4A4

6-150. Enter the date of the original survey and the surveyor's name, grade, telephone number, and unit of assignment. The surveyor signs above his typed name.

Block 4B

6-151. The surveyor enters an "A" (if approving) or "D" (if disapproving) for each drop category. He must complete all of the printed categories. He uses the blank column for special, additional approvals.

Block 4C

6-152. The ground operations approval authority verifies the survey by signing in this block.

Block 4D

6-153. The chief of group tactics or whoever the OG/CC or equivalent assigns to do so completes a safety-of-flight review.

Block 4E

6-154. The reviewer's (OG/CC's or ACC's) signature in this block authorizes the aircraft to operate over the DZ. If operational requirements dictate, he then sends the survey to HQ AMC/DOKT, 402 Scott Drive, Unit 3A1, Scott AFB, IL 62225-5302, so they can add that DZ to their ZAR database. The group tactics offices keep DZ surveys.

Blocks 5A through 5E

6-155. Enter the controlling agency responsible for scheduling the DZ. If the DZ is within a controlled or monitored area, enter the range control data for that location. If the DZ is not located on government owned property. If applicable, the requesting unit must obtain a land use agreement (LUA) or memorandum of understanding (MOU), checks the block (5A through 5E) that applies, and attaches a copy of the memorandum. If the DZ falls within a controlled area, enter the range control data for that location.

Block 6A through 6C

6-156. Enter the DZ dimensions using either meters or yards. For a circular DZ, enter the radius.

Blocks 6D through 6F

6-157. Enter the distance from the leading edge of the DZ to each PI in either meters or yards.

Blocks 7A through 7D

6-158. Enter the primary DZ axis in magnetic, grid, and true North, and include the source and date of the variation data. Use the current year when obtaining the information from a GPS. If DZ is circular, enter "NA."

Note: List any applicable DZ axis restrictions in the remarks block.

Block 8A through 8D

6-159. Enter the elevation in mean sea level (MSL) for each PI and for the highest point on the DZ.

Block 9A

6-160. Enter the spheroid used to compute coordinates for the DZ. You can find this information on the map legend. If the GPS is set to operate in WGS-84 mode, then enter "WGS-84" in this block.

Block 9B

6-161. Enter the MGRS datum used to compute the coordinates. You can also find this information in the map legend. Again, if you are using a GPS, enter "WGS-84."

Blocks 9C through 9E

6-162. Enter the grid zone, Easting, and Northing obtained from the map.

Block 9F

6-163. Place an "X" in the appropriate block.

Block 9G

6-164. Enter the grid zone designator, grid square identifier, and the ten-digit MGRS coordinates. Briefly describe an easily recognized point on or near the DZ, such as a road intersection, benchmark, or pond, that can be used by the DZ party to find the PIs. Include a distance and azimuth from this point to the nearest PI. If needed, continue the point of origin remarks in Remarks.

Block 9H

6-165. Enter the ten-digit MGRS coordinates in local datum and spheroid and the WGS 84 latitude/longitude coordinates to the nearest one-hundredth minute for each indicated point.

Block 9I

6-166. For each corner of the DZ, enter the ten-digit MGRS coordinates in local datum and spheroid and the WGS-84 latitudinal and longitudinal coordinates to the nearest one-hundredth minute.

Block 10

6-167. Enter the name of the DZ and clearly sketch it manually or using a computer program. Include all obstacles or prominent features within the DZ boundaries. Add an arrow for magnetic north to orient the user. Enter the name of the DZ.

Block 11

6-168. Comment on pertinent operations here. Describe safety hazards such as towers. Describe all charted or observed bodies of water and power lines within 1,000 meters of the DZ boundaries.

Block 12

6-169. State whether photographs of the DZ and approaches to it are available, and whether a low-level route is associated with the DZ. Whoever completes the safety-of-flight review should know this information and mark this block accordingly.

Drop Zones

DROP ZONE SURVEY	AIRBORNE UNIT ASSUMES RESPONSIBILITY FOR PERSONNEL INJURY AND EQUIPMENT DAMAGE ON DZ			
	1A. DZ NAME FRYAR DZ	1B. ZAR INDEX NO. 88	2A. COUNTRY USA	2B. STATE ALABAMA
	3. MAP SERIES/SHEET NUMBER/ EDITION/ DATE OF MAP V 745-S FORT BENNING MIM 1986			

4. SURVEY APPROVAL/DISAPPROVAL DATA

| 4A1. DATE SURVEYED
20050824 | 4A2. TYPED NAME AND GRADE OF SURVEYOR
MARIANO L. PIDLAOAN, TSgt, USAF | 4A3. PHONE NUMBER (DSN)
835-5218 | 4A4. UNIT
HHC 1/507TH PIR |

4B. DROP ZONE APPROVAL/DISAPPROVAL A = APPROVED D = DISAPPROVED		FOR	CDS/CRL/CRS	PER	HE	MFF	SATB	CRRC	HSLLADS	HVCDS
	DAY	A	A	A	A	A	D	A	A	A
	NIGHT	A	A	A	A	A	D	A	A	A

4C. DATE APPROVED FOR GROUND OPERATIONS	NAME, GRADE AND SERVICE OF APPROVAL AUTHORITY PAUL BINION, Capt, USAF	PHONE NUMBER (DSN) 731-4432	SIGNATURE Paul Binion
	UNIT AND LOCATION 21 STS/DO POPE AFB, NC 28308		
4D. DATE SAFETY OF FLIGHT REVIEW APPROVED 19950131	NAME AND GRADE OF REVIEWING OFFICER GEORGE E. MORGAN, Maj, USAF	PHONE NUMBER (DSN) 673-1376	SIGNATURE
	UNIT AND LOCATION 437 OSS/OSK CHARLESTON AFB, SC 29404		
4E. DATE OF MAJCOM APPROVAL	NAME AND GRADE OF APPROVING AUTHORITY DEREK A. MOORE, Col, USAF	PHONE NUMBER (DSN) 673-2231	SIGNATURE
	UNIT AND LOCATION 437 OG/CC CHARLESTON AFB, SC 29404		

5. COORDINATING ACTIVITIES

A. DZ CONTROLLING AGENCY OR UNIT LAWSON ARMY AIR FIELD, FT. BENNI, GA	B. MEMORANDUM OF UNDERSTANDING/LAND USE YES ☐ NO ☒ ATTACHED ☐	C. PHONE NUMBER (DSN) 835-9135
D. RANGE CONTROL RANGE CONTROL FM 01.10 / UHF 111.5 (SKYWATCH)		E. PHONE NUMBER (DSN) 835-1102

6. DZ DIMENSIONS (YDS/MTRS) (FOR CIRCULAR DZ, ENTER RADIUS ONLY)

A. LENGTH 2500 YDS	B. WIDTH 1300 YDS		C. RADIUS N/A	
POINT OF IMPACT DISTANCES FROM DZ LEADING EDGE	D. CDS PI 275 YDS	E. PE PI 350 YDS		F. HE PI 550 YDS

7. DZ AXIS DATA (OPTIONAL FOR CIRCULAR DZ)

A. MAGNETIC 350.5	B. GRID (MGRS) 347.2	C. TRUE 348	D. SOURCE/DATE OF VARIATION DATA

8. GROUND POINT ELEVATION	A. CDS PI 300'	B. HE PI 300'	C. PE PI 300'	D. HIGHEST 323'

9. DZ COORDINATES

A. SPHEROID 1866 CLARKE	B. DATUM 1927 NA	C. GRID ZONE 16 S	D. EASTING 6	E. NORTHING 35
F. GPS DERIVED COORDINATES YES ☒ NO ☐	G. POINT OF ORIGIN FL 92963 72166 SW corner of bus parking pad. PPI 1069 yds at 221 degrees.			

H. POINT	MGRS COORDINATES	WGS84 LATITUDE (D-M.MM)	WGS84 LONGITUDE (D-M.MM)
DZ CENTERPOINT	FL 92196 72200	32 16.317' N	084 57.561' W
CDS PI	FL 92383 71383	32 15.844' N	084 57.452' W
PE PI	FL 92368 71396	32 15.881' N	084 57.487' W
HE PI	FL 92331 71574	32 15.977' N	084 57.482' W

I. DZ CORNERS MGRS COORDINATES

LEFT LEADING EDGE FL 91855 70958	RIGHT LEADING EDGE FL 93017 71207
LEFT TRAILING EDGE FL 91240 73150	RIGHT TRAILING EDGE FL 92538 73442

AF IMT 3823, 20021001, V2   PREVIOUS EDITIONS ARE OBSOLETE.

Figure 6-20A. Example completed AF IMT 3823 (front).

Chapter 6

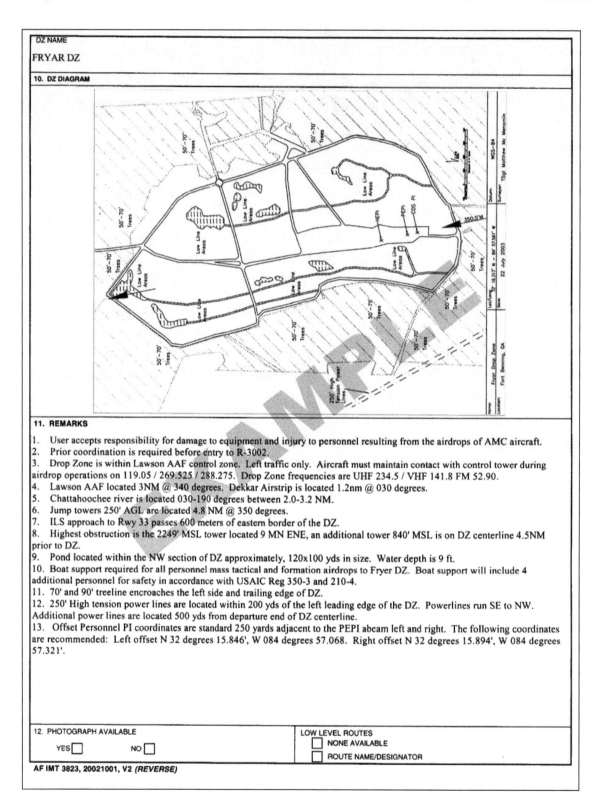

Figure 6-20B. Example completed AF IMT 3823 (back).

AF IMT 4304, DROP ZONE/LANDING ZONE CONTROL LOG

6-170. The AF IMT 4304, *Drop Zone/Landing Zone Control Log*, Figure 6-21, page 6-57, is a scorecard for the Air Force. Since the aircrew computes the air release point on the DZ, the Air Force needs documentation of the crew's performance. The DZSTL ensures this form is complete and accurate based on the instructions that follow:

DATE

6-171. Enter either calendar or Julian date and year. When time is required, use local or GMT consistent with the date.

LOCATION

6-172. Enter DZ name.

CCT AND UNIT

6-173. Enter your (the DZSTL's) name and unit.

DZ/LZ CONTROL OFFICER AND UNIT

6-174. Enter the name of the person controlling the DZ.

DROP ZONE SAFETY OFFICER AND UNIT

6-175. Enter the names of the people (you or someone else) who is acting as the DZ safety officer and the unit safety officer. If you are doing both, then write in your name for both.

LINE NO

6-176. Enter the mission sequence number of each aircraft. Each line number on any given drop zone mission represents an individual pass over the DZ. If you have a multiple aircraft DZ, you should still use a separate line number for each aircraft. For example, use three line numbers for a three-ship operation. Assign a line number to no-drop passes also. Write the reason for each no-drop in remarks.

TYPE ACFT

6-177. Enter the mission design series.

UNIT

6-178. Enter the aircraft's (using) unit.

CALL SIGN

6-179. Enter the call sign of the lead aircraft and, if applicable, formation position numbers.

TYPE MSN

6-180. See the legend for abbreviations of the types of missions.

Chapter 6

ETA

6-181. Enter the estimated time of arrival, estimated TOT, or S3 air brief. Use the same unit of time throughout the form.

ATA/ATD

6-182. Enter the actual time of each pass or the actual time of departure.

STRIKE REPORT

6-183. The strike report yards or clock is the actual purpose of this form. Observe the first parachute-suspended item from the control center, and then determine the distance in yards and the clock direction relative to the PI. Use 12 o'clock as the magnetic drop heading. If the first parachute lands within 25 yards of the PI, then write "PI" here to indicate a PI strike. If you were unable to maintain visual contact with the first parachute, especially during a multiple aircraft operation, then score the drop "S" (satisfactory) or "U" (unsatisfactory). If 90 percent of the parachutes land on the DZ, score the drop as satisfactory. If less than 90 percent hit the DZ, score it unsatisfactory. If you maintain radio communications with the drop aircraft, then relay strike reports to them so they can adjust their subsequent passes accordingly.

YDS

6-184. If the first jumper, container, or pallet lands within 25 yards of the PI, write "PI." If it lands farther from the PI, enter the distance from the PI in yards.

CLOCK

6-185. Use the direction of flight as 12 o'clock and its back azimuth as 6 o'clock. Estimate the direction from the PI to the first jumper, container, or pallet. If you can, enter the actual measurement.

LZ

6-186. Mark the "S" (satisfactory) box if a landing occurred in the first 500 feet of the LZ. If the aircraft had to go around again, if the drop fell short of the touchdown zone, or was more than 500 feet from the beginning of the touchdown zone, mark the "U" (unsatisfactory), and comment in Remarks.

SURF WIND

6-187. Enter the surface wind direction in degrees. Enter the highest wind velocity measured during the 10 minute window for that pass.

SCORE METHOD

6-188. Select from the Legend the abbreviation for the method you use to determine the distance between the PI and the first parachute.

- E = Estimated (You made a calculated guess).
- P = Paced (You paced off the distance).
- M = Measured (You used a calibrated measuring device to determine the distance).

MEAN EFFECTIVE WIND

6-189. Enter the time you measured the wind and the altitude where you measured it.

TIME

6-190. This is self-explanatory.

ALT

6-191. Enter the drop altitude.

DIR & LVL

6-192. Enter the wind direction in degrees and the velocity in knots.

REMARKS

6-193. Enter anything about the DZ operation that could help the Air Force during pilot debriefing. The DZSTL forwards AF IMT 4304 (Figure 6-21) to the air operations officer, who submits it through the chain of command to the USAF representative. If the DZSTL has radio communication with the aircraft, he transmits the strike report directly to the aircraft, for example--

"Lifter one-six, strike report, three o'clock two-hundred yards."

or

"Lifter one-six, strike report, PI."

Chapter 6

LINE NO	TYPE ACFT	UNIT	CALL SIGN	TYPE MSN	ETA	ATA / ATD	STRIKE REPORT YDS	STRIKE REPORT CLOCK	LZ S	LZ U	SURF WIND	SCORE METHOD	MEAN EFFECTIVE WIND TIME	MEAN EFFECTIVE WIND ALT	MEAN EFFECTIVE WIND DIR & VEL	REMARKS
1	C-130	317	27CO	HE	1000	1000	250	5			0209	E	0945	1100	158/09	
2				PE		1012	DRY	PASS								
3				PE		1025	50	6								
4				PE		1029	600	5								
5																
6	C-17	437	52BA	CD	1100	1100	250	6			0210	E	1045	600	150/11	
7			54			1105	150	6								
8			55			1110	200	4								
9			59			1115	200	6								
10																
11																
12																
13																
14																
15																

DROP ZONE/LANDING ZONE CONTROL LOG
DATE: 20050823
LOCATION: FALCON DROP ZONE
CCT AND UNIT: SSGT MOORE / SRA PERRY 1721 CCS
DZ/LZ CONTROL OFFICER AND UNIT:
DROP ZONE SAFETY OFFICER AND UNIT: Maj JOHNSON 2FSSO

LEGEND
AH-Airland (Heavy)
AL-Airland
CD-CDS/CRL/CRS
GM-GMRS
HE - Heavy Equipment
HO - HALO/HAHO
IL - Inverted "L"
LS-Instrument Landing System
PE-Personnel
RB-Radar Beacon Drop

SCORE METHOD
M - Measured
P - Paced
E - Estimated

AF IMT 4304, 20020903, V1   REPLACES AMC 168, DEC 92

Figure 6-21. Example completed AF IMT 4304.

Appendix A
Close Air Support and Close Combat Attack

This appendix does not change existing doctrine, tactics, techniques, or procedures for employing pathfinder teams and elements. It just introduces a vision of how CAS affects pathfinder teams.

DEFINITIONS

A-1. Close air support (CAS) is an air action by fixed and rotary wing aircraft against hostile targets that are in close proximity to friendly forces and require detailed integration of each air mission with the fire and movement of those forces.

A-2. Close combat attack (CCA) is a technique to control attack helicopters (AH-64 or OH-58D) in a close air support role, usually very near friendly troops in contact. It helps the pilot see the same target you see.

PURPOSE

A-3. The main purpose of CAS/CCA is to provide support to ground unit commanders. Other purposes of CAS include the following:

AIR INTERDICTION

A-4. Air interdiction (AI) is very useful to the ground unit commander planning an assault. Air superiority is essential in accomplishing the mission. AI assets will own the air in the area of operation, eliminating the possibility of the friendly forces being hit by enemy CAS.

SECURITY AND RECONNAISSANCE

A-5. Close air support aircraft can pull security during airmobile operations, as well as reconnoiter the air before any mission to remove any air threats.

ATTACK

A-6. CAS/CCA aircraft can attack targets without actually being on a support mission. CAS/CCA can commence bombing runs or strafing runs on one of many different target types.

THEATER MISSILE DEFENSE

A-7. CAS/CCA aircraft can provide missile defense.

SPECIAL OPERATIONS

A-8. Certain CAS/CCA aircraft are set aside strictly for special operations units and missions.

SUPPORT BY FIRE

A-9. Though not the main purpose of CAS/CCA, support by fire is the most common.

Appendix A

SUPPRESSION OF ENEMY AIR DEFENSES

A-10. Most CAS/CCA aircraft have SEAD capability, and usually conduct SEAD missions before any air mission.

TYPES OF AIRCRAFT

A-11. The following aircraft are the ones that will be most commonly seen by the pathfinder team during a deployment. Table A-1 shows the mission, armaments, capabilities, and limitations of each aircraft in the CAS theater.

Aircraft	Mission	Armaments	Capabilities	Limitations
F15C	Air superiority, to include defensive counterair (DCA), offensive counterair (OCA), and force protection.	Air-to-air missiles (AIM-7, -9, -120). Guns: 20-mm cannon.	Advanced air-to-air capabilities.	No CAS capability (air-to-air only).
F16 (Blocks 30, 40, and 50)	Primary: air superiority. Secondary: SEAD. Block 30 and 40 aircraft can provide CAS.	Air-to-air missiles (AIM-7, -9, 120). Guns: 20-mm cannon, all general-purpose bombs (MK-82, -84), guided bombs (GBU-10, -12, -15, -24, JDAM*), cluster bombs (CBU-87, -89), and the AGM-65 Maverick.	Situational awareness datalink (SADL) provides up-to-date battlefield information. CAS depends on unit proficiency.	More diverse missions equal less CAS training. High speed limits target acquisition. Limited night employment.
A-10	CAS and AI.	30-mm Gatling gun "tank killer," air-to-air: AIM-9, carries up to 16,000 lbs. of ordnance (MK-82, -84, -77), GBU-10, -12, CBU-87, CBU-89, AGM-65 Maverick.	Pilots: highly trained in CAS missions. Aircraft: specially designed to support ground forces, slow speed aids in target acquisition, longer loiter time.	Not all-weather. Slower speed makes it vulnerable to surface-to-air missile attacks.
AC-130 Spectre	CAS for special operations units, urban CAS, and reconnaissance.	25-mm cannon, 40-mm cannon, and 105 Howitzer. 25mm is only on the AC130H.	All-weather, long loiter time, surgical strike.	Vulnerable to threats. Employed normally at night in a low threat environment.
EA-6B Prowler.	SEAD.	AGM-88.	Electronic attack and SEAD.	Limited types of targets such as SAM sites.

Table A-1. CAS theater aircraft.

Aircraft	Mission	Armaments	Capabilities	Limitations
F-14 Tomcat	Primary: fleet defense and air superiority. Secondary: reconnaissance, AI, FAC(A), and CAS.	Air-to-air 20-mm cannons, air-to-air missiles (AIM-7, -9, 120), and 13,000 lbs. of ground ordnance.	Two sets of eyes (the pilot and the RIO).	Pilots: Not all have CAS proficiency. Aircraft: age and carrier operations.
F-18	Air superiority, escort, fleet defense, AI, SEAD, reconnaissance, and CAS.	Air-to-air 20-mm cannons, air-to-air missiles (AIM-7, -9, -120), and 14,000 to 17,000 lbs of ground ordnance.	Highly proficient in CAS.	Diverse missions have lower proficiency levels.
AV-8B Harrier	Primary: CAS. Secondary: AI, antiair warfare, helicopter escort, and reconnaissance.	25-mm cannons and the AIM-9, and up to 9,000 lbs of ground ordnance.	CAS proficient and highly flexible deploy and employ options.	Short range, very small payload, short loiter time, and slow speed make it vulnerable to air defenses.
AH-64 Apache	Tank attack and CAS.	2.75 rockets, hellfire missiles, and 30-mm cannon.	Detect and classify 128 targets, prioritizing the 16 most dangerous.	Not all-weather.
OH-58	CAS, recon, and limited AI.	2.75 rockets, Hellfire missiles, .50 cal MG, and air-to-air Stinger.	Limited AI, recon, and CAS.	Not all-weather. Vulnerable to air defenses.
MH-6 Little Bird	CAS for special operations units.	2.75 rockets, Hellfire missiles, .50 cal MG, and MK-19.	Highly maneuverable.	Not all-weather. Vulnerable to air defenses.
MH-60K Blackhawk	CAS for special operation units.	2x M134 6-barrel 7.62 miniguns and 2.75 rockets.	CAS and transportation of internal loads.	Not all-weather. Vulnerable to air defenses.

Table A-1. CAS theater aircraft (continued).

TARGET TYPES

A-12. Target types include—

- Point (tank, radar antenna).
- Soft (vehicle, personnel).
- Hard (armor, bunker).
- Area (column of armor, troops in the open).

WEAPONS EFFECTS

A-13. The method by which a particular weapon alters a target is called a damage mechanism. The five most commonly encountered damage mechanisms for conventional weapons are as follows:

Appendix A

BLAST

A-14. This effect is caused by tremendous overpressure (up to 700 tons per square inch). The bomb expands to one and a half times its normal size. This effect is maximized with a surface burst. Targets include buildings, machinery, and structures.

FRAGMENTATION

A-15. This effect extends over a greater area than that of a blast (up to 3,000 feet). The fragment size depends on the thickness of case, the case material, and the explosive material. Targets include troops, aircraft, and vehicles.

ARMOR PENETRATING

A-16. Amount of penetration and thickness is determined by the type of round used. Targets include tanks and cement buildings.

CRATERING

A-17. General purpose bombs can make unpassible craters in the ground. Targets include airfields and highways.

INCENDIARY

A-18. Dedicated incendiaries produce an intense, relatively small fireball that is more spectacular than effective. Combined effects weapons include an incendiary element that burns intensely for a longer time period. Maximize by hitting something that burns. Targets include uncovered supplies and combustibles.

AIRCRAFT WEAPONS TYPES

A-19. Aircraft weapons have evolved into complex systems capable of accurately targeting and destroying even the most heavily-armored vehicles on the modern battlefield. Below are some of the most common types of aircraft weapons.

GUNS

A-20. Guns include the 20 mm, 25 mm, 30 mm, 40 mm, and the 105-mm howitzer. They penetrate armor and are highly explosive against soft targets. Guns are simple and cannot be jammed and spoofed.

GENERAL PURPOSE BOMBS

A-21. General purpose bombs include the MK-80 series and penetration bombs. Explosive weight is 10 percent to 30 percent of bomb weight. Heavy, forged-steel case to prevent breakup. Blunt-nosed and flat-sided to prevent ricochet. Best penetration capability. Good fragmentation with fair blast.

AGM

A-22. The AGM-65 Maverick has easy mission planning. Launch and leave, as well as very accurate missile. It has low collateral damage and must have fair weather to engage.

Close Air Support and Close Combat Attack

RISK ESTIMATED DISTANCES

A-23. The casualty criterion is a prone soldier in winter clothing who is unable to function within five minutes after an assault. Troops in contact are friendlies within 1 kilometer of targets. Ordnance delivered inside the 0.1% PI is considered danger close (Table A-2). The forward air controller (FAC) must advise the ground commander by passing the ground commander's initials. This indicates the acceptance of the risk for ordnance. Peacetime numbers are found in ACCR 55-26.

Item	Description	REDs (m) 10.0% PI	REDs (m) 0.1% PI
2.75" rocket	Rocket with various warheads	145	240
5" rockets	Zuni with various warheads	220	340
Hellfire	AGM-114	40	105
GAU-8 (A-10)	30-mm gatling gun	40	65
AGM-65	Maverick	25	95
AC-130	25mm, 40mm 105mm	50/45 95	70/85 230
MK-82 LGB	GBU-12	95	300
MK-84 LGB	GBU-10/24	90	340
CBU-87	CEM or Gator	165	220

Table A-2. Risk estimated distances.

TARGET TO WEAPONS

A-24. Table A-3, page A-6, shows what weapons are used to destroy what targets.

Target	Weapon	Target	Weapon
Soft	GP bomb	Area denial and channelization	CBU-89/CBU-104 Gator
	CBU-52/58/71		AGM-154 JSOW
	CBU-87/CBU-103 CEM	Armor	CBU-87/CBU-103 CEM
	20-/25-/30-/40-/105-mm guns		AGM-65 Maverick
Hard	GP bomb with steel nose plug		30-mm (API)
	BLU-109/113		CBU-97/CBU-105 SFW
	AGM-65 Maverick		CBU-89/CBU-104 Gator
	LGB		LGB
	GBU-15		MK-20 Rockeye
Point	LGB	SAM and AAA site	Antiradiation missiles
	AGM-65 Maverick		PGM
	GBU-15		CBU
	20-/25-/30-/40-/105-mm guns		GP bomb

Table A-3. Target to weapons.

Appendix B
Operational Formats

Pathfinder leaders can use the operational formats described in this appendix to plan and carry out pathfinder operations. These formats are intended as guides and should be modified as required.

PLANNING FORMAT

B-1. The pathfinder leader uses the operation planning format shown in Figure B-1, page B-3, to organize an operation. This format consolidates information about each person or element. The leader can refer to this information during his planning and briefing. This format provides columns for writing in—

ACFT NO

B-2. Write in either the chalk number or the last three digits of the number painted on the tail of the aircraft that will transport the pathfinder.

NAME

B-3. Write in the name of each pathfinder.

LOAD TIME

B-4. Write in what time the pathfinder must be on the aircraft with all of his equipment.

TO TIME

B-5. Write in what time the aircraft will depart the staging area (the takeoff time).

DUTY AND LOCATION

B-6. Write in each pathfinder's mission assignment and location within the operational area.

CALL SIGN AND FREQUENCY

B-7. Write in the radio call sign and frequency for each person operating a radio.

EQUIPMENT

B-8. List all equipment, other than individual equipment, that each pathfinder element will carry.

REMARKS

B-9. Write in any other pertinent information.

LANDING ZONE AND DROP ZONE CONTROL RECORDS

B-10. The leader can make up an LZ/DZ control record based on the example formats shown in Figure B-2, page B-4. He uses this to record aircraft arrivals, departures, and load types. This record provides information for both ground and aviation commanders. It helps account for personnel and equipment. It can also help leaders initiate or conduct search-and-rescue operations for overdue or downed aircraft. The pathfinder internal radio net(work) operator, located at the control center, normally maintains this record.

FORMAT HEADINGS

B-11. Format headings include the following:

PATHFINDER UNIT

B-12. Enter the pathfinder unit's code or number designation.

SUPPORTED UNIT

B-13. Enter the name of the main ground or aviation unit.

PERIOD

B-14. Enter the date and time the operation will start and finish. Enter 0001 for the start time of a succeeding day. Enter 2400 for the end time if the operation will continue the next day.

OPERATION (AFLD LZ, DZ)

B-15. Enter the name or number of the operation. Cross out items that do not apply. Add any special designation used.

RECORDER

B-16. Enter the name of the person who records data on this form.

Operational Formats

PATHFINDER OPERATION PLANNING FORMAT

CLASSIFICATION

SUPPORTED UNIT: 1.188TH INF
LIFT UNIT: A/21ST AVN BN
ACL: 8 PAX
LZ TIME: 31 0600 MAR
DACOS: 53 AIR, 1:188TH INF, DFKK STRIP
TYPE ACFT: UH.1H
ARTY PREP AT LZ MACON AND ALBANY COMMENCES
H.20 MIN: LIFTED H.5 MIN.
ARTY PREP FIRED FROM GL 035725
CCP: GL 956696
RP: GL 015692

SIGNAL
1.188TH INF, RIGHT HALF: 47.00
A/21ST AVN BN: DEADLY SERPENT, 39.00
PFDR: DEKKAR CONTROL, 34.50
ALBANY CONTROL, 40.20
MACON CONTROL, 51.30
RESERVE, 37.30

ACFT NO	NAME	LOAD TIME	TO TIME	DUTY AND LOCATION	CALL SIGN AND FREQUENCY	EQUIPMENT	REMARKS
NA	HEITER	NA	NA	SECTION CO, STAGE FLD DEKKAR STRIP, GL 934730	11B85,34:50	2-PRC-112 RADIOS 1-DWYER METER	BE PREPARED FOR MIXED TRAFFIC AND NIGHT OPERATIONS UNTIL RELIEVED
NA	MARSONNER	NA	NA	GTA RATELO, STAGE FLD	11B85R,34:50	1-AN/PMQ-3A ANEMOMETER	
NA	COFFIN	NA	NA	INTERNAL NET RATELO, STAGE FLD	11B39,66:20	2-PRC-113 RADIOS 3-PRC/77 RADIOS 1-AN / PRC 41A	HOMING BEACON FREQ 1750KC.
NA	CASCALASIPA	NA	NA	SIGNALMAN, STAGE FLD	18B67,66:20	1-AN / TRN 30 (EX.1) 24-VS / 17 PANELS	
NA	LEACH	NA	NA	SIGNALMAN, STAGE FLD	11B29,66:20	35MX / 290 LANTERNS 3 SETS OF BATONS 1-SE / 11 LIGHT GUN 3 COLORED JACKETS EXTRA SMOKE	
750	PRUITT	0540	0545	SITE CO, LZ ALBANY GL 055713	J7G38,40:20	1-PRC 41 RADIO 1-PRC 41A RADIO	ACCOMPANY B 188TH ON MOVEMENT TO CONTACT OPERATION UNTIL COMPLETED
750	HODGES	0540	0545	GTA RATELO, LZ ALBANY	J7G38R,40:20	2-PRC/77 RADIOS 12 MX/290 LANTERNS 1-SE/11 LIGHT GUN	
750	CHURCHY	0540	0545	PATHFINDER, LZ ALBANY	NA	1 SET OF BATONS 6-VS/17 PANELS 8 SMOKE GRENADES	
777	CARTER	0535		SITE CO, LZ MACON GL075720	A5W38,51:30	SAME AS FOR LZ ALBANY	
777	DARGSECK	0535		GTA RATELO,LZ MACON	A5W38R51:30		
777	BOWER	0535		PATHFINDER, LZ MACON	NA		
NA	CARMEL	NA	NA	SITE CO, STANDBY RESERVE VIC DEKKAR STRIP	J4038, 37:30	SAME AS FOR LZ ALBANY	REMAIN WITH C 1 118TH (RESERVE) AT DEKKAR STRIP COMMITTED ON ORDER CALL SIGN WILL CORRESPOND WITH NAME OF LANDING SITE IF RESERVE IS COMMITTED
NA	KENFIELD	NA	NA	GTA RATELO, STANDBY RESERVE	J4038R, 37:30		
NA	KEMP	NA	NA	PATHFINDER, STANDBY RESERVE	NA		
NA	CASSIE	NA	NA	NONDUTY			(REFER TO GLOSSARY FOR ACRONYMS)

CLASSIFICATION

Figure B-1. Example format for operation plan.

Appendix B

PATHFINDER UNIT					21ST AVN BN PATHFINDER SECTION		
SUPPORTED UNIT					1. 188TH INF		
PERIOD					210001-212400 MARCH		
OPERATION (AFLD LZ, DZ)....................					MACHER		
					(NAME OR LOCATION OF SITE)		
RECORDER					PFC ROY S. COBB		
FLT OR ACFT NO	TYPE ACFT	TIME COMM ESTAB	TIME		TYPE LOAD		REMARKS
			ARR	DPRT	DELIVERED	EVAC	
(EXAMPLE FOR AFLD OPERATION)							
S7M50	U-1A	0600	0610	0625	RATIONS	2W1A	
L8M82	U-1A	0605	0615		AMMO		DAMAGED PROPELLER TO DISPERSAL AREA
C6E91	C-123	0610	0620	0635	AMMO	4W1A	
(EXAMPLE FOR DZ OPERATION)							
F1Y11	C-7A	1705	1710		3 BUNDLES AMMO		
T3M34	U-6A	1715	NA				ABORTED 2 MILES OUT
B6M78	U-6A	1720	1725		3 BUNDLES RATIONS		
(EXAMPLE FOR HELICOPTER DZ OPERATION)							
A2Y41	UH-1D	1230	1235	1236	PERSONNEL		CONTACTED CONTROL CENTER WITH A FLIGHT OF FOUR
D3S32	UH-1D	1230	1235	1236	PERSONNEL		
E4C23	UH-1D	1230	1235	1236	PERSONNEL	4W1A	
H1Y14	UH-1D	1230	1235	1236	MORTAR AMMO		
J1P67	CH-47	1245	1250	1252	AMMO		

Figure B-2. Example formats for the LZ/DZ control record.

COLUMN HEADINGS

B-17. Column headings include the following:

FLT OR ACFT NO

B-18. This means "flight or aircraft number," so enter the flight or aircraft's radio call sign.

TYPE ACFT

B-19. This means "type aircraft," so enter the Army or Air Force aircraft model designation.

TIME COMM ESTAB

B-20. This means "time communication established," so enter what time the aircraft acknowledges contact (radio, visual, or both, as applicable).

TIME (ARR, DPRT)

B-21. Enter the time the aircraft arrives or when the first of the flight lands. Enter the aircraft's departure time, or the time the last of the flight clears the ground.

TYPE LOAD (DELIVERED, EVAC)

B-22. Enter what type of load the aircraft delivered or evacuated (supplies, equipment, or personnel).

REMARKS

B-23. Write in any other pertinent information.

TROOP-LEADING PROCEDURES

B-24. From the moment he receives an order to conduct a pathfinder operation, the pathfinder leader does his best to use the following troop-leading procedures (TLPs):

SECTION WARNING ORDER

B-25. Issue a section warning order, including—

- Roll call.
- A brief statement of the enemy and friendly situations.
- The mission.
- Chain of command and section structure.
- Individual uniform and equipment (if not in SOP).
- Equipment required.
- Time schedule to complete work priorities (state who must show up, and where and when they must show up).
- Specific instructions and attached personnel.
- Time hack.

TENTATIVE PLAN

B-26. Make a tentative plan of the operation.

- Study the map.
- Check the weather.
- Study the unit SOP.
- Make a quick estimate of the situation. Will you need extra personnel from the supported unit, other equipment or materiel, or additional communications resources?
- Begin planning.

MOVEMENT AND COORDINATION

B-27. Arrange for movement and coordination.

- Arrange to move unit and inform second in command.
- Coordinate with ground and aviation units. Cover the ground tactical plan, the landing and unloading plan, the air movement plan, and the loading plan. Arrange for any extra people or equipment needed from the supported unit.

TENTATIVE OPERATION PLAN

B-28. Prepare a tentative operation plan.

- Reconnoiter when time permits (map, ground, air).
- Continue the estimate and receive recommendations.
- Complete the plan (work out details, formulate orders). Present the tentative plan to the supported unit commander or his staff. Prepare the final plan based on the desires of supported unit commander and on his final order.
- Issue section order (normally an oral order).
- Join supported unit.
- Rehearse and inspect (if time and terrain permit).

Appendix C
Army Helicopter Specifications

For pathfinders to help select landing sites they must know the dimensions of Army aircraft that US Army active and reserve units could employ. The art in this appendix shows helicopters currently in use as of this manual's publication date.

Appendix C

OBSERVATION HELICOPTERS

C-1. This category currently includes only the OH-58D Kiowa. Table C-1 shows specifications for the Kiowa; Figure C-1 shows the aircraft from three angles.

Rotor Diameter	35'
Length:	
Rotor Operating	42' 2"
Blades Removed	33' 10"
Height to Top of Turret	12' 9 ½"
Tread of Skids	6' 2"
Main Rotor:	
Disk Area	0.962 sq ft
Blade Area	38.26 sq ft
Clear Area Needed for Rotor	12.5 m
TDP #1	25 meters diameter

Table C-1. Specifications for the OH-58D Kiowa.

Army Helicopter Specifications

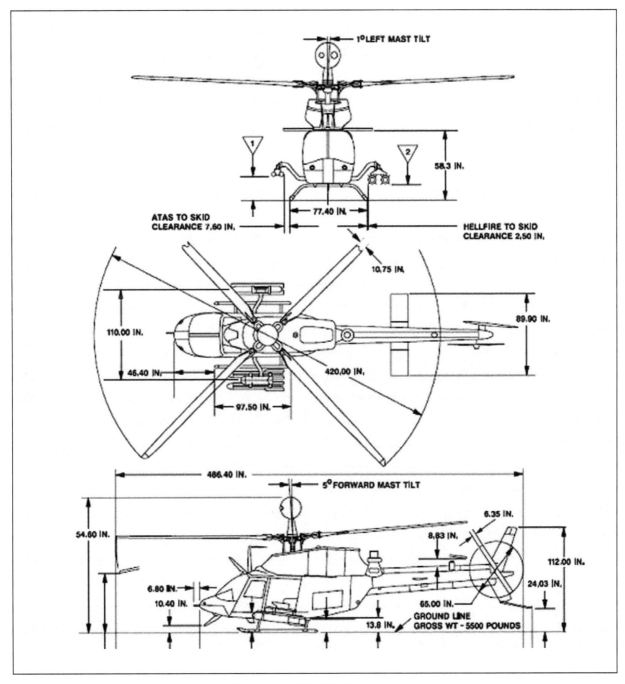

Figure C-1. OH-58D Kiowa.

Appendix C

ATTACK HELICOPTERS

C-2. This category of helicopters includes the AH 64A Apache and the AH 64D Longbow Apache.

AH 64A APACHE

C-3. Table C-2 shows specifications for the AH 64A Apache; Figure C-2 shows the aircraft from three angles.

Rotor Diameter .... 48'

Length:
   Rotors Operating .... 58' 3 ⅛"
   Rotors Static .... 57' 4"
   Fuselage .... 48'

Height .... 15' 3 ½"
Clear Area Needed for Rotors .... 17.9 m
Minimum TDP without   commander's approval is #3 .... 50 meters diameter

Table C-2. Specifications for the AH 64A Apache.

Army Helicopter Specifications

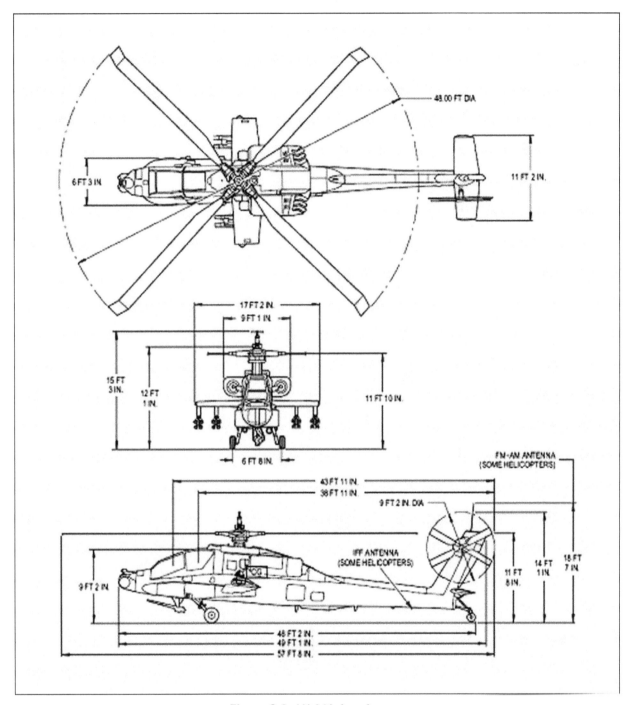

Figure C-2. AH 64A Apache.

Appendix C

AH 64D LONGBOW APACHE

C-4. Table C-3 shows specifications for the AH 64D Apache; Figure C-3 shows the aircraft from three angles.

Rotor Diameter	48'
Length: 　Rotors Operating 　Rotors Static 　Fuselage	 58' 3 ⅛" 57' 4" 48'
Height	15' 3 ½"
Clear Area Needed for Rotors	17.9 meters
Minimum TDP without commander's approval is #3	50 meters diameter

Table C-3. Specifications for the AH 64D Apache.

Army Helicopter Specifications

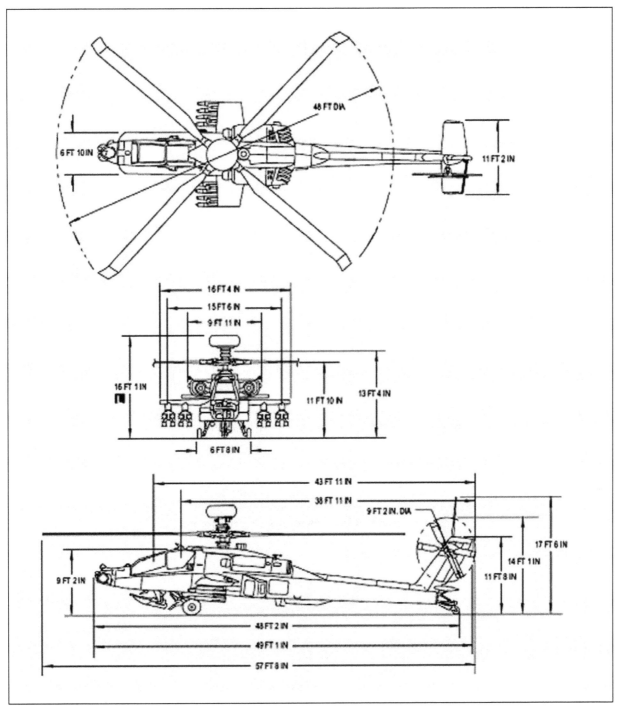

Figure C-3. AH 64D Apache.

UTILITY HELICOPTERS

C-5. This category of helicopters includes the UH-1H Iroquois and the UH-60A/L Blackhawk.

UH-1H IROQUOIS

C-6. Table C-4 shows specifications for the Iroquois; Figure C-4 shows the aircraft from three angles.

Rotor Diameter	48'
Length: Rotors Operating Rotors Static Fuselage	57' 1" 57' 1" 41' 10 ¾"
Span, Maximum Lateral	9' 4"
Height	14' 6"
Tread	8' 6 ½"
Main Rotor Ground Clearance, Static Against Stops	6' 6"
Clear Area Needed for Rotors	17.4 meters
TDP #2	35 meters diameter
Cargo Hook Capacity	4,000 lb

Table C-4. Specifications for the UH-1H Iroquois.

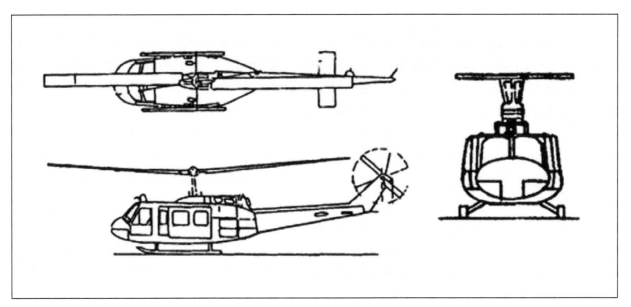

Figure C-4. UH-1H Iroquois.

Appendix C

UH-60A/L BLACKHAWK

C-7. Table C-5 shows specifications for the UH-60A & L Blackhawk; Figure C-5 shows the aircraft from above and from the left side.

Rotor Diameter	53' 8"

Length:
    Rotor Operating
    Rotor Folded
    Fuselage
	
	 64' 10"
	 64' 10"
	 50' 7 ½"

Span, Maximum Lateral	9' 8 ½"
Height	16' 5"
Tread	8' 10 ½"
Main Rotor Ground Clearance, Static Against Stops	 8' 9"
Clear Area Needed for Rotors	19.5 meters
TDP #3	50 meters diameter

Cargo Hook Capacity
    A Model
    L Model
	
	 8,000 lbs
	 9,000 lbs

Table C-5. Specifications for the UH-60A Blackhawk.

Army Helicopter Specifications

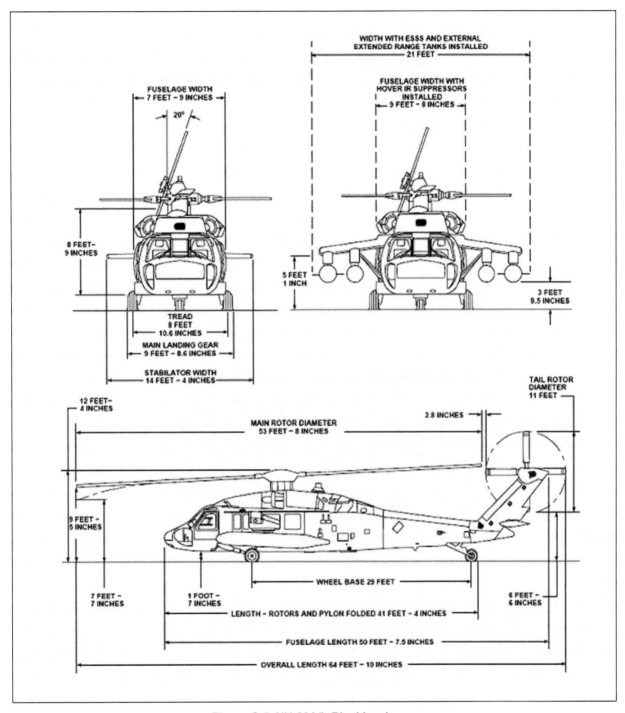

Figure C-5. UH-60A/L Blackhawk.

Appendix C

CARGO HELICOPTERS

C-8. This category of helicopters includes only the CH-47 D Chinook. With slingload, cargo helicopter TDP is #5 (100-meter diameter); without slingload, it is #4 (80-meter diameter). Table C-6 shows specifications for the CH-47 D Chinook; Figure C-6 shows it from three angles.

Rotor Diameter	60'
Length:	
Rotors Operating	98' 10 ¾"
Rotors Folded	51'
Fuselage	51'
Height (Overall)	18' 7 $^{13/16}$ "
Tread	11' 11"
Rotor Ground Clearance:	
Static Forward	7' 10 $^{5/8}$ "
Idling Forward	11' $^{7/8}$ "
Clear Area Needed for Rotors	30.4 meters
TDP #4	80 meters diameter
Allowable Cargo Load:	
Forward Hook	17,000 lb
Center Hook	26,000 lb
Aft Hook	17,000 lb
Fore & Aft Hooks combined	25,000 lb

Table C-6. Specifications for the CH-47 D Chinook.

Army Helicopter Specifications

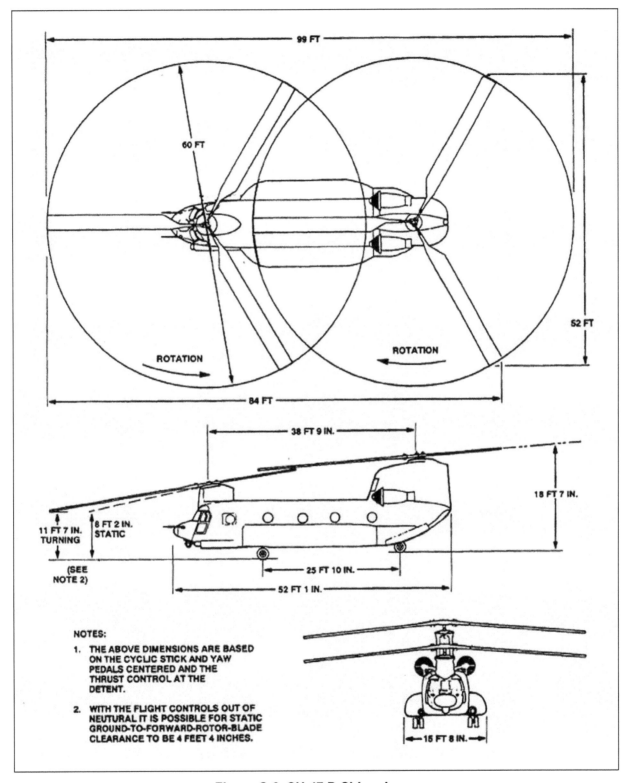

Figure C-6. CH-47 D Chinook.

Appendix D
Digitization Supplement

This appendix does not change existing doctrine, tactics, techniques, or procedures for employing pathfinder teams and elements. It just introduces a vision of how digitization will affect pathfinder teams.

DEFINITION

D-1. "Digitization" refers to the ongoing effort to integrate the Army's diversified battlefield operating systems into a network in which leaders and Soldiers can share and interchange current information about the battlefield environment for immediate or later use. Digitization is the near real-time transfer of battlefield information between diverse fighting elements to permit a shared awareness of the tactical situation. Accelerated operational tempo, instant communications, and immediate response times will characterize the digital environment.

D-2. Digitization is based on advancements in computers, communications, satellite navigation, and own-the-night (OTN) vision and sighting capabilities. Satellite navigation, digital communications, and digital mapping will allow leaders and Soldiers to share a common, digital picture of the battlespace environment in real time.

D-3. New computer capabilities will allow leaders to decisively concentrate their battlefield combat power. High-speed digital data exchange, the simultaneous display of intelligence data to leaders at all levels, and the rapid exchange of targeting data from sensors to shooters power this increased effectiveness.

D-4. New OTN capabilities enhance the ability to detect, identify, and engage targets during limited visibility. They also increase accuracy and control of fires, which reduces the risk of fratricide.

PURPOSE, ADVANTAGES, AND CAPABILITIES

D-5. The main purpose of digitization is to provide access to common, current data about friendly and enemy forces. Leaders and Soldiers collect these data through networks of sensors, CPs, processors, and weapons platforms. Every leader and Soldier will have immediate access to relevant information. All Soldiers will know what is happening around and among them. Other purposes of digitization include the following:

INFORMATION

D-6. To provide an integrated digital information network that will improve information flow; increase command and control; support battlefield fire and maneuver; and give leaders (decision makers), Soldiers (shooters), and supporters customized information. Leaders, Soldiers, and supporters need--

- To make the decisions necessary to prevail in any campaign.
- To share vital battlefield information (friendly and enemy) rapidly, if not instantly, rather than by slow voice radio or even slower liaison efforts.
- To act on information faster than the enemy does.
- To win the information war against any adversary.
- To use common data collected through the digitized network.

Appendix D

SITUATIONAL AWARENESS

D-7. To achieve near real-time situational awareness at all times and at all levels. This will allow leaders and Soldiers to collect, share, and use relevant information at once.

OPERATIONAL AWARENESS

D-8. Greater situational awareness leads to increased operational awareness, which is better understanding the "big picture."

OPERATIONAL TEMPO

D-9. A greater grasp of the "big picture" enables leaders and Soldiers to set and maintain an increased operational tempo, which will help in overwhelming the enemy.

LETHALITY, ACCURACY, AND SURVIVABILITY

D-10. To enhance the effectiveness and combat power of a force comprised of fewer and smaller units, so it can execute its missions with greater lethality, accuracy, and survivability in an environment characterized by an accelerated operational tempo, instant communications, and immediate response times.

PLANNING AND PREPARATION

D-11. To streamline and support mission planning, preparation, and execution, and to do so by providing critical information to every leader at the same time. Having earlier access to needed information compresses the mission planning and preparation cycles.

EFFECTIVENESS

D-12. To increase the pathfinder team's effectiveness in conducting pathfinder operations for its parent unit.

FIREPOWER

D-13. To synchronize direct and indirect fires more effectively. To mass the effects of dispersed firepower. This replaces the existing way of fighting that relies on physically massing weapons and forces.

DECENTRALIZATION

D-14. To support more decentralized operations, thereby improving the effectiveness of team- and element-level operations.

BATTLESPACE

D-15. To maintain a clear, accurate, simultaneous, and appropriate vision of the battlespace at each echelon, from Soldier to commander, and to enhance the mission capabilities needed in a multidimensional battlespace.

FRATRICIDE

D-16. To minimize fratricide.

SIGNATURE

D-17. To reduce the team's signature on the battlefield.

NAVIGATION

D-18. To improve navigation.

LINKUP

D-19. To improve linkup.

Appendix E
Air Force Instruction

Air force instructions are used primarily in the establishment of CARP drop zones and used in certain cases for GMRS drop zones.

AIRDROP AIRSPEEDS

E-1. The airdrop airspeed is used to determine additional size requirements on VIRS and GMRS drop zones using the D=RxT and T=D/R formulas. It is also used to determine the forward throw for rotary wing aircraft. See Table E-1 for the airdrop airspeeds for various aircrafts.

Type of Aircraft	Type of Load	Drop Speed (Knots Indicated Airspeed)
UH-1	All	50 to 70 knots (optimum 70 knots)
UH-60	All	65 to 75 knots (optimum 70 knots)
CH-46 (USMC)	All	80 to 90 knots
CH-47	All	80 to 110 knots (optimum 90 knots)
CH-53 (USMC)	All	90 to 110 knots
CH/HH3 (USAF)	All	70 to 90 knots
C-130	Personnel (Static Line)	130 knots
	Personnel (HALO & HAHO)	110 to 150 knots (optimum 130 knots)
	Equipment/Combination **	130 to 140 knots
	CDS*/Combination **	130 to 140 knots
	Door Bundle	130 knots
	SATB	Same as load simulated
C-17	Personnel (Static Line)	130 to 135 knots
	Personnel (HALO and HAHO)	138 to 145 knots
	Equipment/Combination **	145 knots +/- 5 knots
	CDS*/Combination **	145 knots +/- 5 knots
	Door Bundle	130 to 135 knots
	SATB	N/A
C-141/C5A	Personnel (Static Line)	130 to 135 knots
	Personnel (HALO and HAHO)	130 to 180 knots
	Equipment/Combination**	150 knots
	CDS*/Combination**	150 knots
	Door Bundle	130 to 135 knots
	SATB	Same as load simulated

* Includes free fall, high velocity CDS, wedge, Ahkio (military cold weather, squad-sized) sled, and combat rubber raiding craft (CRRC).
** Combination airdrops (for example, heavy equipment followed by personnel) use the highest airdrop airspeed.

Table E-1. Airdrop airspeeds.

Appendix E

DROP ZONE SIZE

E-2.   The airlift mission commander is normally responsible for airdrop accuracy and safety-of-flight for all drop zones meeting Air Force minimum size criteria. Standard DZ sizes are shown in Table E-2. For more information, see AFI 13-217.

Altitude (AGL)	Width [1,2]	Length [3]		
Container Delivery System (CDS), Container Release System (CRS), and Container Ramp Loads (CRL): C-130				
To 600 feet	400 yards/366 meters	Single Containers	Double Containers	
		1	1 to 2	400 yards/366 meters
		2	3 to 4	450 yards/412 meters
		3	5 to 6	500 yards/457 meters
		4	7 to 8	550 yards/503 meters
		5 to 8	9 or more	700 yards/640 meters
Above 600 feet	Add 40 yards/36 meters to width and length for each 100 feet above 600 feet (20 yards/18 meters to each side of DZ, 20 yards/18 meters to each end).			
CDS: C-141, C-17				
To 600 feet	450 yards/412 meters	Single Containers	Double Containers	
		1	1 to 2	590 yards/562 meters
		2	3 to 4	615 yards/540 meters
		3	5 to 6	665 yards/608 meters
		4 to 8	7 to 16	765 yards/700 meters
		9 to 14	17 to 28	915 yards/837 meters
		15 to 20	29 to 40	1,065 yards/974 meters
Above 600 feet	Add 40 yards/36 meters to width and length for each 100 feet above 600 feet (20 yards/18 meters to each side of DZ, 20 yards/18 meters to each end).			
CDS: High Velocity (HV) (Using 12-, 22-, or 26-Foot Ring Slot Parachutes)				
To 3,000 feet	580 yards/530 meters	660 yards/604 meters		
		Add 50 yards/46 meters to trailing edge for each additional row of containers.		
Above 3,000 feet	Add 25 yards/23 meters to each side and 100 yrds/91 meters to each end for every 1,000-foot increase in drop altitude.			
CDS: High Altitude Airdrop Resupply System (HAARS)				
To 3,000 feet	500 yards/457 meters	1 to 8 containers	1,200 yards/1,098 meters	
		9 or more containers	1,900 yards/1,739 meters	
Above 3,000 feet	Add 25 yards/23 meters to each side and 50 yards/46 meters to each end for every 1,000-foot increase in drop altitude.			
High Speed Low Level Aerial Delivery System (HSLLADS)				
Unknown	300 yards/274 meters	600 yards/549 meters		
Personnel (Static Line)				
To 1,000 feet	600 yards/549 meters	1 parachutist	600 yards/549 meters	
		Additional parachutists	Add 75 yards/69 meters the trailing edge for each additional parachutist (PI for ST/para-rescue personnel).	
Above 1,000 feet	Add 30 yards/28 meters to width and length for each 100 feet above 1,000 feet (15 yards/14 meters to each side of DZ, 15 yards/13 meters to each end).			

Table E-2. Standard drop zone size criteria.

Altitude (AGL)	Width [1, 2]	Length [3]	
Heavy Equipment			
To 1,100 feet	600 yards/549 meters	One platform	1,000 yards/915 meters
		Additional platforms	Add 400 yards/366 meters (C-130), 500 yards/457 meters (C-141/C-17/C-5) to the trailing edge for each additional platform.
Above 1,100 feet	Add 30 yards/28 meters to the width and length for each 100 feet above 1,100 feet (15 yards/14 meters to each side of DZ, 15 yards/14 meters to each end).		

[1] This does not apply to AFSOC assigned or gained, to aircraft OPCON to USSOCOM, or to a theater special operations command:

   a. For day visual formations, increase width by 100 yards/92 meters (50 yards/46 meters on each side).

   b. For C-141, C-130 station-keeping equipment (SKE) AWADS formation, increase width by 400 yards/366 meters (200 yards/184 meters on each side).

   c. At night, increase width by 100 yards/92 meters for single ship visual drops (50 yards/46 meters on each side). Increase 200 yards/184 m for visual formations (100 yards/92 meters on each side).

[2] C-17 DZ width adjustments. You might need to adjust more than once:

   a. For visual formations (day or night), increase width by 100 yards/92 meters (50 yards/46 meters each side).

   b. For night pilot-directed airdrops, increase width an additional 100 yards/92 meters (50 yards/46 meters each side). This does not apply to aircraft performing GPS drops.

   c. For SKE HE/CDS formation, increase width by 400 yards/366 meters (200 yards/183 meters each side).

   d. For personnel formations, minimum DZ basic width using center PIs is 1,240 yards for 2-ship elements and 1,800 yards for 3-ship elements. When using offset PIs, minimum basic width is 1,100 yards for 2-ship elements and 1,300 yards for 3-ship elements.

[3] This does not apply to AFSOC assigned or gained, to aircraft OPCON to USSOCOM, or to a theater special operations command. At night, increase length by 100 yards/92 meters for visual drops (50 yards/46 meters on each end). This also does not apply to a C-17 doing GPS drops.

Table E-2. Standard drop zone size criteria (continued).

GROUND MARKED RELEASE SYSTEM

E-3. The GMRS is mainly used for small unit insertion and aerial resupply operations. It is the most tactical drop zone because communication with the drop aircraft is not necessary. Table E-3 shows the constants for different airdrop loads. Table E-4, page E-4, shows the forward throw distance for various aircraft. Forward throw distance is how far a parachutist or cargo container travels along the aircraft flight path. It begins after the person or cargo exits the aircraft, and continues until the parachute fully opens and the load descends vertically. (For more on the GMRS, see AFI 13-217.)

Type Drop	K (Load Drift Constant)
Personnel (static line)	3.0
Heavy equipment	1.5
CDS/CRL/CRS	1.5
Door bundle	1.5
SATB	2.4

Table E-3. Ground marked release system load drift constants (K).

Appendix E

Type Drop	C-130	C-17	C-141	C-5
Personnel (static line)/door bundle	250 yards (229 meters)	250 yards (229 meters)	250 yards (229 meters)	250 yards (229 meters)
Personnel (MFF)	328 yards (300 meters)	328 yards (300 meters)	328 yards (300 meters)	328 yards (300 meters)
Heavy equipment	500 yards (458 meters)	700 yards (640 meters)	730 yards (668 meters)	730 yards (668 meters)
CDS/CRS/CRL	550 yards (503 meters)	725 yards (663 meters)	750 yards (686 meters)	N/A
SATB	160 yards (147 meters)	N/A	160 yards (147 meters)	N/A

Table E-4. Ground marked release system forward throw distance.

POINT OF IMPACT

E-4. The point of impact is the location where the first piece of equipment or first personnel is planned to land on the DZ. These are used in computing the release point on CARP drop zones and for tactically assessed GMRS DZs for CDS or heavy equipment. For more information, see Table E-5 and AFI 13-217.

Type Drop	Distance From Sides (See Note 4)	Distance from Approach End	
C-130/C-141/C-5 *(See Notes 1 and 2)*		*Day*	*Night*
CDS C-130 *(See Note 3)*	*(See Note 4)*	200 yards/183 meters	250 yards/229 meters
CDS C-141 *(See Note 3)*	*(See Note 4)*	225 yards/206 meters	275 yards/251 meters
Personnel	*(See Note 4)*	300 yards/274 meters	350 yards/320 meters
Equipment	*(See Note 4)*	500 yards/457 meters	550 yards/503 meters
C-17 *(See Notes 1 and 2)*		*Day*	*Night*
CDS *(See Note 3)*	*(See Note 4)*	225 yards/206 meters	275 yards/251 meters
Personnel	Offset PI=250 yds left or right of calculated center PI (or see Note 4)	300 yards/274 meters	350 yards/320 meters
Equipment	*(See Note 4)*	500 yards/457 meters	550 yards/503 meters

1 PI location may be adjusted to meet specific mission requirements. Participants must be briefed.

2 PI location may be adjusted for aircrew PI acquisition training. The PI may be located anywhere within the surveyed DZ boundaries as long as the minimum required DZ size for that type airdrop and aircraft formation fits within the boundaries, and provided the distance from the leading edge listed above is complied with. For lateral placement, the PI must be located at least one-half the width of the minimum size DZ (based upon type airdrop and aircraft formation) from the closest side of the DZ. All participants must be briefed when using this option.

3 For high velocity (HV) CDS and HAARS, laterally position the PI in the center of the DZ.

4 PI distance from sides of DZ must be at least one-half the minimum width for that type airdrop.

Table E-5. Standard point-of-impact placement.

Glossary

acft load	aircraft load; refers to cargo suspended below a slingload
ACL	allowable cargo load
ACP	air control point
ADS	aerial delivery sling
AEL	Army Electronic Library
AF	Air Force
AFB	Air Force base
AFI	Air Force Instruction
AFSOC	Air Force Special Operations Command
aft	to the rear, behind, or toward the tail of the aircraft
AGL	above ground level
AH	attack helicopter
Ahkio sled	a squad-powered sled for operations in extreme cold
AI	air interdiction
airdrop	delivery of cargo or personnel by parachute from an aircraft in flight
AL	airland
ALO	air liaison officer
alt	altitude
AM	amplitude modulation
AMC	Air Mobility Command
AO	area of operations
apex fitting	the uppermost point (clevis, shackle, ring, or loop) that gathers the sling tension members and attaches to the cargo hook
apex fitting pin	A headed pin that extends through the two ends of the apex fitting-clevis, retained in place by a bolt and nut apex fitting spacer (an hourglass-shaped bushing that fits over the apex fitting pin), causing the apex fitting to stay centered on the cargo hook
approach azimuth	the direction of an aircraft's approach to the landing point, usually expressed in degrees and measured clockwise from a reference point
arr	arrival
ASIP	advanced system improvement program
ATA	actual time of arrival
ATC	air traffic controller
ATD	actual time of departure
AWADS	All-Weather Aerial Delivery System
AZAR	assault zone availability report
basket hitch	a type of attachment in which a flat web nylon strap is formed in the shape of the letter "U" with the two ends connected side-by-side
basket leg	the cable on a pallet sling that encircles the load

becket	a short length of rope with an eye on one or both ends, used to secure items such as eyelets or coils of rope
bight	a formed loop in a rope or cable
BIT	built-in test
blivet	A rubber or fabric storage bag, transportable by air or ground, that holds fuel or water
breakaway technique	use of material with a low breaking strength, such as tape or cotton webbing, to temporarily restrain the sling equipment from becoming entangled on the load as the helicopter puts tension on the sling
breaking strength	resistance to breaking, commonly measured in pounds. (Refers to tensile strength.)
brownout	a loss of orientation with respect to the horizon, caused by blowing sand, dust, or dirt
CA	combat assault
cable	a suspended external cargo sling system. Cargo hook attached to the bottom of the fuselage by a system of cables
CAPES	Chemlight-Assisted Personnel Exit System
cargo hoist	a device used to raise, lower, or winch cargo
cargo hook	a suspension hook device on which the apex fitting is placed to transport an external load
cargo hook keeper	a spring-loaded device used to prevent the apex fitting from sliding off the cargo hook load beam
cargo hook loading pole	also called a "shepherd's hook," with a hook on one end, which an aircrew member uses to pick up the apex fitting and connect it to the cargo hook. Used when the hookup team cannot stand on top of the load
cargo net	a meshed arrangement of straps or cords that have been knotted or woven together at regular intervals and used to transport supplies and equipment
cargo sling	consists of multiple tension members which, when properly rigged, enable aircrew to suspend cargo and equipment under a helicopter
CARP	computed air release point
CAS	close air support
castle nut	a hexagon-shaped nut with a slot in each of its six sides and secured in place by a cotter pin
CBRN	chemical, biological, radiological, or nuclear
CBU	cluster bomb unit
CC	control center
CCA	close combat attack
CCP	communications checkpoint
CDS	container delivery system
cellulose	a cushioning or padding material used to protect the load or sling legs
center (main) cargo hook	a cargo hook located in the center of the helicopter
center of balance	location where an item would balance if it were possible to support the load at that point

centerline	an imaginary line that extends lengthwise and bisects the bottom of the helicopter fuselage
CG	center of gravity
CH	cargo helicopter
chemiluminescent light	a plastic tube filled with a liquid chemical and a glass vial that when activated produces a glowing light known as chemiluminescence
choker hitch	a knot formed by placing a strap or cord around an item and passing the free end of the strap or cord through the loop formed by the other end
clevis	a "U"-shaped yoke device with a bolt or pin through the two ends
COMSEC	communications security
connector link	a metal link device that joins the ends of a nylon web loop together, such as used on the web ring of the 15,000-pound capacity multileg sling
constant power	the point at which a helicopter engine produces a fixed level of performance
CONUS	Continental United States
CP	command post
CRC	control and reporting center
CRL	container ramp load
CRS	Container Release System
DCA	defensive counterair
dep	departure
det	detachment
DF	direction finding
down wash	also called "rotor wash." High-velocity air movement under a hovering helicopter
downslope	downhill; descending; a slope that lies downward
downwind	in the direction that the wind is blowing
drawbar	a beam across the rear of a vehicle or aircraft to which implements are hitched
drop-off	a very steep or perpendicular descent
DS	direct support
DTG	date-time group
dual-point load	cargo or equipment rigged and suspended from two cargo hooks
DZ	drop zone
DZSO	drop-zone safety officer
DZST	drop-zone support team
DZSTL	drop-zone support team leader
ECCM	electronic countercountermeasures
ECM	electronic countermeasures
EMT	emergency medical technician
end bar	the removable side of a connector link
energy-dissipating material	artificial cardboard packing material. In parachute operations, protects equipment by dissipating shock or energy when the package lands
ETA	estimated time of arrival

Glossary

EW	electronic warfare
exit path	the track or course of an aircraft departing the landing point
ext	extracted
external air transport	movement of supplies or equipment that is rigged and suspended from a helicopter cargo hook
external load	consists of supplies or equipment properly rigged with either one or more slings, cargo bags, or cargo nets
eye sock	a loop formed at both ends of a sling leg
EZ	extraction zone
FAARP	forward area arming and refueling point
FB	Fort Benning
FEBA	forward edge of the battle area
field-expedient pendants	individual slings or sling legs used as a vertical riser or pendant
field-expedient static-discharge wand	a device fabricated from readily available material to discharge the helicopter's static electrical charge
field-expedient drogue device	any device locally fabricated to connect to an external load for the purpose of increasing the stability of the load
FLA	frontline ambulance
flat web nylon	a flat nylon strap or sling fabricated in either concentric loops or single lengths
floating web keepers	(*see* sliding keepers)
FM	frequency modulated
FOC	flight operations center
forward cargo hook	a cargo hook located forward of the center or main cargo hook
forward slope	ground whose surface forms an upward angle or incline with the horizon
FRAGO	fragmentary order
free-swinging cargo hook	a cargo hook attached to the end of a pendant or cable instead of attached directly to the helicopter fuselage
ft	feet
fuselage	the central body portion of a helicopter, which accommodates the crew, passengers, and cargo
fwd	forward
GAIL	glide angle indicator light
GCA	ground-controlled approach
glide angle indicator light	(GAIL) A device that emits a three-color light beam that indicates a safe glide path over approach obstacles onto a landing site
glide path angle	the helicopter's angle of approach to the landing point
GMRS	Ground Marked Release System
GMT	Greenwich Mean Time
GP	general purpose
grabhook	a hook for grabbing (as the links of a chain)

ground crew	personnel on the ground who help prepare and rig loads, guide the helicopter, and connect the load to the helicopter
GSI	glide slope indicator
GTA	ground-to-air
GUC	ground unit commander
GWT	gross weight
HAARS	High Altitude Airdrop Resupply System
HAHO	high-altitude, high-opening
HALO	high-altitude, low-opening
handheld	designed to be operated while held in the hand
HE	heavy equipment
HEAT	helicopter external air transport
HLZ	helicopter landing zone
HMMWV	high-mobility, multipurpose wheeled vehicle
HO	HALO or HAHO
HSLLADS	High-Speed, Low-Level, Aerial Delivery System
HVCDS	High-Velocity Container-Delivery System
IAW	in accordance with
ID	identification
ILS	Instrument Landing System
immediate mission	a task or support mission that arises during the course of a battle and which by its nature cannot be planned in advance
INR	internal net recorder
ins	inserted
ISA	international standardization agreement; *see also* QSTAG, STANAG
JAAT	joint air attack team
JP	jet petroleum
keeper	a device that holds something in position such as an apex fitting on the helicopter cargo hook
KIAS	knots indicated airspeed
knotless nylon cord cargo net	a cargo net manufactured from braided nylon cord joined by a knotless intersection method
kt	knot(s)
landing point	a point within a landing site where one helicopter can land
landing site	a site within a landing zone that contains one or more landing points. This is also known as the touchdown point
landing zone	any specified area used for the landing of aircraft
lanyard	a short piece of rope or cable used to fasten something or an extension of a shorter device
lashing straps	a flat-web nylon strap with a D-ring on one end. Used to lash equipment together
latch bar	the movable top part of the pallet sling tensioner

lateral slope	ground whose surface forms an angle oriented from either right to left or left to right with the horizon
lb	pound(s)
lifting eye	a loop in a cable, rope, or other device used to lift an object
lifting leg hook	a hook on the end of a sling leg, usually used with a hoisting sling
lifting point/ lifting provision	an integral part of the equipment, commonly called a lug, eye, shackle, or ring that provides a means of attaching a sling for safe lifting
lifting shackle	a ring or clevis that provides a means of attaching sling for safe lifting
liftoff	a vertical takeoff by an aircraft or a rocket vehicle or a missile
LIN	line item number
load beam	a structural member of the cargo hook that supports the weight of the external load
load binders	a locking device used to tighten and secure
load oscillation	the swinging movement of an external load
locking detent	a slot in the pallet sling tensioner stirrup that engages the release knob assembly on the latch bar
low-response, external cargo sling system	a cargo hook attached to a suspension frame below the fuselage by a system of cables and pulleys
lunette	the towing eye on the trailer drawbar
LZ	landing zone
MAC	Military Airlift Command
MAF	Military Airlift Facility
main cargo hook winch	a mechanical drum with a cable attached to raise and lower the cargo hook
manual release knob or lever	a lever, knob, or other device that, when actuated by either the ground crew or aircrew member, causes the cargo hook to open
mean effective wind	the average wind speed from the ground to drop altitude
MEDEVAC	medical evacuation
METT-TC	mission, enemy, terrain, troops, time, and civil considerations
MEW	mean effective wind
MFF	military free fall
MGRS	military grid reference system
MK 100	(Mark 100) the designation given to the pallet sling that can accommodate a pallet load 48 to 70 inches high
MK 86	(Mark 86) the designation given to the pallet sling that can accommodate a pallet load 29 to 40 inches high
MOGAS	motor gasoline
MPS	meters per second
MSL	mean sea level
multileg-pole pendant	A reach pendant that has one or more removable sling legs
NATO	North Atlantic Treaty Organization

Glossary

NAVAID	navigation aid
NCO	noncommissioned officer
night vision goggles	an image-intensification device that improves visibility in low light situations by amplifying available light
NLT	not later than
NM	nautical miles
no-load condition	a situation in which the sling legs are under no tension
no-sew fitting	a web keeper secured in place by a locking fork
NSN	national stock number
NVD	night vision device
NVG	night vision goggles
nylon donut	a ring formed by joining two ends of a flat, web-nylon strap using a Type IV link or two-point link connector
OCA	offensive counterair
OPCON	operational control
OPORD	operation order
oscillate	to swing back and forth like a pendulum
OTN	own the night
overfly	to fly over; to pass over in an airplane
pendant	a releasable swivel hook. That is, a high-strength sling constructed of multiple plies of nylon webbing with a remotely operated, manually released, full 360-degree swivel hook
pendant cargo hook	a cargo hook that is connected to the end of a strap and suspended below the fuselage
PEPI	personnel point impact
permanent keeper	a web keeper that encircles all of the loops of a nylon web strap and is either sewn or otherwise retained in place
phraseology	a manner of organizing words and phrases into longer elements; a choice of words
PI	point of impact
PIBAL	pilot balloon
pickup zone	landing site designated where an aircraft picks up passengers or cargo
piggyback load	cargo suspended below a slingload such as a cargo net carried beneath a howitzer
POL	petroleum, oils, and lubricants
port side	the left-hand side (as one looks forward)
preclude	to make impossible by necessary consequence; to rule out in advance
preplanned mission	a task or support in accordance with a program planned in advance of the operation
proword	procedure word; a word or phrase limited to radio telephone procedure used to facilitate communication by conveying information in a condensed standard form.
PSP	perforated steel planking
PZ	pickup zone

Glossary

QSTAG	quadripartite standardization agreement
quick-fit strap fasteners	metal, V-shaped device with a double bar and a friction-grip crossbar. Used with lacing straps
racetrack	to fly in an oval flight pattern over a drop zone or point of impact
RAM	raised-angle marker
RB	radar beacon
reach pendant	braided fabric rope assembly with an attached, stiffened reach tube and a loop on each end
reach tube	a length of tubing that encases the braided rope portion of a reach pendant
receiving unit	a unit receiving the transported supplies and equipment
recon	reconnaissance, reconnoiter
relative humidity	the ratio of absolute humidity to the maximum possible density of water vapor in the air at the same temperature
rendezvous point	a clearly defined and visible point or assembly area for the ground crew during helicopter operations
retainer strap	nylon web loop interwoven on the web ring of the 15,000-pound capacity multileg sling that retains the sling legs on the lower part of the web ring
retention pins	metal devices used to secure objects such as clevises or shackles to the vehicle frame
RIO	radar intercept officer
rope lay	an individual grouping of wire strands woven or twisted together, which when braided together form a cable
rotor wash	(See down wash.)
RP	release point
SADL	situational awareness datalink
safe working load	the greatest capacity of a lifting device used in helicopter external load operations
SAM	surface-to-air missle
SATB	simulated airdrop training bundle
SATCOM	satellite communications
SEAD	suppression of enemy air defenses
SIGINT	signals intelligence
signalman	A person who signals or who works with signals, or a member of the ground crew who communicates with the pilot by means of arm-and-hand signals
SIGSEC	signal security
SINCGARS	Single-Channel, Ground and Airborne Radio System
single-point load	cargo or equipment rigged and suspended from one cargo hook
SKE	station-keeping equipment
sliding keeper	a web keeper located near the ends of a flat web strap that encircles all of the loops and acts as a cinch
sling leg	An individual tension member of the sling set
slingload	Consists of supplies or equipment properly rigged with either one or more slings, cargo bags, or cargo nets

sling-to-clevis attachment	Connecting a flat web nylon strap to a lift provision by means of inserting a clevis through the loop on the end of the strap and attaching the clevis to the provision
SOI	signal operating instructions
SOP	standing operating procedure
SPIES	Special Patrol Insertion Extraction System
spreader bar	A device that prevents the sling legs from bearing against the load, which could cause damage
STANAG	standard NATO agreement
starboard side	The right-hand side (as one looks forward)
static discharge wand crewman	A member of the ground crew responsible for discharging the static electricity from the helicopter. Also called "static probe crewman."
static electricity	A electrical charge produced and stored in the helicopter fuselage during flight
STOL	short takeoff and landing
STT	special tactics team
supported unit	A unit requesting the mission to transport supplies and equipment
swage stops	Short lengths of metal tubing crimped on the pallet sling cables
tandem load	An external load consisting of two pieces of equipment joined together, such as a prime mover and a howitzer
TDP	touchdown point
tensioner	A locking device on the pallet sling cables used to adjust the overall length of the cable
tensioner stirrup	The fixed body of the pallet sling tensioner
theodolite	A surveyor's instrument for measuring horizontal and, usually, also vertical angles
tie-down provision	An integral part of the equipment commonly called a lug, eye, shackle, or ring that provides a means of attaching a hook, strap, or cable to restrain equipment during shipment
tie-down strap	A device consisting of a flat web nylon strap with hooks on one or both ends and a ratchet device used to secure items
TOT	time on target
touchdown hover	a helicopter landing with only part of the landing gear positioned on the ground
TOW	tube-launched, optically tracked, wire-guided missile
transit	to pass across
TSC	Training Support Center
TTB	tactical training bundle
TTB/CDS	tactical training bundle/Container Delivery System
TTB/HE	tactical training bundle/heavy equipment
turbo meter	an instrument for measuring ground wind speed
turnaway	the act of refusing admittance
turnout	an act of turning out
two-point link connector	a device used to connect two ends of a flat web nylon strap together

Type III nylon cord	a thin rope made of several strands of Type III nylon woven together
Type IV link connector	a device used to connect two ends of a flat web nylon strap together
Type X sling	a nylon aerial delivery sling consisting of two, three, or four consecutive loops of Type X nylon webbing
Type XXVI sling	a nylon multiloop-line sling consisting of two or more consecutive loops of Type XXVI nylon webbing
UH	utility helicopter
UHF	ultra-high frequency
upslope	a slope that lies upward; uphill
upwind	the direction from which the wind is blowing
USAF	US Air Force
USCG	US Coast Guard
USMC	US Marine Corps
USSOCOM	United States Special Operations command
VAPI	visual approach-path indicator
VDC	volts of direct current
vertical pendant	a high-strength sling or strap used to increase the clearance between the helicopter and the load
vertical riser	a suspension member oriented in a vertical direction
VHF	very high frequency
VIRS	Verbally Initiated Release System
VMC	visual meteorological conditions
V-shaped approach path	the area within a designated arc or sector measured outward from the center of the landing point
web ring	the apex fitting of the 15,000-pound capacity, multileg sling set
web ring connector bar	a metal connecting link that joins the two ends of the web ring strap on the 15,000-pound capacity, multileg sling
web ring strap	a nylon web loop that forms the web ring on the 15,000-pound capacity, multileg sling
whiteout	a loss of orientation with respect to the horizon due to caused by blowing snow, the sun reflecting on the snow, or an overcast sky
windchill factor	the cooling effect of moving air
yd	yard(s)

References

SOURCES USED

These are the sources quoted or paraphrased in this publication.

ARMY PUBLICATIONS

FM 3-21.220. *Static Line Parachuting Techniques and Tactics.* 23 September 2003.

FM 1-02. *Operational Terms and Graphics.* 21 September 2004.

FM 10-450-3. *Multiservice Helicopter Slingload: Basic Operations and Equipment.* 10 April 1997.

FM 21-60. *Visual Signals.* 30 September 1987.

FM 24-18. *Tactical Single-Channel Radio Communications Techniques.* 30 September 1987.

FM 24-24. *Signal Data References: Signal Equipment.* 29 December 1994.

TM 9-1370-206-10. *Operator's Manual for Pyrotechnic Signals.* 31 March 1991; with Change 1, 10 March 1992.

AIR FORCE INSTRUCTIONS

AFI 11-231. *Computed Air Release Point Procedures.* 7 July 2004.

AFI 11-410. *Personnel Parachute Operations.* 20 May 2004.

AFI 13-217. *Assault Zone Procedures.* 1 May 2003; with four supplements published between 1 October 2003 and 15 May 2004.

DOCUMENTS NEEDED

These documents must be available to the intended users of this publication.

AIR FORCE FORMS

AF IMT 3823. *Drop Zone Survey.*

AF IMT 4304. *Drop Zone Control Log.*

ARMY PUBLICATIONS

FM 3-97.6. *Mountain Operations.* 28 November 2000.

FM 90-3. *Desert Operations.* 24 August 1993.

FM 90-4. *Air Assault Operations.* 16 March 1987.

FM 90-5. *Jungle Operations.* 16 August 1982.

DEPARTMENT OF THE ARMY FORMS

DA Form 2028. *Recommended Changes to Publications and Blank Forms.*

DA Form 7382-R. *Sling Load Inspection Record.*

DA Form 7461-R. *Internal Net Record.*

References

INTERNATIONAL AGREEMENTS*

QSTAG 585. *Marshaling Helicopters in Multinational Land Operations.* 23 April 1981.

STANAG 2863. *Navigational and Communication Capabilities for Helicopters in Multinational Land Operations.* 26 September 1988.

STANAG 3117. *Aircraft Marshaling Signals.* 17 October 1985.

STANAG 3281. *Personnel Locator Beacons.* 3 April 1978.

STANAG 3570. *Drop Zones and Extraction Zones--Criteria and Markings.* 26 March 1986.

STANAG 3619. *Helipad Marking, Third Edition.* 20 March 1997.

INTERNET WEB SITES

Some of the documents listed in these References may be downloaded from Army websites:

U.S. Army Publishing Directorate (USAPD)
http://www.usapa.army.mil

Army Doctrine and Training Digital Library (ADTDL)
http://www.adtdl.army.mil

Air Force Publishing
http://afpubs.hq.af.mil/

NATO Online Library (for International Standardization Agreements [ISAs])
http://www.nato.int/docu/standard.htm

---

* To requisition copies of standardization agreements, send a completed DD Form 1425 (*Specifications and Standards Requisition*) to Naval Publications and Forms Center (NPFC), 5801 Tabor Avenue, Philadelphia, PA 19120.

Index

360-degree turnout (*illus*), 3-9

ACL. *See* allowable cargo load

ADS. *See* aerial delivery slings

advanced system improvement program (ASIP), 6-23

advisories, 1-1, 2-6, 3-8, 3-15 (*illus*), 4-3, 4-11

aerial delivery slings, 5-3 (*illus*), 5-10 (*illus*)

aerial marker, distress, 6-22

AF forms. *See* forms

air assaults, 2-6, 4-10, 4-14

air control points, 2-9, 4-24

aircraft
    drag coefficient, 5-21
    load limitations, 5-16
    points of attachment, 5-12
    separation requirements, 3-10
    taxiing, 3-10

airdrop, 6-1, 6-3 (*illus*), 6-4, E-1 (*illus*)
    accuracy, E-2
    airspeeds, E-1
    static line, 6-12, 6-19, E-1
    surface wind limits, 6-29
    tactically assessed drop zones, on, 6-48 (*illus*)

Air Force, 1-2
    computed air release point, 6-40
    drop zone sizes, E-2
    forms. *See* forms
    instruction, E-1
    support of, 2-8
    Verbally Initiated Release System (VIRS), 6-31 (*illus*), 6-40 (*illus*)

airlift, 5-19, 6-2, 6-9 (*illus*), 6-10 (*illus*), 6-18, 6-48, E-2

air medical evacuation,
    coordination, 2-2, 5-29
    plan, 2-3 (*illus*)
    requests, 3-1

air movement table, 2-2 (*illus*)

air routes, 2-10, 2-11 (*illus*)

air traffic control, 3-1
    aircraft separation requirements, 3-11
    assault, in an, 2-6
    communications, 3-12
    electronic warfare, 3-12
    establishment of, 2-7
    external loads and, 5-2
    light, 6-27
    phrases, 3-4 (*illus*)
    positive, 2-6
    safety, 3-1
    spacing techniques, 3-9
    taxiing aircraft, 3-10
    terms, 3-5 (*illus*)
    traffic pattern legs, 3-8
    visual signals, 3-12, 3-13 (*illus*)
    voice control, 3-1

allowable cargo load (ACL), 4-31, 5-16, C-12

alternate landing sites, 4-10

altitudes,
    airdrop, 2-2, 6-3 (*illus*)
    civil, 3-6
    density, 4-9
    drop, 6-2
    modes, 2-10
    terrain flight, 3-17, 4-23 (*illus*)

AN/PRC-119A (SINCGARS) radio, 6-22

anemometers, 6-19

approach path, 4-7, 4-34, 6-18

arrival record, 3-12, 3-16, 4-10, 4-29, 5-29, 6-55, B-2

artillery, 1-2, 2-7, 5-19, 5-20 (*illus*)

ASIP. *See* advanced system improvement program

assaults, 2-6, 4-14

assault zone availability report (AZAR), 6-47

assembly
    aids, 1-3, 2-1, 2-13, 4-141
    points, 4-14

base leg (approach), 3-8 (*illus*), 3-9 (*illus*), 3-10

briefing
    aids, 2-2
    aircrew mission briefing, 6-37
    DZST, 6-18, 6-37
    initial preparation, 2-1
    landing site party, 4-12
    operation plan, 4-8, B-3 (*illus*), B-6
    radio operator, 4-12
    site team leader, 4-12
    weather and operational, 2-4

brownouts, 4-3, 4-32, 5-29

capabilities, pathfinder, 1-2

cargo
    aircraft, 4-26
    bag, 5-5 (*illus*)
    bulk, 4-22
    containers, 5-4
    emergency release, 5-19, 5-28
    helicopters, 4-34
    hooks, 5-7, 5-16 thru 5-18 (*illus*), 5-26
    landing site, 3-14 (*illus*), 4-18 (*illus*)
    loads, external, 4-27, 5-1
    nets, 5-4, 5-5 (*illus*), 5-20
    safety, 3-12
    slope, 4-5
    straps, 5-10
    tie-downs, 5-11, 6-20

Index

"V" formation, 4-8 (*illus*), 4-18 (*illus*)

CARP. *See* computed air release point

CCP. *See* communications checkpoint

CDS. *See* container delivery system

civil altitude, 3-6

clearance, 3-1, 4-7
    departure, 3-4 (*illus*)
    horizontal, 4-7, 6-36 (*illus*)
    instructions, 3-3
    obstacles, 2-7, 4-27, 6-36 (*illus*), 4-6
    phrases, 3-4 (*illus*)
    ratio, 6-36, 6-37 (*illus*)
    to drop, 6-30
    to ground level, 4-3
    to land, 3-2 (*illus*), 3-10

close air support, A-1

close combat attack, A-1

closed traffic, 3-4 (*illus*), 3-6

cold weather, 4-28, E-1

communications, 2-8
    checkpoint (CCP), 2-4, 3-12, 4-22
    code letters, 6-30, 6-43 (*illus*)
    cold weather, 4-28, E-1
    compatibility, 1-2, 2-8
    desert, 4-32
    equipment, 1-2, 3-17
    formats, 3-2
    ground to air, 1-2, 3-2, 3-12, 6-23, 4-9, 4-12
    jamming of, 1-5, 2-8
    jungle, 4-31
    mountain, 2-10, 3-8, 4-33
    net, 3-12, 3-17, 4-13, 4-23, 4-24
    radio, AN/PRC-119A (SINCGARS), 6-22
    terrain, 4-28, 4-31, 4-33

communications security, 1-5, 3-17, 6-23

computed air release point (CARP), 6-4

Air Force, 6-40

computed air release point (*continued*)
    drop zone, 6-9 (*illus*), 6-10 (*illus*), 6-13 (*illus*), 6-21 (*illus*)
        additional platforms, 6-11
        Air Force instructions and, E-1
        bundles, 6-13
        container delivery system (CDS), 6-10
        heavy equipment, 6-9
        parachutists, 6-13
        personnel, 6-9
        point of impact, E-4
        raised angle marker, 6-21
    markings, 6-28
    personnel, 6-9
    sunset to sunrise, 6-9 (*illus*)

COMSEC. *See* communications security *and* signal security.

conduct of operations, 2-6

container delivery system, 6-2 (*illus*), 6-4 (*illus*), 6-5 (*illus*), 6-10 (*illus*), 6-45, E-2 (*illus*)

contour, terrain, 4-35

control
    center, 3-12, 4-1, 4-10, 6-29
    log, 6-54
    method of delivery and, 6-4 (*illus*)

conversion charts, PIBAL, 6-16 (*illus*), 6-17 (*illus*)

coordination. *See also* signals
    air movement phase, 2-2 (*illus*), 4-10
    checklist, 6-24 (*illus*)
    electronic warfare, 3-12
    final, 2-4, 4-10
    linkup with supported unit, 2-4

premission, 6-27
    release point, 2-2 (*illus*), 4-1, 6-4, 6-28, 6-31 (*illus*), 6-40, 6-54

coordination (*continued*)
    signalmen, 3-10, 4-14, 4-27, 4-34, 5-22, 5-26,
    times, 2-1
    troop-leading procedures, B-5
    warning order, 2-1

DA Forms. *See* forms

danger statements. *See* safety

daylight assault. *See* assaults

debriefing, 6-56

decentralized operations, D-2

deception, 1-5, 2-8

density altitude, 4-9, 4-31

departure
    clearance, 3-4 (*illus*)
    commander, 4-11
    directions, 4-7
    final coordination, 2-4
    instructions, 3-15
    internal net record, 4-11
    lights, 3-15
    log, 4-11
    obstacle ratio, 4-32
    obstacles, 3-15
    record, B-2
    routes, 4-10, 4-34, 6-18, 6-
    time, 6-54, B-5
    traffic patterns and, 3-6

desert terrain, 4-32

direction-finding systems, enemy, 1-5

distress marker, aerial, 6-22

drift scale, 6-22

drop altitude, 6-2

drop heading, 6-31

drop zone
    airdrop airspeeds, 6-1
    control records, B-2, B-4 (*illus*)

Index

coordination checklist,
6-24 (*illus*)
estimation of time,
6-13 (*illus*), 6-20, 6-25
obstacles, 6-6
placement, 6-42 (*illus*)
selection factors, 6-1

drop zone (*continued*)
size, 6-9, E-2 (*illus*)
survey, 6-47, 6-49 (*illus*)

Drop Zone/Landing Zone Control Log. See forms

drop zone support team
(DZST), 6-18
assault zone availability
report (AZAR), 6-47
computed air release
point, Air Force, 6-40
control group, 6-25
coordination checklist,
6-24 (*illus*)
ground marked release
system (GMRS), 6-32
leader, 6-28
missions, 6-19

Drop Zone Survey. See forms

electronic warfare, 3-12

emergency. *See also* safety
cargo release procedures,
5-28
codes, 4-23
conduct, 5-25
in-flight, 3-16
landings, 2-5
lighting, 4-26 (*illus*)
mayday, 3-5
medical technician, 1-1
procedures, helicopter,
5-29
signal mirror, 6-22
tactical, 2-10

environment
cold weather, 4-28, E-1
desert terrain, 4-32
high threat, 2-9
jungle terrain, 4-31
mountainous, 2-10, 3-8,
4-33

equipment, 1-2, 1-4, 2-1, 2-4,
3-12
airdrop airspeeds, E-1

airdrops, 6-47
assembly aids, 1-3, 2-1,
2-13, 4-141
circular drop zones and,
6-44
drop zone support team,
6-18

equipment (*continued*)
external loads, 4-27, 5-1,
5-18 (*illus*)
favorable conditions for
forward throw distances,
3-18
heavy, 6-2, 6-4, 6-5
(*illus*),
6-9 (*illus*)
drops, 6-18
operations, 6-14

escape routes, 4-35

estimate of the situation, 4-1,
B-5

extension, traffic pattern, 3-9,
3-10 (*illus*)

external loads, 4-27, 5-1, 5-18
(*illus*)

extraction, 2-7, 4-2

final glide, 3-11

format
control record, B-4 (*illus*)
operation plan, B-3 (*illus*)

formations, "V" type, 4-8
(*illus*), 4-18 (*illus*)
flight, 4-3, 4-13

forms
AF IMT 3823, *Drop Zone
Survey*, 6-31, 6-46,
6-51 (*illus*), 6-52 (*illus*)
AF IMT Form 4304, *Drop
Zone/Landing Zone
Control Log*, 6-54,
6-57 (*illus*)
DA Form 7382, *Sling Load
Inspection Record*,
5-29, 5-30 (*illus*)
DA Form 7461-R, *Internal
Net Record*, 4-11,
4-12 (*illus*)

formulas
D=KAV, 6-14 (*illus*)
D=RT, 6-12 (*illus*)
T=D/R, 6-13 (*illus*)

forward throw, 6-18 (*illus*),
E-1, E-4 (*illus*)

glide path, final, 3-11 (*illus*)

go-around, 3-4

ground
crew, 4-30
slope, 4-5, 4-6 (*illus*),
4-28
tactical plan, 4-1, 4-13,
B-5
to air (GTA), 3-2, 3-12,
3-13, 6-23

ground marked release system
(GMRS), E-3 (*illus*)
Air Force Instructions
and,
E-1
control center, 6-29
drop zone, 6-12
forward throw distances,
E-4 (*illus*)
load drift constants, E-3
markings, 6-37
release point, 6-31 (*illus*),
6-32

helicopters, A-1 (*illus*)
AH-64A (Apache), C-4,
C-5 (*illus*)
AH-64D (Longbow
Apache), C-6,
C-7 (*illus*)
CH-47D (Chinook), C-12,
C-13 (*illus*)
OH-58D (Kiowa), C-2,
C-3 (*illus*)
UH-1H (Iroquois), C-8,
C-9 (*illus*)
UH-60AL (Blackhawk),
C-10, C-11 (*illus*)

hitches, 5-4 (*illus*)

hooks, cargo, 5-7, 5-16 to
5-18 (*illus*), 5-26

Index

hookup and release, 5-22

hookup men, 5-26

horizontal clearance, 4-7, 6-36 (*illus*), 6-37 (*illus*)

initial
    assembly points, 4-14
    contact, 3-14, 4-11
    preparation, 2-1

insertion, 2-5, 4-2, E-3

intercept heading, 4-13, 4-22 (*illus*)

Internal Net Record. See forms

internal net recorder (INR), 4-11, 4-12 (*illus*), 4-24

inverted "Y," 4-14, 4-25 (*illus*)

jungle terrain, 4-31

landing, 3-6
    clearance for, 3-2 (*illus*), 3-10
    formation(s), 2-4, 2-7, 4-3,
        4-4 (*illus*), 4-13, 4-23, 4-29 (*illus*)
    instructions, 3-10, 3-15, 4-13

landing point (debarkation point), 2-5, 3-12, 3-14, 4-1, 4-2 (*illus*), 4-3 (*illus*), 4-7 (*illus*), 4-8 (*illus*), 4-9 (*illus*), 4-13, 4-19 (*illus*), 4-25, 4-26 (*illus*), 4-28, 4-35, 5-1
    desert operations, 4-32
    separation requirements, 3-11 (*illus*)

landing site(s), 4-1. *See also* obstacles, landing zone, slingloads
    alternate, 4-10
    approach and departure directions, 4-7
    attached personnel, duties of, 4-12
    communications, 4-13
        checkpoint, 2-4, 2-7, 3-12, 3-17, 4-22, 4-31

control center, 4-10, 6-29
control records, B-2
density altitude, 4-9, 4-31, 4-34
ground slope, 4-5, 4-6 (*illus*)
leader, 4-14
lighting, 4-25, 4-26 (*illus*)
marking, 2-3, 4-10, 4-13, 4-14, (*illus*), 4-28
    patterns, 6-32
    safety, 6-7
    "V" formation, 4-8 (*illus*), 4-18 (*illus*)
multiple, 4-30
operations, 4-13

landing (*continued*)
    party, 4-12
    prevailing wind, 4-7
    security personnel, 4-24
    selection of, 4-3
    symbols, 4-21 (*illus*)

landing zone operations, 4-22 *See also* landing site

leg (approach), 3-6, 3-8 (*illus*)

liaison, 2-2, 2-7, 3-12, 5-29, D-1

light
    AN/PRC-77, 6-21
    baton (M-2), 6-22
    emergency, 4-21 (*illus*)
    gun, 4-23
    signals, 3-1, 3-13 (*illus*)
    Whelen, 6-21

limitations
    aircraft, 5-1, 5-16
    pathfinder, 1-2

linkup, 2-4, D-3

loads, 5-1
    external, 3-15, 4-1, 4-9, 4-27, 5-1, 5-19 (*illus*)
    limitations, aircraft (ACL), 5-1, 5-16
    safe, 5-9 (*illus*)
    sling. *See* slingload

M-2 light baton, 6-22

mask clearance, 6-37 (*illus*)

mean effective wind, 6-14, 6-22, 6-55
    measuring, 6-14

medical evacuation (MEDEVAC), 3-1, 3-10, 6-28

metal air items, 5-4, 5-11

methods of delivery, 6-4

methods of entry, 3-6

minimum separation requirements, 3-11 (*illus*)

mirror, signaling, 6-22

mountains, 2-10, 3-8, 4-33

movement overland, 2-5

multiple
    helicopter operations, 4-34
    landing sites, 4-30

NATO landing "T," 4-14, 4-25 (*illus*)

navigation, 4-31
    aids, 1-2, 4-24

night, 2-5, 4-8, 4-9, 4-23, 4-24, 6-22, 6-42
    airdrop altitudes, 6-3
    approaches, 4-8 (*illus*), 4-30
    assault, 2-6
    cargo landing site, 4-18 (*illus*)
    communications, 2-7
    control center, 4-11
    drop zone support team, 6-18
    emergency lighting, 4-26 (*illus*)
    external loads, 4-27, 5-1, 5-18 (*illus*)
    flight leader, 3-15
    formations, 4-20 (*illus*), 6-9 (*illus*), E-3 (*illus*)
    helicopter landing zones, 4-1
    infrared navigation aids, 1-3
    insertion by parachute, 2-5
    landing lights, 4-25 (*illus*)
    landing sites, 4-19 thru 4-20 (*illus*)

Index

landing symbols, 4-21
   (*illus*)
lighting unit, 6-22
multihelicopter operations,
   4-34
pilot balloon (PIBAL),
   6-14 to 6-17 (*illus*)
rotary-wing aerial
   delivery, 5-3 (*illus*),
   6-4 (*illus*)
signals, 4-19, 6-29
site team leader, 4-13
slingload operation site,
   4-17 (*illus*)
spacing, 5-1
tactical landing lights,
   4-25
touchdown point
   markings, 4-25 (*illus*)

night (*continued*)
   vision, 4-27
   visual navigation aids, 1-3

night operations, 2-6, 4-7, 4-8
   (*illus*), 4-9, 4-14, 4-17 to
   4-21 (*illus*), 4-22, 4-23,
   4-24, 4-25 (*illus*), 4-26
   (*illus*), 4-30, 6-9

night vision goggles, 1-3,
   4-3 (*illus*), 4-27, 6-27

numbers, transmittal of, 3-3
   (*illus*)

obstacles, 4-10, 6-6
   advisory information, 3-15
   advisory services, 3-8
   air assaults, 4-10
   approach path, 4-7, 4-34,
      6-18
   checkpoint, 4-22
      ground to air, 1-2, 2-8,
      3-12, 3-14, 4-11, 4-24
   clearance, 2-7, 4-27, 6-36
      (*illus*), 4-6
   communications, 3-12
   control center, 3-12, 4-1,
      4-10, 6-4, 6-29, B-2
   coordination, 4-7 (*illus*)
   departure, 2-2, 3-15
   drop heading, 6-31
   height, 3-6, 4-35
   identification of, 4-9
   jungle, 4-31

marking, 2-3 (*illus*), 4-14,
   6-36
ratio, 4-7, 4-31
reconnaissance, 6-28
removal of, 2-4, 2-6, 4-3,
   4-5
risk assessment and, 6-26
snow, 3-15, 4-3, 4-28,
   4-29 (*illus*), 5-24
spacing between loads,
   5-1
terrain contour, 4-35
operation
   decentralized, D-2
   ground, 2-7, 4-28, 6-48
   landing site, 4-13
   landing zone, 4-22
   mixed, 2-7
   multihelicopter, 4-27
   night, 2-5, 4-8, 4-9, 4-23,
      4-24, 6-22, 6-42
operation (*continued*)
   plan, format, B-1,
      B-3 (*illus*)
   plan, tentative, B-6
   stay-behind, 2-6
organization
   combat, 2-4
   helicopter landing zone,
      4-10
   drop zone support team,
      6-18
overland movement, 2-5

panel markers, VS-17, 4-14,
   6-6, 6-20, 6-21 (*illus*),
   6-27, 6-32, 6-37
path, final glide, 3-11
pathfinder. *See also*
   communications, control
   center, equipment,
   organizational
   capabilities, 1-2
   duties, 2-2, 4-10, 5-26,
      6-27
   ground unit(s), 1-6, 2-1,
      2-4, 3-1, 3-12, 3-16,
      4-14
   commander, 2-2 thru
      2-3 (*illus*), 2-4, 2-7,
      2-9, 4-1, 4-10, 4-28,
      4-32, 6-1, 6-43, A-3

initial preparation, 2-1
insertion, 2-4
internal net, 4-11
limitations, 1-2
night assault, 2-6
stay-behind operations,
   2-6

patterns,
   air traffic, 3-7 (*illus*)
   legs, 3-8, 3-9 (*illus*)

personnel drops, 6-5 (*illus*),
   6-19, 6-25, 6-29

phrases, air traffic control, 3-2,
   3-4 (*illus*)

PIBAL. *See* pilot balloon

pilot advisories, 1-1, 2-6, 3-8,
   3-15 (*illus*), 4-3, 4-5, 4-10,
   4-11

pilot balloon (PIBAL), 6-15,
   6-16 (*illus*), 6-17 (*illus*)

planning, 2-1
   coordination, 2-2 thru
      2-3 (*illus*), 3-12
   checklist, 6-24 (*illus*)
   decentralized operations,
      D-2
   direction finding, 1-5
   final, 2-4, 4-10
   initial preparation, 2-1
   liaison, 2-2, 2-7, 3-12,
      5-29, D-1
   linkup, 2-4, D-3
   reorganization, 2-1, 2-7
   security, 1-5, 3-17, 4-24,
      6-23

position of the sun, 4-35

preparations, 2-1

prevailing wind, 4-7

radios
   AN/PRC-77, 6-21
   AN/PRC-113 (Have
      Quick), 6-23
   AN/PRC-119A
      (SINCGARS), 6-22

raised angle marker (RAM),
   6-21 (*illus*)

Index

ratio
    mask clearance, 6-36
    obstacle, 4-7, 4-31

reach pendant, 5-7

reconnaissance party, 4-10

release point,
    computed air, 6-4, 6-9, 6-40
    location, 2-2, 6-31 (*illus*)
    party, 4-10

reorganization, 2-1, 2-7

reporting points, 3-9

rescue boat, 6-26

rigging supplies, 5-20

rotary-wing aerial delivery, 5-3 (*illus*), 6-4 (*illus*), 6-10 (*illus*)

roundsling, 5-8, 5-9 (*illus*)

route(s), 2-2, 2-4, 2-9
    air, 2-10, 2-11 (*illus*)
    approach and departure, 4-7, 4-34, 6-18
    escape, 4-35

safety
    advisories, 3-8
    air traffic control, 3-1
    airdrop, 6-4, 6-29, 6-48
    cargo hook, 5-15, 6-18
    cold weather, 4-28, E-1
    continuous support, 2-4, 2-7
    desert, 4-32
    drop zone, 1-6
    emergency cargo release, 5-28
    equipment, 5-22
    evacuation to rendezvous point, 5-29
    flight formation, 4-13
    frostbite, 4-30
    high drag coefficient, 5-20
    hookup and release, 5-22
    night vision goggles, 4-27
    obstacles, 6-8
    overflight of personnel, 3-12
    power lines and poles, 6-7
    rotor wash, 4-30
    simultaneous exit, 6-4

sling set, 5-13
straight-in approach, 3-7
suspended loads, 5-26
tactical light set, 4-27

search and rescue, 3-12

security, 1-2, 2-2, 3-16, 4-13, 4-24, 4-32, A-1. *See also* signal security

separation requirements, 3-11 (*illus*)

signal lights, 3-13 (*illus*)

signal security, 1-5, 3-17, 6-23

signal(s), 1-3, 1-5, 2-3 (*illus*), 3-3 (*illus*), 3-12, 3-13 (*illus*), 4-23, 5-24, 5-26
    arm and hand, 2-8, 4-24, 5-24
    mirror, 5-22

signal(s) (*continued*)
    no drop, 6-27
    visual, 3-12, 4-23, 6-30

signalman, 3-10, 4-14, 4-25, 4-28, 4-30, 4-34, 5-22, 5-25

SIGSEC. *See* signal security

site assessment, 4-34

sling sets, 5-3, 5-7, 5-12 (*illus*)
    coupling link, 5-14 (*illus*)
    grabhook, 5-14, 5-15 (*illus*)
    safety, 5-13

slingload theory, 5-21

slingload, 4-17 (*illus*), 4-19 (*illus*), 5-1. *See also* hitches
    cargo helicopters, C-12
    equipment, 5-2
    Inspection Record. See forms
    operations, 4-30
    safety, 3-12, 5-26
    theory, 5-21
    types, 5-1, 5-3 (*illus*)

snow, 3-8, 3-15, 4-3, 4-28, 4-29 (*illus*), 5-24, 5-29

spacing techniques, 3-9

specific tactics team, 1-2

staging areas, 2-7

static discharge wand, 5-24

static electricity, 4-31, 5-22

supplies, 2-6, 4-5, 4-14, 4-30
    rigging, 5-2, 5-10, 5-19

support
    Army aviation, 2-7
    ground operations, 1-5, 2-7, 4-28, 6-48
    ground-to-air communications, 3-12, 6-23
    mixed operations, 2-7
    terminal guidance, 1-5, 2-9
    requirements, DZST, 6-25

supporting unit, 5-2

surface wind, 6-14, 6-28 (*illus*), 6-32, 6-54

suspended loads, 2-5, 5-27, 5-54

tactical
    assessment, 6-31, 6-47 (*illus*)
    instrument flight, 2-9
    landing lights, 4-25

taxiing aircraft, 3-10

team(s), 2-9, 3-1, 6-29

terminal guidance, 2-9

terms, air traffic control, 3-4 (*illus*) and 3-5 (*illus*)

terrain, 2-2, 2-5, 2-10, 3-8, 3-16, 4-10, 4-13, 4-22, 4-23 (*illus*), 4-25, 4-28, 4-31, 4-34, 5-29, 6-18, 6-36, 6-42, 6-46, B-6
See also communication types, 4-31

theater missile defense, A-1

threat. *See also* advisories
    environment, 2-9, 2-11 (*illus*), A-2 (*illus*)

touchdown point, 3-14, 4-1, 4-14, 4-25 (*illus*), 4-26

traffic patterns, 3-4 (*illus*), 3-5 (*illus*), 3-6, 3-7 (*illus*), 3-8 (*illus*), 3-10 (*illus*)

training, 1-5, 3-1, 3-12, 4-14, 4-32, 6-1, 6-2 (*illus*), 6-3 (*illus*), 6-18, 6-26, 6-28 (*illus*), 6-46, A-2 (*illus*), E-4 (*illus*)

turnout, 3-9 (*illus*)

unit responsibilities, 5-2

vector count, 6-39

Verbally Initiated Release System (VIRS), 6-31 (*illus*), 6-40 (*illus*)

vertical air currents, 4-34

"V" formation, 4-14 (*illus*)

voice control, 2-9, 3-1

VS-17 panel marker, 4-14, 6-6, 6-20, 6-21 (*illus*), 6-27, 6-32, 6-37

warning order, 2-1, B-5

warning statements. *See* safety

weight
    aircraft, 4-3
    external slingload, 5-15
    load, 4-10, 5-5
    rough, 5-1
    safe working, 5-9
    sling set capacity, 5-12
    standard, 5-18 to 5-19 (*illus*)

Whelen light, 6-21

whiteouts, 4-29 (*illus*)

wind, 4-32, 4-33, 6-14
    anemometer, 6-19
    approach path, 4-34
    conditions, 2-5, 4-14
    departure path and, 4-7
    direction, 1-2, 3-6, 3-10, 5-25, 5-29, 6-32
    drift scale, 6-22
    erratic, 6-40
    limits, 6-7
    mean effective, 6-14, 6-22, 6-54
    measurement, 6-14, 6-19, 6-25

signal(s) (*continued*)
    monitoring of, 6-28
    PIBAL. *See* pilot balloon
    prevailing, 4-7
    shear, 6-40
    speed, 3-3 (*illus*)
    surface, 6-28 (*illus*), 6-54
    traffic pattern legs, 3-8 (*illus*)
    turbulence, cause of, 3-8, 4-33, 6-45
    velocity, 1-2, 3-10

wind streamer vector count, 6-39

INTERNAL NET RECORD

For use of this form, see FM 3-21.38; the Proponent Agency for this form is TRADOC.

PFDR DET		OPERATION	
SUPPORTED UNIT		DESIGNATION	
PERIOD		RECORDER	

NO. A/C	TYPE A/C	CONTACT TIME	CALL SIGN	TIME		LOAD TYPE		DESTINATION	REMARKS
				ARR	DEP	INS	EXT		

DA FORM 7461-R, SEP 2002

USAPA V1.00

FM 3-21.38
25 April 2006

By Order of the Secretary of the Army:

PETER J. SCHOOMAKER
General, United States Army
Chief of Staff

Official:

JOYCE E. MORROW
Administrative Assistant to the
Secretary of the Army

0609401

Official:

Distribution: *Active Army, Army National Guard, and U. S. Army Reserve:* To be distributed IAW IDN 115893 for FM 3-21.38 (110401, AKA quantity requirement block, that is, requirements for FM 3-21.38).

Printed in the USA
CPSIA information can be obtained
at www.ICGtesting.com
LVHW081700111023
760837LV00014B/436

9 781974 428816

ABOUT THE *EXPLORE* SERIES

Since 1888, *National Geographic* magazine has provided its readers a wealth of information and helped us understand the world in which we live. Insightful articles, supported by gorgeous photography and impeccable research, bring the mission of the National Geographic Society front and center: to inspire people to care about the planet. The *Explore* series delivers National Geographic to you in the same spirit. Each of the books in this series presents the best articles on popular and relevant topics in an accessible format. In addition, each book highlights the work of National Geographic Explorers, photographers, and writers. Explore the world of *National Geographic.* You will be inspired.

ON THE COVER
Panthera leo, the king of beasts

BIG CATS

A lightning-fast, young male cheetah

4   **Letter from the Editors**

5   **Big Cats Initiative: Causing an Uproar**
Big cats strike fear into the hearts of their prey, but they are threatened by an even more powerful species—humans. National Geographic's Big Cats Initiative seeks to raise awareness and help humans and big cats to live together.

12 **Politics Is Killing the Big Cats**
By George B. Schaller
Biologist George Schaller has studied big cats in the wild for almost 50 years. He explains how politics is getting in the way of protecting these endangered animals.

16 **Explorers' Journal with Dereck and Beverly Joubert** *By Dereck and Beverly Joubert*
These National Geographic Explorers have studied big cats in Botswana's Okavango Delta for 30 years. Learn why the Jouberts believe big cats must be saved.

24 **Living with Lions** *By David Quammen*
Humans must learn to share the land with lions if these iconic cats are to survive. Find out about the strategies people who live among them are using to make peace with and protect lions.

30 **A Cry for the Tiger** *By Caroline Alexander*
Get up close and personal with tigers. This account tells of the writer's journey to see the striped cats in the wild in India, Myanmar, and Thailand.

36 **Cheetahs on the Edge** *By Roff Smith*
Sleek, elegant, and built for speed, the exotic cheetah is rare and getting rarer. Considered by some to be the most beautiful of all the big cats, the cheetah is under pressure in Africa and Asia.

42 **Nat Geo WILD: On Location with Boone Smith** *By Andrea Alter*
Big cat tracker Boone Smith's passion for preserving big cats is contagious. Read about his latest adventure on location in South Africa.

46 **Document-Based Question**
What are some of the successes and challenges of the Big Cats Initiative?

LETTER FROM THE EDITORS

In our cover photograph, we see close up just how magnificent the lion is. His full mane and steely look show why he is sometimes referred to as the king of the big cats. But the majestic lion is not the only big cat that enchants us. Mountain lions, tigers, leopards, cheetahs, jaguars—these fierce felines all captivate us with their beauty and strength. Artists and poets have celebrated their grace and skill as hunters. Big cat exhibits at zoos are always among the most popular, and sports teams are named after them. We yearn to possess a lion's power or a leopard's poise.

Though we may admire the big cats, we have not done enough to protect them. There are 37 species of big cats that inhabit our planet, and every year, their numbers fall at an alarming rate. The threat from humans has been on the rise for decades. As human populations grow, they spread into big cat habitats. With this expansion, it's inevitable that humans and cats clash. And when they do, the cats often lose. We've seen Africa's lion population decline 90 percent in the last 75 years. Cheetahs have disappeared from more than 75 percent of their range. And there are more tigers in captivity than there are in the wild.

There is hope, however. Many programs have been launched to protect endangered big cats. This book will introduce you to the National Geographic Society's Big Cats Initiative and the dedicated Explorers who helped start it. Through articles adapted from *National Geographic* magazine, you will get closer than ever before to these fascinating cats and their natural habitats. Read the story of how one leopard cub grows up. See a cheetah chasing after its prey. Visit some of the last places that tigers roam, and find out what it's like to have lions in your backyard.

You will also meet some of the scientists, conservationists, and ordinary people who are trying to help big cats as they face growing threats. Together we can save these amazing creatures from disappearing before it's too late.

HIDDEN SPOTS
Though it appears solid black, this leopard does indeed have spots. Look closely to see the brown spots hidden in its sleek black coat.

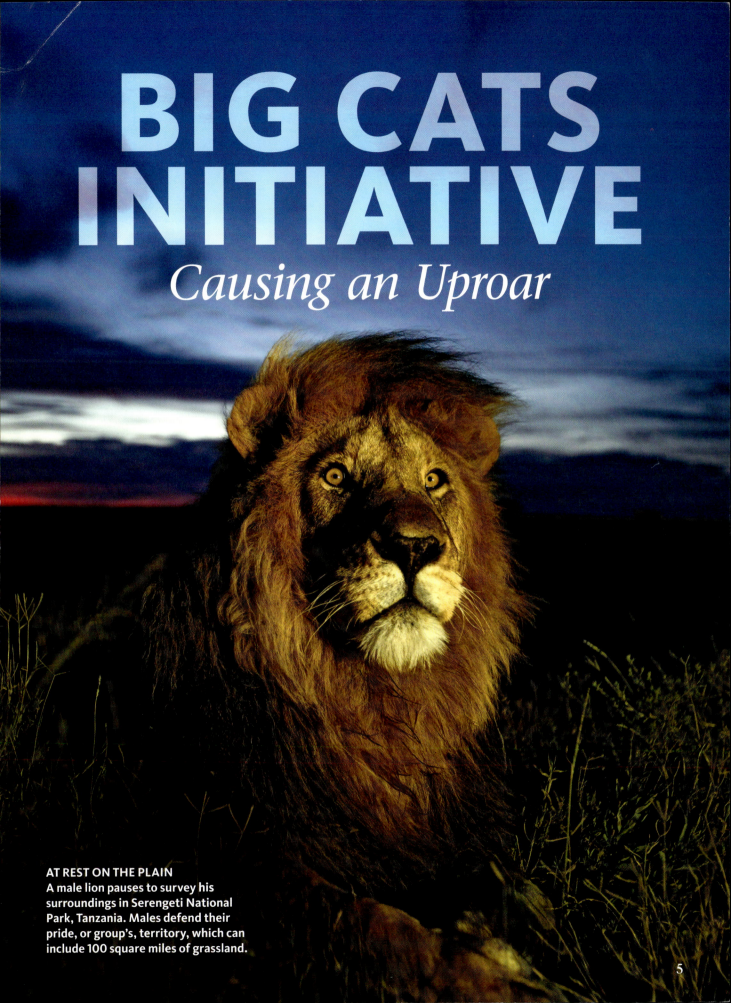

BIG CATS INITIATIVE
Causing an Uproar

AT REST ON THE PLAIN
A male lion pauses to survey his surroundings in Serengeti National Park, Tanzania. Males defend their pride, or group's, territory, which can include 100 square miles of grassland.

In 2009, National Geographic Explorers Dereck and Beverly Joubert launched the Big Cats Initiative (BCI), an organization dedicated to saving endangered cats and finding ways for humans and big cats to live together. The BCI celebrated its five-year anniversary in 2014, and it is just getting going.

A TIPPING POINT

The main objective of this **initiative** is to halt the decline of big cats around the world. According to information gathered by BCI, the downward spiral of big cat numbers is alarming. Fewer than 3,000 tigers, 7,500 snow leopards, 10,000 cheetahs, and 30,000 lions exist in the wild worldwide. These numbers signal a tipping point. If humans don't address the problem now, some species of big cats may become extinct.

Why are big cats in crisis? One of the reasons is an increase in human population. As humans grow in numbers and spread out, big cat habitats disappear. Sometimes big cats are killed because they hunt livestock. Other reasons include people hunting big cats for sport or killing them for supposed "cures" made from their bones. It is possible, too, that climate change events such as flooding may harm lion populations in parts of sub-Saharan Africa.

The good news is that it's not too late, and projects under the BCI are already showing signs of progress. The BCI has grown since the Jouberts set it up in conjunction with the National Geographic Society. It funds more than 60 projects in 23 countries that focus on the conservation of big cats and their habitats. The group's approach is not to swoop into a community and demand change. Instead, the BCI works with and within communities in vastly different areas of the world to bring about awareness and change.

HIGH-ALTITUDE CATS
Snow leopards like this one in India are well-equipped for life in cold mountain climates. Their thick fur keeps them warm, and well-padded paws and strong lungs make them quick on their feet.

CATS IN CRISIS

LION
Panthera leo

Lions are the only wild cats that live in large family groups. They once roamed all of Africa and into Asia. Today, the greatest number of lions lives in Tanzania.

Estimated wild population: 20,000 to 30,000

Status: Vulnerable

CLOUDED LEOPARD
Neofelis nebulosa

Clouded leopards are the smallest of the big cats, but they have canine teeth as long as a tiger's. These acrobatic climbers hunt in trees as well as on the ground in forests across Southeast Asia.

Estimated wild population: 10,000

Status: Vulnerable

JAGUAR
Panthera onca

Revered as a god by the Aztec and Maya, the most powerful predator in Central and South America weighs up to 250 pounds. The jaguar is the third largest cat, after tigers and lions.

Estimated wild population: At least 10,000

Status: Near threatened

SNOW LEOPARD
Panthera uncia

The snow leopard, known as the "ghost of the mountains," lives in the Himalaya and surrounding ranges of Central Asia. In 1971, *National Geographic* was the first magazine to publish photos of the elusive cat taken in the wild.

Estimated wild population: 4,000 to 6,500

Status: Endangered

All wild population estimates are uncertain.

WHY SAVE BIG CATS?

Africa's lion population has **DECLINED 90%** in the last 75 years.

Cheetahs have disappeared from **MORE THAN 75%** of their range.

There are **MORE TIGERS IN CAPTIVITY** than there are in the wild.

> "We no longer have the luxury of time when it comes to big cats. If there was ever a time to take action, it is now."
>
> — DERECK JOUBERT

PUMA
Puma concolor

Cougar, mountain lion, panther. The cat of many names ranges from Canada to the tip of Chile. The cougar is returning to its former lands in the U.S. Midwest, but its population is thought to be falling.

Estimated wild population: 30,000 (U.S. only)

Status: Least concern

LEOPARD
Panthera pardus

The most widespread of big cats—found from Africa to Southeast Asia—leopards are most abundant in sub-Saharan Africa. Black leopards are often called black panthers.

Estimated wild population: No reliable data

Status: Near threatened

TIGER
Panthera tigris

No cat is bigger than the tiger, with males topping 600 pounds. Three tiger subspecies have gone extinct since the 1930s. The Malayan and four or five other subspecies hang on in Asia.

Estimated wild population: Fewer than 4,000

Status: Endangered

CHEETAH
Acinonyx jubatus

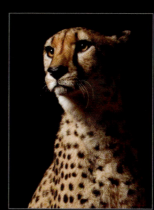

The cheetah is the fastest mammal and can sprint 60-plus miles per hour. East and southwest Africa are its remaining strongholds. Targeted by lions and hyenas, only a few cubs reach adulthood.

Estimated wild population: 7,000 to 10,000

Status: Vulnerable

FOR MORE INFORMATION

To learn more about big cats, the Big Cats Initiative, and what you can do to help, visit **www.causeanuproar.org.**

TRACKING CHEETAHS
Radio collars worn by these cheetahs in Namibia will help a conservation organization protect them by tracking their movements.

THE BCI APPROACH

The BCI uses a three-pronged approach in its work: reducing the threat, keeping the peace, and community outreach and engagement. The BCI and the communities with which it works are coming up with workable solutions for people and big cats alike.

REDUCING THE THREAT Biologist and BCI Grantee Florian Weise works for the Naankuse Foundation in Namibia. This organization is dedicated to reducing conflict between humans and **carnivores**, particularly cheetahs and leopards. Landowners and herders want to protect their livestock without having to resort to killing big cats.

Solutions that this BCI project has put into action include using guardian animals and herders to protect grazing livestock, constructing thorn bush fences to keep predators out, and using GPS tracking devices on big cats in the area to make landowners aware of their movements. Weise's team has often seen livestock losses decrease by up to 88 percent, sometimes even stop altogether, with a combination of these preventive strategies. By reducing the threat to livestock and herders, this BCI project helps pave the way for sustainable solutions.

KEEPING THE PEACE High in the Himalaya Mountains in northern Pakistan, National Geographic Explorer Shafqat Hussain's goal is to protect the elusive snow leopard. In 1998, Hussain started Project Snow Leopard, which provides livestock insurance to Pakistani herders.

With BCI support, Project Snow Leopard is able to help more people in more villages. Basically, if livestock are killed by a snow leopard, herders can be reimbursed the value of their livestock. In this way, herders' economic wellbeing is not threatened, and they are much less likely to carry out **retribution** killings on snow leopards. Project Snow Leopard helps keep the peace among herders and snow leopards, and it provides a new way for the big cats and humans to coexist.

BIG CAT PARTNERS Shivani Bhalla and members of Ewaso Lion's Warrior Watch program collect data on lion movements by using GPS technology.

COMMUNITY OUTREACH National Geographic Explorer and BCI Grantee Shivani Bhalla, founder of Ewaso Lions, works with the Samburu people in her native Kenya. Ewaso Lions partners with various communities to promote coexistence with big cats. Its Warrior Watch program focuses on reducing livestock loss by tracking lion movements. The work has paid off. Lion numbers have increased in the area from fewer than half a dozen to more than 40 in only a few years.

Another BCI Grantee who focuses on community outreach and engagement is Laly Lichtenfeld, co-founder and executive director of the African People and Wildlife Fund (APW). Located in northern Tanzania, the APW trains community members and empowers them to act as patrols, conservationists, and Warriors for Wildlife. The APW also helps the Maasai build "living walls" made of thick branches and trees woven through chain link fences to create enclosed spaces for livestock, safe from predators. By engaging with the community, the APW achieves an important partnership with the Maasai people and, ultimately, both big cats and humans benefit.

THINK ABOUT IT!

1. **Identify Problems and Solutions** According to the Big Cats Initiative, what are some of the main threats facing big cats worldwide?

2. **Compare and Contrast** How are some BCI-supported projects similar and different?

BACKGROUND & VOCABULARY

carnivore *n.* (KAHR-nuh-vohr) a meat-eating animal

initiative *n.* (ih-NIHSH-uh-tihv) a strategy, plan, or approach to resolve a problem or situation

retribution *n.* (reh-truh-BYOO-shun) punishment considered to be right or deserved

RARE BEAUTY
This tiger is protected inside Bandhavgarh National Park, in India.

POLITICS *is* KILLING *the* BIG CATS

BY GEORGE B. SCHALLER

Adapted from "Politics is Killing the Big Cats," by George B. Schaller, in *National Geographic*, December 2011

George B. Schaller has studied big cats in the wild and is the vice president of Panthera, an organization for big cat conservation and a Big Cats Initiative partner. In this article, he makes a plea for a new approach to saving these endangered animals.

THEN AND NOW

When I began to study the big cats nearly half a century ago, their magnificence thrilled me. Tigers striding on velvet paws through the forests of India, secure in their power, dignity, and dramatic beauty. Prides of Serengeti lions lying in the shade, poured like honey over the golden grass. Today I worry about these symbols of wilderness because their future depends on us.

Back in the 1960s and 1970s, I did not think the wilderness would disappear so quickly. The number of people has more than doubled since then, forests have become fields, and **livestock** herds have replaced wildlife in many areas. Lions were once numerous but now are disappearing outside of protected areas. They are poisoned, shot, and trapped by farmers because they kill cattle and sometimes people. Tigers now live in only about seven percent of their former ranges. Fewer than 4,000 may be left in the wild.

Tigers and leopards in Asia are threatened by **poachers** who sell skins, bones, and other body parts. Some people falsely believe that these parts can be used to treat illnesses. No wonder two of India's protected areas lost all their tigers, even though they were guarded. How can the world watch while natural treasures such as this vanish, country by country?

When I first began observing big cats, I wanted to make sure they were safe within a protected area. But I have had to change my thinking since then. Most countries do not have the space to set aside large new areas to support a big population of snow leopards or tigers. Most protected areas now are small, able to support only a few big cats, and even those cats may disappear due to disease or accidents.

Instead of focusing just on protected areas, conservationists now look at whole landscapes. The goal is to connect protected areas without human populations, where a leopard or jaguar can have cubs. Thin paths of habitat connect the main protected areas, so the cats can travel from one safe place to another. People use the

FOREST CAT
The forests of Belize, in Central America, were once home to thousands more jaguars like this one.

remaining area. Because the cats do not have to travel through areas with humans, both are safer.

Most countries, however, have not had the political will and public support to save their wildlife. Even the protection of wildlife in **reserves** is weak. Poaching of animals, as well as other activities such as illegal logging and mining, are common. Each country needs a guard force supported by police and even the army. Each country also needs the help of its own people to stop illegal trade of big cat skins and bones. Poachers must face quick legal action. This will only happen if politicians pass laws to make sure big cats are protected. Conservation is **politics** and politics is killing the big cats.

PROTECTING SURVIVORS

I wonder if a positive approach might be the best one. Perhaps governments could pay communities to protect healthy big cat populations. After all, it is painfully clear that good science and good laws do not always mean that big cats are protected. People who share their land with big cats must be directly involved in conservation.

We still have much to learn. We know how to manage lions and tigers in national parks and other protected areas. It is harder to manage them in areas that are shared with people. The number of cats in an area depends on the animals they can eat. It is difficult to count prey animals, especially in forests, and little is known about how many prey animals a habitat can support.

I have recently focused less on studying cats in the wild and more on protecting them. I love watching cats in the wild, but preserving them is more important. I have tried to spread the word about them, balancing knowledge and action. Our greatest challenge is to get individual countries to promise to protect big cats. It's everyone's job.

Ultimately, conservation is based on moral values, not scientific ones. The big cats are a test of our willingness to share this planet with other animals. We must act now to offer them a bright and secure future, because they are among the most wonderful expressions of life on Earth.

THINK ABOUT IT!

1. **Summarize** Explain how the system of reserves that Schaller describes could benefit big cats.

2. **Draw Conclusions** What must individual countries do to protect big cats?

BACKGROUND & VOCABULARY

livestock *n.* (LYV-stahk) the animals raised for food and other products

poacher *n.* (POH-chur) a person who illegally kills wildlife

politics *n.* the way that laws are passed and people are governed

reserve *n.* a protected area designated for wildlife, especially endangered wildlife

EXPLORERS' JOURNAL
with Dereck and Beverly Joubert

BY DERECK AND BEVERLY JOUBERT

Adapted from "Explorers Journal: Protecting Predators," by Dereck and Beverly Joubert, in *National Geographic*, December 2010; and "Lessons of the Hunt," by Dereck Joubert, in *National Geographic*, April 2007

National Geographic Explorers Dereck and Beverly Joubert have devoted their lives to saving big cats. In this article, they explain why.

CATS, ONE-ON-ONE

The amazing animal that changed our lives was still a wobbly, half-blind cub when we came upon her with her mother in Botswana's Okavango Delta in 2003. We had been working for many years with big cats in Africa and had developed ideas about the big picture of conservation. Then we met this baby leopard we called Legadema, which means "light from the sky" in Setswana, a language spoken by people in southern Africa.

We followed Legadema for nearly five years, and she taught us something that is true of all big cats. While we try to protect these species, because of the number of animals that are killed, we often forget that they are individuals with personalities and lives of their own. As their numbers decline, conservation becomes more about saving these individual animals.

Legadema grew up to be beautiful. She is seven now, and doing well. She has become mother to at least two sets of cubs. We still visit her from time to time. But in the years we've known her, other leopards have not been as lucky. The 1973 agreement called the Convention on International Trade in Endangered Species (CITES) has set rules that allow people from other countries to take home up to 2,653 leopard trophies a year. Poaching and the trade for skins have hurt leopard numbers as well. Although exact numbers are difficult to pin down, we believe there has been a drop in the number of leopards left in the wild.

‹ AT HOME WITH LIONS
The Jouberts work in Botswana's Okavango Delta, which they consider one of the best preserved wilderness areas in Africa.

Working with Legadema and becoming National Geographic Explorers led us to spread the word about big cats. It inspired us to start National Geographic's Big Cats Initiative (BCI) as an effort to save these top predators. Big cats are **keystone species** that support the African and Asian ecosystems. Without these animals, important wilderness areas may collapse as the balance of life becomes hopelessly upset.

Africa's majestic lion is one example of a keystone species at high risk of extinction. If humans were trying to drive these animals to extinction on purpose, we could not be doing a better job. Most people think many lions are left and that someone is taking care of their conservation. The truth is we've seen a major drop in lion numbers in our lifetimes. At this rate, we fear that lions could soon disappear. Without lions, the whole ecosystem falls apart. If we can't protect this species, what hope is there for the rest?

LIVING WITH BIG CATS

For 30 years, we have made our home in Botswana's Okavango Delta, a part of the world that is hidden to most people. Most of the time, it's just the two of us living in a tent, filming and researching cats, away from what most people consider civilization. The rewards are great. We've captured amazing video of lions attacking an elephant, and we have unlocked the mysteries of the relationships between lions and hyenas, and between leopards and baboons. By getting to know animals up close, we have helped break down misunderstandings about the world's greatest predators.

If you look into the eyes of a leopard, for example, you can feel the deep, ancient connection between humans and this animal. We admire big cats and we fear them. We are at war with them in so many places on Earth. But there's one thing of which we're certain. Without them, the world will be a worse place.

We felt that profound connection with Legadema. By following her as she grew toward adulthood and independence, we learned priceless lessons about how leopards interact with each other and with their surroundings. Watching her was a deeply moving experience.

Legadema was eight days old when we spotted her. Her eyes were still milky gray. Stepping into the sunlight from her den, she seemed curious and bold, taking no notice of the squirrels that screamed in fright when they saw her.

ON THE PROWL
A group of lions crosses a small stream in the Okavango Delta.

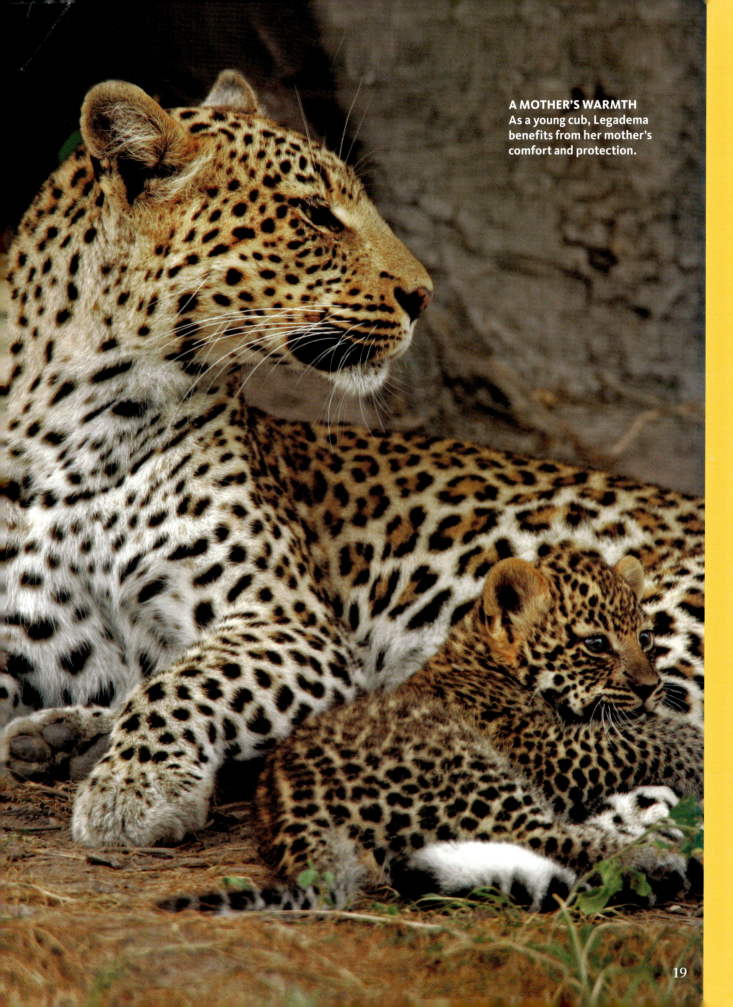

A MOTHER'S WARMTH
As a young cub, Legadema benefits from her mother's comfort and protection.

MIRROR IMAGE
Legadema bonds with her mother as they patrol their territory together.

Her mother had lost five cubs to hyenas, baboons, and other predators. What would happen to this one? Unlike lions or cheetahs, leopards are secretive cats that live alone. Without a family to depend on, they hunt by themselves, hiding in the shadows. They survive on **stealth** and intelligence. Finding any leopard is difficult, so when we discovered this mother and cub in the thick stands of trees in Botswana's Okavango Delta, we decided to follow the little one as she grew up.

From her first days, Legadema was always in danger. Whether it was a group of baboons that tried to drag both mother and daughter out of their den, or the waiting hyenas, death was never far away. Lions, a big threat to young leopards, are common in this part of the Moremi Game Reserve. But none of this kept Legadema from exploring the forest on her own when her mother left her alone for days at a time to bring back meat. Wherever Legadema went, monkeys spotted her a mile off, and squirrels set up alarm calls. In time, these experiences only made her better at hiding and hunting.

Her mother, ever the patient teacher, instructed Legadema in the skills she would need to survive as a predator, such as how to pin down prey and where to bite their throats to kill them. Only after learning these and many other lessons would young Legadema become a solitary hunter.

CLOSE CALL
Scrambling to save her cub from a 60-foot fall during horseplay, Legadema's mother wrestles the cub back onto a branch—a tricky move for an animal equipped only with teeth, claws, and determination.

STAYING CLOSE
Growing more independent, Legadema prepares for the day when she will stake her own claim in the forest. But the six-month-old, right, still seems reassured by the touch of her mother's tail.

When she was five months old, her mother brought her a live baby **impala**. At first Legadema was not sure what to do, playing curiously, then trying to attack. Her mother guided her patiently through every step of the kill, until at last Legadema learned that living animals can become a meal. As her skills improved, Legadema turned her attention to squirrels, chasing the small creatures for hours—even playing games of hide-and-seek with them. Over time, Legadema got the hang of hunting and began killing hundreds of squirrels, as well as larger prey such as baby warthogs.

At 13 months old, still a teenager, Legadema got into a fight with her mother that led to them to part ways. Legadema had refused to share a kill with her. Although they had been growing apart for some time, Legadema was now showing her independence, and her mother drove her off.

Eventually, Legadema found her own hunting grounds and had cubs of her own. If she and her young stay within Moremi, they will be safe from harm by humans. But in other places in Africa, leopards are not as lucky. Some 2,500 a year are allowed to be shot by hunters and at least as many are killed by poachers. As conflicts with people and livestock continue, fewer and fewer leopards are likely to enjoy a life as free as young Legadema's. This is why we are dedicated to saving the big cats.

THINK ABOUT IT!

1. **Make Generalizations** Why are keystone species important?

2. **Pose and Answer Questions** What questions would you like to ask the Jouberts about their lives among the big cats?

3. **Sequence Events** What were the first animals that Legadema hunted? What do you think she hunts now?

BACKGROUND & VOCABULARY

impala *n.* (ihm-PAH-luh) a species of antelope, a hoofed animal that eats plants

keystone species *n.* a species that is essential for the survival of a certain ecosystem

stealth *n.* (STEHLTH) the ability to move quietly, without being noticed

LIVING WITH

BY DAVID QUAMMEN

Adapted from "Living with Lions," by David Quammen, in *National Geographic,* August 2013

LIONS

GUARDING THE HERD
This young Maasai in Ngororo, Kenya, keeps a watchful eye on his cattle herd.

When people and lions collide, both suffer. Can lions and humans share the land? Writer David Quammen explores the issue with the people who study lions and those who live among the big cats.

LOSING LIONS

Lions are complicated creatures, magnificent at a distance yet fearsomely inconvenient to the people who live among them. These lords of the wild **savanna** are not compatible with farming. It is no wonder their luck has decreased as humans have succeeded.

There is evidence across at least three continents of the lions' glory days and their decline. Chauvet Cave in southern France is filled with vivid paintings of wildlife, showing us that lions inhabited Europe along with humans 30,000 years ago. The Book of Daniel in the Bible suggests that lions still lived near Babylon in the sixth century B.C. There are reports of lions surviving in Syria, Turkey, Iraq, and Iran until the 19th or 20th centuries. During the long decline of the lions, only Africa has remained as a reliable heartland.

But that has changed too. New estimates suggest that the lion has disappeared from about 80 percent of its African range. No one knows how many lions survive today in Africa because wild lions are difficult to count. There may be only as many as 35,000.

The decline has multiple causes. Humans have taken lions' habitat. Their prey is hunted by humans or displaced by domestic animals. They may become ill and die. Humans kill lions for killing livestock or people, and lions may become caught in **snares**. Tribes such as the Maasai, who live in Kenya and Tanzania, kill them as part of their cultural traditions. Wealthy Americans hunt them for trophies.

Counts compiled by scientists from the big cat conservation organization Panthera, Duke University, and the Big Cats Initiative indicate that African lions now live in nearly 70 distinct areas. The largest and most secure areas can be considered **strongholds**. The smallest contain only tiny populations. That is, the African lion

RAISED FOR SPORT
These lions were raised on a South African ranch that breeds lions specifically for private hunts.

inhabits many separate patches of **refuge**, not all of which are connected. More than a few of these populations may soon go extinct.

What can be done to stop the losses? Some experts say we should focus efforts on the areas with large populations. These include the Serengeti ecosystem in Tanzania and Kenya, the Selous ecosystem in southeastern Tanzania, the Ruaha-Rungwa in western Tanzania, the Okavango-Hwange in Botswana and Zimbabwe, and the Greater Limpopo in Mozambique, Zimbabwe, and South Africa. Those five ecosystems alone hold about half of Africa's lions.

PROBLEMS OR SOLUTIONS?

Craig Packer, biologist and director of the Lion Research Center, has offered a drastic suggestion for further protecting some areas: fence them, or at least some of their borders. He says fences are the best way to prevent herders, their livestock, and poachers from entering and lions from leaving.

Other experts strongly disagree. Many conservationists have long thought habitat patches must be connected. Packer knows that. Even he wouldn't put a fence across a valuable route of wildlife migration. However, fencing the western boundary of the Serengeti, where it meets the farmlands beyond, might work. If you fly over that area, you will see the border, along which runs a red clay road. East of it lies the rolling green terrain of Maswa, covered with woods and savanna. West of the road, you will look down on mile after mile of cotton fields, cornfields, teams of oxen plowing bare dirt, and cows standing in pens. Packer believes that a fence along that border could do no harm and possibly some good. It's an idea worth discussing, at least.

Trophy hunting is also controversial. Does it negatively affect lion populations? Or does it make the lions valuable, bringing cash to countries where they live? Does that give some people a good reason to protect lions' habitat? The answer depends on where the lions are hunted, on whether old or young lions are killed, and on how well the program is managed. In some countries, hunting rights are not granted fairly. Situations exist in which little of the money from trophy hunting reaches the local people who pay the real costs of living with lions, and areas remain where too many lions are killed.

BLACK MARKET BONES
Poachers sell lion bones like these to dealers in Asia for use in traditional medicines.

THE STATE OF LIONS

80 PERCENT — Lions have vanished from more than 80 percent of their former range.

1 MILLION — In 1750, 1 million lions roamed the savannas of Africa.

35 THOUSAND — By 2012, fewer than 35,000 lions remained.

PROTECTORS
These Lion Guardians use GPS units and radio transmitters to monitor movements of lions that have been fitted with radio collars. This technology protects lions by helping prevent conflicts with herders and cattle.

For example, in places such as Maswa Game Reserve, hunts are closely watched. There, a ban on hunting would not make sense because the organization that oversees the hunts helps to save wildlife habitat as well.

Sport hunting of captive lions released into fenced areas on private ranches raises a whole different set of questions. There are about 200 lion ranches in South Africa, home to more than 3,500 lions. Some argue that allowing captive lion hunts may help lion conservation because fewer wild lions will be hunted. Others fear it may affect the profits of legal hunting of wild lions by offering cheaper and easier ways to put a lion head on your wall.

Then there's the matter of what happens to the rest of the lions. South Africa ships lion bones to Asia. There they are sold as an alternative to tiger bones, which are thought to have medicinal value. This could increase the demand for lion bones and, in turn, cause even more lions to be killed. Lion conservation is a complicated project. It must now reach across borders, across oceans, and across different branches of science.

LION GUARDIANS

Ultimately, conservation begins at home, among people who live close to the beautiful and terrifying lion. One group, the Maasai, lives on ranches on the plains of southern Kenya. Since 2007, a program there called Lion Guardians has recruited young Maasai men. Before, they killed lions as part of a cultural tradition. They now protect lions instead. These men are paid and trained in radio tracking and GPS use. They follow lions on a daily basis and prevent lion attacks on livestock. The program seems to be succeeding. Lion killings have decreased, and the Lion Guardians now play an important role in those communities.

I spent a day recently with a Lion Guardian named Kamunu. He was about 30 years old, serious and steady. He wore a beaded necklace, beaded earrings, and a red cloth wrapped around him. He carried a dagger on his belt at one side and a cell phone on the other. Kamunu had killed five lions, he told me, but he didn't intend to kill any more. He had learned that lions were more valuable alive. Lions brought in money from tourism and from Lion Guardians. He could pay for food and education for his family.

We walked a long way that very hot day, winding through the bush, crossing a dry river, Kamunu following lion tracks in the dust and me following him. We probably walked about 16 miles. In the morning we tracked a lone adult that Kamunu recognized from its giant footprints. It was known to kill cattle. When we met a long line of cows headed for water with several Maasai boys, Kamunu warned them to stay clear of the lion.

Around midday he picked up a different trail, very fresh, left by a female with two cubs. We saw the place where she had rested in the grass beneath a bush. We traced her path into a grove of trees that grew thicker as we went. Kamunu moved quietly. Finally we stopped. I saw nothing but plants and dirt.

"They're very close," he explained. "This is a good spot. No livestock nearby. We don't want to push any closer. We don't want to disturb them."

"No, we don't," I agreed.

"We think they are safe here," he told me. It's more than can be said for many African lions, but at that moment, in that place, it was enough.

THINK ABOUT IT!

1. **Make Inferences** Why might Lion Guardians be respected in Maasai communities?

2. **Form and Support Opinions** Do you think trophy hunting of lions should be allowed? Why or why not?

BACKGROUND & VOCABULARY

refuge *n.* (REH-fyooj) a safe place such as a national park or game reserve

savanna *n.* (suh-VAN-uh) an area covered by grasslands and patches of trees

snare *n.* a trap made of wire loops set by poachers to catch wild animals

stronghold *n.* a place where a type of animal is plentiful

A CRY for the TIGER

BY CAROLINE ALEXANDER

Adapted from "A Cry for the Tiger," by Caroline Alexander, in *National Geographic,* December 2011

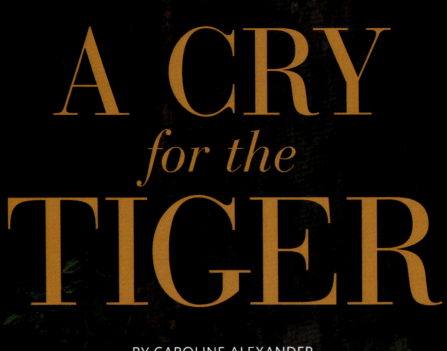

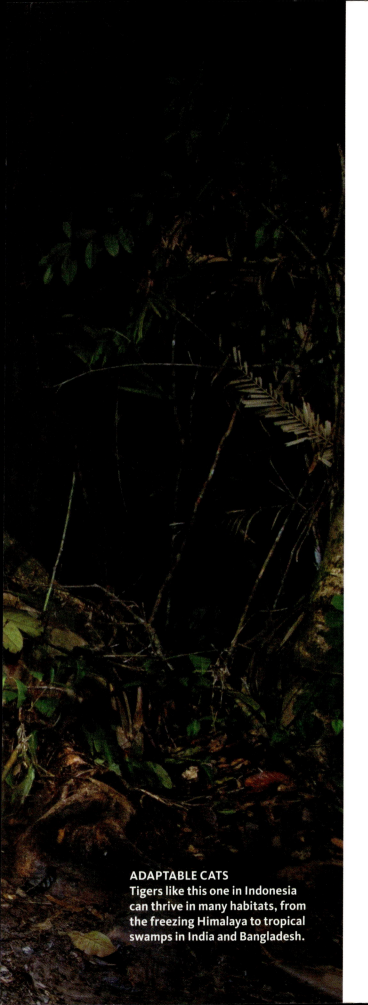

ADAPTABLE CATS
Tigers like this one in Indonesia can thrive in many habitats, from the freezing Himalaya to tropical swamps in India and Bangladesh.

We have the means to save the mightiest cat on Earth. But do we have the will? Journalist Caroline Alexander travels to some of the last places on Earth where tigers live.

BEAUTIFUL CARNIVORE

It is dawn, and mist holds the forest in India's Ranthambore National Park. Only a short stretch of red dirt road can be seen. A tigress walks into view. She stops to rub her whiskers against a tree and then turns to inspect us with a bored look.

The tiger is the largest of all the big cats. One of the fiercest carnivores on the planet, it has claws up to four inches long and teeth that can crack bone. Yet, with its golden coat and pattern of black flames, it is also one of the most beautiful creatures. While able to reach 35 miles an hour, the tiger is built for strength, not speed. Short, powerful legs help it pounce on its prey. In fact, a tiger was captured on video jumping from the ground to attack a ranger riding an elephant. The roar of the tiger can carry more than a mile.

For weeks I had been traveling through some of the best tiger habitat in Asia, but never before had I seen a tiger. Partly this was because of the animal's secretive nature. The tiger is powerful enough to kill and drag prey five times its weight, yet it can move in total silence. Those who have seen an attack often remark that the tiger "came from nowhere."

Today, tigers in the wild face extinction. The tiger's enemies include the loss of habitat to humans, the hunting of prey animals, and above all, the dark threat of the Chinese black market for tiger parts. People first started to worry about the fate of tigers in 1969. In the 1980s about 8,000 tigers remained in the wild. Now, the tiger population is probably fewer than 4,000 animals, spread through the 13 tiger countries of Asia.

FRAGILE HABITATS

I wanted to see a wild tiger in my lifetime. This quest brought me to Ranthambore Tiger Reserve, one of 40 reserves in India. I spotted my first tiger within ten minutes. In four days, I had nine sightings. I even saw the first tiger, a three-year old female, twice. She stalked with such focus and patience—each paw raised in slow motion and placed so gently down—that it was possible to *see* her stealth.

It didn't matter that I shared my experience with a line of other cars. Seeing tigers in the wild is now mostly a tourist experience in India. The Bengal tiger is not only India's national animal but also one of the country's biggest attractions. India is home to 50 percent of the world's wild tigers. In 2010, there were about 1,900 in the country, up 20 percent from the previous estimate. Forty-one of these tigers were living in Ranthambore. But tiger counts, in India or elsewhere in the world, are still at best only estimates.

Tiger hunting was legal in India until the early 1970s. Though the tigers of Ranthambore are now protected, between 2002 and 2004, 20 tigers were poached—half of the reserve's population. This was better than the fate of the nearby Sariska Tiger Reserve, found to have no tigers at all. Professional gangs had killed every single one.

Ranthambore and Sariska highlight a major problem in tiger conservation. Many reserves are islands of fragile habitat in a sea of humanity, yet tigers can range over a hundred miles seeking prey, mates, and territory. Nearly a third of India's tigers live outside tiger reserves, which is dangerous for both humans and animals. Prey and tigers can only travel to other safe areas if there are paths of land between protected areas. But over the next ten years about $750 billion a year will be spent on building roads and other development projects, which will likely destroy habitat along these paths.

Long-term conservation must focus on all aspects of a tiger landscape. After years of experience and failures, conservationists have come up with a strategy that allows any site or landscape to increase its tigers. Central to this method are guarding and monitoring both the tiger and its prey.

RANGERS VS. POACHERS

My first encounter with the Hukawng Valley Wildlife Sanctuary in northern Myanmar was not encouraging. The level of human activity within its borders amazes me. Large bites have been taken from the zone that surrounds the wildlife sanctuary. Land for a farm was cleared so quickly that the shrinking of the forest could be seen not over weeks but days. A gold-mining settlement in the west is home to 50,000 people. Yet the 6,708-square-mile tiger reserve is large enough that even these human disturbances do not prevent wildlife from thriving.

The Hukawng Valley, in between three mountain ranges, is filled by dense, dark jungle. As recently as the 1970s, people who lived in Hukawng came across tigers in the course of daily life, hearing their roars at night. Rarely did a tiger harm a human, though tigers did sometimes take cattle. Myanmar youth now know the tiger more from educational programs than from life.

In Hukawng, teams of rangers do the hard and often discouraging work of guarding and tracking tigers. Two days after I arrived, I joined the Myanmar Forest Department's tiger and guard teams as they headed up the Tawang River. The sun had burned off the morning mist. Close to shore, banana trees cast green shade on the water. Flocks of ducks flew ahead and waited, while an occasional heron sailed by.

Upriver, at a guard post, the head ranger gave a summary of the teams' work for the season. The tiger team spent a third of each month looking for the tracks of tigers and their prey as well as signs of human activities. "Sometimes if it is sunny, you can see the sky," a ranger said, describing what it was like to work in the dark forest for up to six weeks. The worst days are when it rains, and the trees spill water from their leaves and dripping mists chill the bone. Then the **leeches** get bigger. **Malaria** has killed team members. In all, 74 people are responsible for patrolling a 700-square-mile area of dense forest.

There may be 25 tigers in the Hukawng Valley according to a former tiger poacher. Official evidence of the tigers' existence is harder to come by. Between 2006 and 2007 the only trace was several paw prints of a single tiger, and in the 2007–2008 season, traces of only three tigers

PUTTING ON A SHOW
A tiger leaps for a plastic bag tied to a pole while tourists watch at Tiger Temple in Kanchanaburi, Thailand.

HUNTING FOR PREDATORS
Patrollers search for poachers in Thailand's Western Forest Complex, habitat for up to 200 tigers.

were found. The following season a clean line of prints by the river was cause for celebration. Measurements and plaster casts of the tracks were made and three camera traps were placed in the area. About the same time, fresh tracks were discovered nine miles upriver, which proved to belong to the same tiger.

Later I spoke with Alan Rabinowitz, who worked with the Myanmar Forest Department to create the Hukawng Sanctuary. Was spending so much time worth it for so few tigers?

As part of his answer, he pointed to a map that showed Hukawng's key position in the northern web of tiger landscapes. "Hukawng's potential is so huge," he argued. Rabinowitz has seen habitats that have been turned around before. He continued, "Huai Kha Khaeng was in terrible shape when I was there in the 1990s, and now it's one of Asia's best tiger reserves."

THE EDGE OF SURVIVAL

"I first worked here in 1986, when every night there were gunshot noises, every day dead animals," Rabinowitz told the group of rangers gathered at the headquarters of the Huai Kha Khaeng Wildlife Sanctuary in western Thailand. The scene Rabinowitz described was one his audience could no longer recognize.

"What you have done here," Rabinowitz said, "is you have turned Huai Kha Khaeng from a site whose future was in grave doubt into one of the world's best tiger sites." Two decades ago, there were maybe 20 tigers in Huai Kha Khaeng. There are now about 60 in the reserve alone and about 100 in nearby protected forests. The improved health of the forest and the rise in prey suggest that the tiger population could continue to grow.

NO SAFE PLACES
Dara Arista, 8, holds a photo of Sheila in front of her cage in Jambi, Indonesia. Poachers had slaughtered the tiger during the night.

Bringing tigers back from the edge of survival relies not only on human actions in the immediate future but also on the tiger's own adaptable nature. Tigers are not picky about diet or habitat. Tiger tracks have been found in the mountains of Bhutan in territory overlapping the land of the snow leopard, while tigers in the mangrove swamps of India and Bangladesh, are powerful swimmers and have learned to eat fish. Tigers can increase their numbers if given a chance. A female can raise six to eight cubs over her 12-year lifespan. This helped the population at Huai Kha Khaeng triple in 20 years.

At the ranger meeting, I watched each of the 20 patrol leaders step up and make a report of his team's work. They showed us maps of the patrol area, the paths they followed, and locations of trouble spots. The rangers also showed video and photographs of other wildlife. They were clearly proud of their work. In many tiger landscapes, rangers make do with old clothes and equipment, but the rangers of Huai Kha Khaeng were dressed in sharp new uniforms. Their jobs are seen as important and are respected in their communities. Thailand's biggest asset is a national commitment to pay for tiger conservation. It pays for two-thirds of the work at Huai Kha Khaeng.

Following the meeting I joined Rabinowitz and a tracker for a walk in the forest. Far below the canopy, we stepped through towering bamboo. Twice we stopped to listen to the call of an elephant. After a few miles, we ran into a stream. On the opposite bank we found a long line of tiger tracks, four inches wide, among the bird scratches and footprints left by elephants.

"Lean all your weight on your hands," Rabinowitz said. Then he measured the depth of the print my hand made in the sand. "One and a half centimeters," he announced. Just over half an inch. The tiger's **pugmark** was an inch and a half deep. It was made by a male weighing more than 400 pounds.

"There is 1.1 million square kilometers of tiger habitat remaining," said Eric Dinerstein, chief scientist and vice president of conservation science of the World Wildlife Fund. "Assuming two tigers for every 100 square kilometers, that's a potential 22,000 tigers." For now the task is to save the few tigers that actually exist.

In November 2010 the 13 tiger countries attending the St. Petersburg Global Tiger Summit in Russia pledged to "double the number of wild tigers across their range by 2022." In March 2010 a mother and two cubs were poisoned in Huai Kha Khaeng, the first to be killed in two years. The deaths led the Thai government to offer a $3,000 reward for capture of the poachers. In the same month two young tigers were poisoned in Ranthambore, though two new cubs were later born. In Hukawng, a new male tiger was caught by camera trap, a lone reminder of what this great wilderness could hold. Most authorities agree that the fight to save the tiger can be won, but it will require effort and commitment.

THINK ABOUT IT!

1. **Make Predictions** Do you think there will be any tigers left in the wild in 20 years? Why or why not?

2. **Compare and Contrast** How are working conditions in the Hukawng Valley Wildlife Sanctuary different from those of the Huai Kha Khaeng Wildlife Sanctuary?

3. **Draw Conclusions** Why is it so important to keep track of the animals that tigers prey upon?

BACKGROUND & VOCABULARY

leech *n.* a type of worm that feeds on the blood of animals and humans

malaria *n.* (muh-LAIR-ee-uh) a disease carried by mosquitos

pugmark *n.* a mammal's paw print

CHEETAHS ON THE EDGE

BY ROFF SMITH

Adapted from "Cheetahs On the Edge," by Roff Smith, in *National Geographic*, November 2012

CHEETAH AT REST
A female cheetah stands in the tall grass of the Maasai Mara Reserve in Kenya.

Cheetahs are remarkable animals: sleek, lightning fast, and able to live in wildly different environments. But even these adaptable creatures are in danger of extinction. What pressures do cheetahs face? What is being done to protect them?

BUILT FOR SPEED

Anticipation ripples through the crowd. Fingers tighten around binoculars. Cameras snap into focus. Eleven **safari** buses, bright with tourists and bristling with long lenses, huddle near an acacia tree in Tanzania's Serengeti National Park. For the past half-hour a mother cheetah named Etta has been sitting in the shade with her four young cubs. She has been eyeing a herd of gazelles on a nearby rise. Then she is up and moving, sidling toward the herd with a seeming indifference that fools no one.

Suddenly the gazelles break and run and Etta launches into an explosive sprint. The sleek cat is too fast for the eye to follow. She blurs through the grass like a bullet. The drama is over in seconds, ending with a luckless young gazelle in a stranglehold. As Etta drags the animal back to her cubs, they come out of the brush eager for the feast. The safari buses are only seconds behind, the drivers trying for the best camera angles.

Cheetahs occupy a curious place in the human imagination. Beautiful, exotic, and sports-car fast, they are media stars, the darlings of filmmakers and advertisers.

You might get the impression that cheetahs are as secure in nature as they are in popular culture. They are not. In fact, cheetahs are the most **vulnerable** of the world's big cats. They are rare and growing steadily rarer. A few centuries ago cheetahs roamed from the Indian subcontinent to the shores of the Red Sea and throughout much of Africa. Fast as they are, though, they could not outrun the long reach of humanity.

Today, the Asiatic cheetah, which once graced the royal courts of India, Persia, and Arabia, is all but extinct. In Africa, cheetah numbers decreased by more than 90 percent during the 20th century. Farmers, ranchers, and herders crowded the cats out of their habitat. Hunters shot them for sport. Poachers captured cubs for the illegal trade in exotic pets. In all, fewer than 10,000 cheetahs survive in the wild today.

Even within Africa's great game parks, cheetahs are under heavy pressure. Shy and delicately built, they are the only big cats that cannot roar. They are bullied by lions, which are far stronger both in body and number. Consider Tanzania's Serengeti National Park and the Maasai Mara Reserve in Kenya. Together, these two parks are home to more than 3,000 lions, 1,000 leopards, and just 300 cheetahs.

Cheetahs are a separate **species** from the other great cats. They belong to a separate **genus** as well, one with just one member: themselves. Among all the cats, they alone have an unusual semi-retractable claw. In contrast, lions and leopards have fully retractable claws designed for tearing flesh and climbing trees. The cheetah's claws are more like the spikes on a track shoe. They serve a similar function, too: solid grip and quick **acceleration**.

Everything about a cheetah is designed for pure, raw speed. Put a cheetah and a fast car side by side and either might smash the speed limit first. Both can go from zero to 60 miles per hour in under three seconds. A cheetah can reach 45 miles per hour in the first couple of strides. Thanks to its flexible spine and long, fluid legs, a cheetah can take bounds that exceed 25 feet.

Such superhuman abilities gave cheetahs an otherworldly aura in ancient times. Egyptians were the first to tame them as pets and carve their images on tombs and temples, nearly 4,000 years ago. In India, Iran, and Arabia, hunting with cheetahs became an immensely popular sport. Favorite cheetahs were adorned with jeweled collars and strode in royal processions.

HOW FAST CAN A CHEETAH RUN?

The fastest cheetah ever recorded, named Sarah, ran 100 meters in 5.95 seconds. Cinematographer Greg Wilson used an ultra high-speed camera to record Tommy T, a cheetah at the Cincinnati Zoo, run 100 meters in 7.19 seconds. These 34 frames show just a half second of Tommy T's run. (And yes, he's faster than 100-meter Olympic gold medalist Usain Bolt, who clocks in at 9.58 seconds.)

CHEETAHS AT RISK

Cheetahs remain highly fashionable in Saudi Arabia and the Gulf states, where a cub can cost more than $10,000. Popularity has led to widespread illegal trafficking. Cheetahs are smuggled into countries and then made to appear as if they had been bred legally in captivity. Proving where a cub came from is difficult. Today, though, scientists can use genetic analysis to connect a cub with cheetahs living in a certain area of the world.

What is the impact of trafficking on the dwindling cheetah population? Evidence suggests that trade in wild cheetah cubs is a large-scale operation. "I suspect the problem is bigger than we imagine," says Yeneneh Teka, an Ethiopian official who is working to protect his country's wildlife. "There is a great deal of money involved," he continues, "and those who smuggle wildlife have well-established networks."

Last year Ethiopian authorities cracked down on wildlife smuggling. They started a training program for border guards and customs officials. The stepped-up enforcement paid off when officials discovered an illegal shipment of cheetah cubs.

"While the border guards were examining the truck's paperwork, they heard scratching sounds coming from [inside a container]," Teka says. "When they opened it up, they found five tiny cheetah cubs in very poor condition." One of the cubs died. The other four were treated and then taken to a wildlife sanctuary where they will spend the rest of their lives.

"They'll never be able to return to the wild," says Mordecai Ogada, a Kenyan wildlife biologist. "Even if you could teach them to hunt, humans can't teach cubs how to recognize and avoid **predators** such as lions and hyenas."

Even mother cheetahs find it difficult to raise cubs in the wild. Death among cubs can run as high as 95 percent. The great majority of cubs may never make it out of the den in which they're born. Some are killed in raids by lions or hyenas. Some die of the cold. Others are abandoned by mothers that are not skillful enough hunters to support them. Many female cheetahs never raise a single cub to adulthood.

A rare few, however, enjoy astonishing success in raising cubs. Some even raise the offspring of other females. These supermoms are superb hunters and wise in the ways of the bush. They manage to make a kill nearly every day while keeping their cubs safe in the wide-open grasslands. One such supermom, named Eleanor, has mothered at least 10 percent of all the adult cheetahs in the southern Serengeti.

"I'm not aware of any other carnivore whose survival relies so heavily on the success of so few females," says Sarah Durant, who directs the Serengeti Cheetah Project. Now in its 38th year, the project has followed the lives of generations of the Serengeti's cheetahs. It is hot, dusty work, involving long hours bouncing over the grasslands seeking out the most **elusive** of Africa's great cats. It was Durant's careful research that revealed the vital importance of supermoms.

The female lines of the Serengeti's cheetah population are now well known. But male lines are another matter. Wildlife biologist Helen O'Neill waits patiently a short distance from where three cheetah brothers—Mocha, Latte, and Espresso, known as the Coffee Boys—lie sprawled in the shade. O'Neill is on "poop patrol," collecting feces dropped by specific, identifiable cheetahs. Scientists are able to extract DNA samples and hope someday to fill in the male side of the Serengeti's family trees.

SURVIVING IN ASIA AND AFRICA

A world away from the sunlit grasslands of the Serengeti, late on a cold, clear afternoon, a lone male cheetah picks his way along a ridge. He pauses briefly, and then slinks out of view of the video camera that has been recording his passage. The concealed camera is one of 80 cameras that have been set up in a remote region in Iran's mountainous central plateau. By using these remotely operated cameras, scientists hope to glimpse one of the world's rarest and most elusive big cats: the Asiatic cheetah.

"These cats are incredibly rare," says Iranian wildlife biologist Houman Jowkar. "We have game wardens who have lived and worked in these mountains for years but have never seen a live cheetah."

The camera program has helped Iranian scientists determine roughly how many cheetahs are left and where they live. This is vital information for developing a conservation strategy. Saving the Asiatic cheetah will be a tall order. Its downfall started long ago in the glory days of the Mogul Empire, which ruled northern India from the 1500s to the mid-1700s. Then, hunting with cheetahs became all the rage. One emperor is said to have collected more than 9,000 cheetahs during his 49-year reign.

Compare then and now. In ten years of setting out cameras, Iranian researchers have so far managed to obtain just 192 fleeting images. Those images document 76 **gaunt** individuals, pretty much all that remains of the noble cheetah that once roamed throughout much of Asia. Today's survivors live a precarious existence, competing with wolves and even humans for the available food supply.

"They are living on a knife edge, at the very limit of what is ecologically possible," says Luke Hunter, president of Panthera, a conservation group dedicated to preserving big cats. "What's intriguing, though, is that these cheetahs have not been pushed into these mountains recently. They've been here for thousands of years. People don't realize how tough cheetahs really are." Indeed they are. Despite their vulnerability, cheetahs are some of the world's shrewdest survivors, enduring bitter winters in Iran and scorching heat in the Sahara.

> "*They are living on a knife edge, at the very limit of what is ecologically possible.*"
> —Luke Hunter

Back in Serengeti National Park, it is late afternoon. The hot taste of dust is in the air. Thunderclouds billow along the horizon. For the past hour Etta has been creeping up on a big male gazelle. She is within 40 yards of him, while he has remained unaware of her presence.

"It's too early to tell if Etta is going to turn out to be a supermum," Durant says. "This is only her first litter. But the fact that she has brought four cubs out of the den and has raised them this far is an encouraging sign."

The gazelle is big, with a lot of meat on him. Etta takes another couple of steps forward, then crouches and waits. She looks like a runner on the starting blocks, poised and ready for the gun.

A tense minute crawls by, then another. Suddenly, and seemingly for no reason, Etta stands up and strolls away. Something feels wrong to her—a whiff of hyena on the breeze or maybe the scent of lions. Whatever it is, to a mother of four young cubs alone on the Serengeti, one fat gazelle is not worth the risk. She beckons to her cubs to come along. Together they trot off into the violet haze.

THINK ABOUT IT!

1 Categorize What are some of the forces working against the survival of the cheetah?

2 Synthesize Imagine you must convince someone that the cheetah is worth protecting. What would you say to that person?

BACKGROUND & VOCABULARY

acceleration *n.* (uhk-sehl-uh-RAY-shuhn) the act of speeding up

elusive *adj.* (ee-LOO-sihv) hard to find or capture

gaunt *adj.* (GAWNT) very thin as a result of suffering or starvation

genus *n.* (JEE-nuhs) in biology, a category of related species

species *n.* (SPEE-seez) in biology, a category of related organisms

predator *n.* (PREHD-uh-tuhr) an animal that gets its food mainly from killing and eating other animals

safari *n.* (suh-FAHR-ee) an organized tour to see wildlife in its natural habitat, usually in Africa

vulnerable *adj.* (VUHL-nur-uh-buhl) at risk of harm; undefended

On Location with
BOONE SMITH

BY ANDREA ALTER

SOUTH AFRICAN DINNER
Special engineers built this box to keep Smith off the menu as he observed a lion feast. In this photo, the partially-built box is missing the strong metal bars that kept him safe from the lions.

Big Cat tracker Boone Smith is no stranger to unusual situations, but his latest project has him a little boxed in.

BIG CAT TRACKER

Boone Smith felt beads of sweat break across his brow, and it wasn't just the heat of the South African night. It was the hot breath of three huge lions just inches away, separated from him only by plexiglass and a few metal bars. For the tenth time, he wondered whether this experiment was such a good idea.

At his day job, Boone Smith is a juvenile detention officer, but his other job brings him into contact with very different clients. Smith grew up on a ranch in Idaho and is a fourth-generation wildlife tracker and capture specialist. He helps conservation groups track endangered animals, and he relocates animals in dangerous situations, including coyotes, bears, and moose.

Because of his experience with mountain lions and bobcats when he was young, Boone Smith developed a soft spot for wild cats. As a passionate ambassador for big cats, he has hosted several shows for Nat Geo WILD's Big Cat Week.

For the show "Hunt for the Shadow Cat," Smith tracked jaguars in Belize. The wetlands there are an important link in the jaguar corridor that extends from Central America into South America. Knowing where jaguars roam helps experts protect safe passages for these elusive cats.

The rugged Himalaya provided the backdrop for "Snow Leopard of Afghanistan." While there, Smith helped teach rangers how to capture snow leopards and fit them with radio collars. Data collected from the collars reveals snow leopard behaviors and the ranges they travel.

In 2013, Smith went to Montana to film "Cougar vs. Wolf." In recent years, wolf packs have encroached on cougar territory, causing these competitive predators to square off in violent skirmishes. Smith wanted to pinpoint where the cougar-wolf battles were taking place to find out more about shrinking cougar habitats.

MAN V. LION

Clearly, Boone Smith's work takes him all over the world. Little did he know he might one day find himself in the middle of a pride of hungry African lions.

In the summer of 2014, Smith traveled to the Nambiti Reserve in South Africa with Nat Geo WILD to film "Man v. Lion" for that year's Big Cat Week. Smith wanted to learn more about the feasting and hunting habits of lions and to showcase their amazing skills, so he put himself into a few daring situations.

While on the reserve, Smith followed a group of three male lions, the Nambiti brothers. He observed their behaviors and learned some unexpected things. When the three brothers encountered a lone female looking for a mate, the story got very interesting. Predictably, the males fought with each other to claim the female. The dominant brother won out. However, the physical skill and social dynamics, or relationships, of the Nambiti lions surprised him.

For one part of the filming, Smith perched in a tree to observe the physical skill of the female lion. He waited until she came along to eat meat that he had strung from a high branch. Smith wanted to see if she would jump for it, and if so, how she would "kill" it. It was his chance to see first-hand how lions go in for the kill: first the paws go around the prey's neck, and then they go in for the kill bite.

Not only did the lion jump much higher than Smith expected—10 feet—but she even adapted to the "hunt" and decided to climb the tree when the meat moved higher than she could jump. Smith experienced a few tense moments as he looked the lion in the eye while she decided whether or not he was part of the meal, too.

During another part of the shoot, Smith climbed inside "Boone's Box," a four-foot high box made of plexiglass, so that he could have a front-row seat for a night at a lion feast. What was he thinking? It's a fair question. For one thing, he wanted to be able to document lion behavior up close. By placing himself in the middle of the action, he would be able to watch the lions interact with each other as they ate. Smith had a hunch he would learn a lot about lions' social dynamics from this unique vantage point.

BOONE IN HIS BOX
While he was in the box, Smith was inches away from the Nambiti brothers. He could even feel the vibration of their roars.

How does one prepare for such an event? "First, you must have a very good understanding of lions. Also, you build a very good box," says Smith. "Once I believed in the box, the adventure and adrenaline kicked in."

To lure the lions to the meal, Smith's team tied a fresh wildebeest carcass to the top of the box and then Smith and his cameraman waited safely inside for the brothers to come to dinner. They didn't know how the lions would react. The lions were immediately curious, and once they decided to eat, they made short work of the wildebeest. One of the brothers even tried to take the meat for himself. He pulled the 300-pound carcass off the top of the box and dragged it for five feet—along with the 900-pound box and two 200-pound men inside.

"To be that close and watch these guys devour that carcass was pretty cool. In about 20 minutes, two brothers had eaten about three-quarters of the wildebeest," Smith recalls.

Smith and his cameraman spent six hours in Boone's Box that night. He remarked, "Their personalities really showed up. It was fun to see the brothers create a coalition to run their pride." What astonished Smith the most is that part way through the feast and the fight over the meat, the dominant male decided to concede the meal to his brothers. He was more concerned about continuing his lineage with the lone female than he was with the wildebeest.

When asked if he would climb into Boone's Box again, Smith exclaimed, "In a second!" He might do crazy things, but Smith's first-hand perspective and passion for his work is contagious. In the spirit of the Big Cats Initiative, Boone Smith is definitely causing an uproar.

ROCKET CAT
Lions are heavy cats, but they can still catch air. Smith tested the vertical limits of this female lion, who eventually jumped 10 feet to snatch the meat dangling from the rope.

Document-Based Question

Big cats face many threats in the wild, and the most dangerous of all are humans. National Geographic teamed with Explorers Dereck and Beverly Joubert to start the Big Cats Initiative (BCI), which funds projects to protect these awesome animals. The BCI focuses on three major goals: community outreach and engagement, keeping the peace, and reducing threats to big cats.

DOCUMENT 1 Primary Source
Community Outreach

Big Cats Initiative Grantee Amy Dickman reaches out to communities in Tanzania to save big cats. Her team helps people gain access to education and other resources in exchange for their knowledge and cooperation. Here, Dickman describes how her crew connected with traditional warriors.

> Traditionally a nomadic group, they don't really like outsiders, so it took a huge amount of time and effort to build trust with this group and actually get some initial communication. For the first year that we lived in the village, they completely ignored us, and then by complete chance we had a solar panel that we put in so that we could charge our computers. These very traditional warriors suddenly turned up the next day and handed me a mobile phone, and they would all turn up then to charge their mobile phones to have out in the bush with them. This was the breakthrough. Modern communication actually brought us together.

from "Resolving Human-Animal Conflict," animals.nationalgeographic.com/animals/big-cats-initiative/projects

CONSTRUCTED RESPONSE
1. Why do you think the local people were so suspicious of Dickman and her crew? What else might conservationists do to connect with communities?

DOCUMENT 2 Primary Source
Keeping the Peace

Shivani Bhalla, a National Geographic Explorer and founder of Ewaso Lions, works with the BCI in Kenya to resolve conflicts between people and lions. She explains in this interview how she convinces people not to kill lions when they eat their livestock.

> I have a great team of elders, warriors, and women from the community who deal with it every day. When livestock is killed by lions they respond immediately. The first thing they do is calm the people down and give them a chance to explain what happened. Usually, lions kill livestock that have been lost. Then they talk about the importance of lions. In our areas rhinos were wiped out in the 1980s, and the elders remember that and talk about it. They say they don't want their lions to disappear, because their kids have never seen a rhino. Then they talk about how to better protect livestock and how reducing conflict will save lions.

from "Q&A: Explorer Shivani Bhalla Helps People and Lions Coexist," by Brian Clark Howard, news.nationalgeographic.com, June 11, 2014

CONSTRUCTED RESPONSE
2. Why do you think it might be difficult for conservationists to convince livestock owners that lions are important?

What are some of the successes and challenges of the Big Cats Initiative?

DOCUMENT 3 Secondary Source
Reducing the Threat

Snares set by poachers are among the many threats to big cats. These easily made wire traps are set to capture other animals for meat, but often catch big cats instead. Wildlife ecologist and National Geographic Grantee Matthew Becker works with the BCI in Zambia to combat this threat by helping to remove snares and providing medical help to cats and other animals that are caught in them.

CONSTRUCTED RESPONSE

3. How might the BCI help protect big cats by working with the poachers who use snares?

SNARE HUNTER Andi Dominic, a member of the snare removal team at Budongo Conservation Field Station in Uganda, shows one of his finds.

PUT IT TOGETHER

Review Think about your responses to the Constructed Response questions and what you have learned from the articles in this book. Consider the threats to big cats and what the Big Cats Initiative is doing to combat them.

List Main Idea and Details Write down the Big Cats Initiative's major goals. List actions the BCI and others are taking to meet the goals.

Write What are some of the successes and challenges of the Big Cats Initiative? Write one paragraph describing a problem the BCI has worked to solve. Write another paragraph about a challenge that still remains.

INDEX

acceleration, 37, 41
African People and Wildlife Fund (APW), 11

Bangladesh, 35
Bhalla, Shivani, National Geographic Explorer, 11, 46
Becker, Matthew, 47
Belize, 14–15, 43
black market, 31
Big Cats Initiative (BCI), 5–11, 13, 18, 26, 44, 46–47
Big Cat Week, 43, 44
Botswana, 17, 18, 20, 27

carnivore, 10, 11, 31
cheetahs, 4, 6, 8, 9, 10, 11, 36–41
  adaptable nature of, 37
  Asiatic, 40, 41
  separate genus and species, 37
  speed of, 37, 38–39
  vulnerability of, 37, 40
climate change, 6
clouded leopards, 8
conservation, approaches to, 5–11, 14–15, 27, 32–34, 41
Convention on International Trade in Endangered Species (CITES), 17
cougars, 9, 43

Dickman, Amy, 46

economics, of protecting cats, 10, 15, 32–35
  see also illegal trade
ecosystem, 18, 27
elusive, 40, 41
Ewaso Lions, 11, 46
extinction, threat/risk of, 6, 18, 27, 31

gaunt, 41
genus, 37, 41
GPS tracking, 10, 11, 28

Huai Kha Khaeng Wildlife Sanctuary, Thailand, 34–35
Hukawng Valley Wildlife Sanctuary, Myanmar, 32, 34
human populations, 4, 26, 37
  adjusting contact with, 14–15
  BCI working with, 10, 11
  big cat space and, 4, 6
  encroaching on land, 14
  protecting lions, 24–29
hunting, 6, 23, 26, 27, 31, 32, 37, 41
  managing rights to, 27, 29
Hussain, Shafqat, National Geographic Explorer, 10

illegal trade, 14, 15, 17, 31, 40
impala, 23
India, 31, 32, 35, 37
initiative, 6, 11
Iran, 40–41

jaguars, 8, 14, 43
jaguar corridor, 43
Joubert, Beverly, National Geographic Explorer, 6, 16–23
Joubert, Dereck, National Geographic Explorer, 6, 9, 16–23

Kenya, 26, 27, 29, 36, 37
keystone species, 18, 23

leech, 32, 34, 35
Legadema, 17, 18–23
leopards, 4, 8, 9, 10, 11, 14, 17, 18
  black, 4
  mother-cub relationship, 18, 20, 22–23
  predators of, 18, 20
Lichtenfeld, Laly, 11
Lion Guardians, 28, 29
lions, 4, 6, 8, 10, 11, 14, 15, 18, 20, 42–45
  lion ranches, 29
  living with and protecting, 24–29
  numbers of, 27
livestock, 6, 10, 11, 14, 15, 26–29, 46
livestock insurance, 10

Maasai, 11, 24–25, 28, 29
Maasai Mara Reserve, Kenya, 36, 37
malaria, 34, 35
Maswa Game Reserve, 29
Moremi Game Reserve, 20
mountain lions, 9, 43
Myanmar Forest Department, 32, 34

Naankuse Foundation, 10
Nambiti Reserve, South Africa, 43
National Geographic Society, 4, 6
Nat Geo WILD, 43

Okavango Delta, 17, 18, 20, 23

Pakistan, 10
Panthera, 13, 26, 41
panthers, black, 9
poacher, 14, 15, 17, 23, 32, 37, 47
  rewards for capture, 35
politics, 12–15
  passing laws for protection, 15
predator, 40, 41
Project Snow Leopard, 10
pugmark, 35
pumas, 9

Rabinowitz, Alan, 34, 35
Ranthambore National Park, India, 31, 32
refuge, 27, 29
reserve, 15, 20, 32, 37, 43
retribution, 10, 11

safari, 37, 41
Sariska Tiger Reserve, India, 32
savanna, 26, 27, 29
Serengeti Cheetah Project, 40
Serengeti National Park, Tanzania, 5, 37, 41
Smith, Boone, 42–45
snare, 26, 29, 47
snow leopards, 6–7, 8, 10, 43
South Africa, 27, 28, 29, 43
species, 37, 41
stealth, 20, 23, 32
stronghold, 26, 29

Tanzania, 8, 11, 26, 27, 37
tigers, 4, 6, 8, 9, 12–13, 14, 15, 30–35
  adaptable nature of, 35
  Bengal, 32
  nature of, 31
  protecting habitats, 34, 35
  Sumatran, 30–31
trophy hunting, 26, 27, 29

vulnerable, 37, 41

Warrior Watch, 11
Weise, Florian, 10
World Wildlife Fund, 35

Zambia, 47

SKILLS

Categorize, 41
Compare and Contrast, 11, 35
Draw Conclusions, 15, 35
Form and Support Opinions, 11, 29
Identify Problems and Solutions, 11
List Main Idea and Details, 47
Make Generalizations, 23
Make Inferences, 29
Make Predictions, 35
Pose and Answer Questions, 23
Review, 47
Sequence Events, 23
Summarize, 15
Synthesize, 41
Write, 47